Peace and all Good, Peter!
— Fr. Robb, OFM

Advance Praise for
The Bad Catholic's Guide
to the Seven Deadly Sins

If you believe that all moral instruction should be undertaken with a grim face, steer clear of this book. The sins he describes may be deadly, but Zmirak's prose is lively. He rants and rambles, jokes and digresses, tells stories about himself—in short, entertains. Only gradually does the reader realize how many serious insights were packed in between the laughs.

> —**Philip Lawler**, author of *The Faithful Departed,* editor of Catholic World News.

Wickedly funny and a sound guide to living a life that won't end in misery but in joy. One of our best writers produces another classic.

> —**Mark P. Shea**, author of *Mary, Mother of the Son.*

What does one say about a book by a polymath who is at the same time gloriously funny and massively serious? What we have here is a thoroughly orthodox and sane treatment of the Seven Deadly Sins by the Tom Wolfe of Catholic apologetics. He capers through the entirety of Catholic doctrine, hagiology, literature, history and contemporary culture in the course of making his case. The book is serious, weighty, and even encyclopedic—but never sententious, never turgid. "Frolicksome" is a word that springs into one's mind here. The reader will be instructed, blessed, and exhilarated.

> —**Thomas Howard**, author of *Evangelical is Not Enough* and *Chance or the Dance?*

Reading this guide to the Seven Deadly Sins is the most fun you can have without actually committing them!

> —**Robert Spencer**, author of *N.Y. Times* bestseller *The Politically Incorrect Guide to Islam (and the Crusades)* and *Religion of Peace.*

John Zmirak is a theological Cyrano de Bergerac. In *The Bad Catholic's Guide to the Seven Deadly Sins* he engages in wordplay like swordplay—sidestepping error and skewering fuddled thinking with razor edged logic and rapier-sharp repartee. Into his learned content he weaves wacky stories, wild illustrations and wonderful anecdotes. Zmirak writes with panache. He makes theology effervescent and vital, and moves you so much that he makes you think.

> —**Fr. Dwight Longenecker**, blogger, broadcaster, and author of *More Christianity, Adventures in Orthodoxy* and *The Gargoyle Code.*

You're in for a treat: John Zmirak is one of the sharpest, funniest, and most gifted Catholic writers of our generation, and this is a must-have book.

> —**Brian Saint-Paul**, editor of *Crisis* magazine, InsideCatholic.com.

If the authors had not given me a free copy of this book, I would have bought it, but I would have done it online or in disguise at a bookstore. I certainly will give it to many friends, but anonymously. Unfortunately, I still have remnants of a respectable reputation to preserve. . . .

 —**Msgr. Lorenzo Albacete**, theologian and author, professor at the John Paul II Institute for Studies in Marriage and Family.

I have long considered it a significant theological point that Our Lord's first public miracle was turning water, a dull liquid in which fish fornicate, into glorious wine. That's my kind of Christianity. These authors understand that the authentically Catholic life is one of fasting and feasting, to the point of cheerfulness, in anticipation of the great wedding banquet in heaven.

 —**Rod Dreher**, Director of Publications, The John Templeton Foundation.

Bad Catholics, beware. The authors have a hidden agenda. . . . Beneath the puns, ribaldry, and hilariously apt (and no doubt delicious) feast-day recipes lie a profound reverence for—and knowledge of—the Church, her saints, her teachings, and her traditions.

 —**Jeffrey Rubin**, editor at Conservative Book Club; former editor at *The Latin Mass* and *Sursum Corda* magazines.

The ideas outlined here for food and fun are zany, sophisticated, and delightful! How many guides to seasonal cooking urge their readers to flambé chickens, smother squirrels, put antidepressants in the punch and sell indulgences? Not nearly enough, if you ask me.

 —**Georges Briguet**, owner of Le Périgord Restaurant, New York City.

What a great book. . . . As a non-Catholic I found it most educational and extremely funny. It is so refreshing, in this politically correct era!

 —**Rabbi Abba Perelmuter**, Shul By The Shore, Long Beach, California.

THE BAD CATHOLIC'S GUIDE TO THE SEVEN DEADLY SINS

THE BAD CATHOLIC'S GUIDE TO THE SEVEN DEADLY SINS

JOHN ZMIRAK

CROSSROAD NEW YORK

The Crossroad Publishing Company
www.crossroadpublishing.com

© 2010 by John Zmirak
Crossroad, Herder & Herder, and the crossed C logo/colophon are registered trademarks of
The Crossroad Publishing Company

In continuation of our 200-year tradition of independent publishing, The Crossroad Publishing Company proudly offers a variety of books with strong, original voices and diverse per-
spectives. The viewpoints expressed in our books are not necessarily those of The Crossroad
Publishing Company, any of its imprints or of its employees. No claims are made or responsibility assumed for any health or other benefit.

Library of Congress Catalog information exactly as it appears in the email received.
Or Library of Congress Catalog information is on file.
ISBN 13: 978-0-82452585-9

Books published by The Crossroad Publishing Company may be purchased at special
quantity discount rates for classes and institutional use. For information, please email
info@CrossroadPublishing.com.

To

Miss Gertrude Best, devoted teacher, who gently guided me and countless others to fidelity in a hostile time and place; to Fr. John Hardon, S.J., the saintly catechist whose weekly classes formed my faith; and to Faye Tatum Ballard, the dearest and best of friends, whose love and support made this whole book possible.

Contents

Acknowledgments

My thanks to the editors at various magazines and Web sites that ran early or partial versions of many of the chapters included in this book. These include Inside-Catholic, TakiMag, *The American Conservative*, *Faith & Family*, FrontPageMag, and GodSpy. I would also like to thank my indulgent colleagues and students at the Thomas More College of the Liberal Arts, and my generous co-workers at the Intercollegiate Studies Institute. I also thank the countless priests and religious and lay activists who have helped me over the years to learn about and deepen the Catholic Faith that comes to us from the Apostles.

Bibliography

This book aims to edify sinners.
(So all of us *sind* Berliners.)
The sources I read
Amassed in my head
And spilled as it went to the printer's.

The erudite Fr. George Rutler
Elocutes like B. Wooster's butler.
His slim *Adam Danced*[1]
Left this reader entranced:
His analyses couldn't be subtler.

The *midrasher* Solomon Schimmel[2]
Goads *sinderkers* back toward *Himl*.
From Aquinas to Freud
All his means were employed
To *lemn* this *kunyehlemel*.

The faith-challenged Henry Fairlie[3]
Approaches iniquity charily.
He's brilliant with sources.
(He yokes them like horses.)
May his Particular Judgment go merrily.

Old *Catholic Encyclopedia!*[4]
Long hours I've thrilled just to be with her.
She's good for the brain,

---

1. George W. Rutler, *Adam Danced: The Cross and the Seven Deadly Sins* (Front Royal, VA: Christendom, 2004).
2. Solomon Schimmel, *The Seven Deadly Sins: Jewish, Christian, and Classical Reflections on Human Psychology* (Oxford, UK: Oxford University Press, 1997). *Midrasher* = one who analyses the meaning of the Torah; *sinderker* = sinner; *Himl* = heaven; *lemn* = teach; *kunyehlemel* = nebbish.
3. Henry Fairlie, *The Seven Deadly Sins Today* (Notre Dame, IN: University of Notre Dame Press, 1979).
4. *Catholic Encyclopedia* (New York: Encyclopedia Press, 1913), available on CD-ROM or at http://www.newadvent.org/cathen.

In the public domain,
And her rhetoric's tinted in sepia.

The prodigious Saint Thomas Aquinas[5]
Made Theology science's dynast.
When he found revealed Truth
He would wrangle a proof,
So for me he's the blanket of Linus.

Fourth-century Spaniard Prudentius[6]
Saw virtue and vice as contentious.
He depicted their feud,
In similes crude,
But at least he was never pretentious.

5. Fathers of the English Dominican Province, trans., *The Summa Theologica of St. Thomas Aquinas*, 2nd and rev. ed. (repr., Westminster, MD: Christian Classics, 1981). Online Edition Copyright © 2008 by Kevin Knight, available at http://www.newadvent.org/summa.
6. "The Battle for the Soul of Man (Psychomachia)," available at http://web.archive.org/web/20020429135514/http://www.richmond.edu/~wstevens/grvaltexts/psychomachia.html

Introduction

One way of describing the Seven Deadly Sins might be "the seven key areas of life where Jesus ruins our fun." By this, I mean the categories of normal human experience that make up the bulk of our lives—where our instincts, habits, and egos have patched together perfectly serviceable habits of schlepping through, day to day. We'd just as soon our coping strategies weren't disrupted by some fish-multiplying, wonder-working God-Man who speaks in riddles. But hey, thanks for thinking of us.

The book that you are holding covers subjects that are near and dear to my heart, as I know they are to yours—namely, Lust, Wrath, Vainglory, Sloth, Envy, Gluttony, and Greed. I've wondered what ordinary (i.e., fallen) human life would be like in their absence. Cable TV would certainly suffer. As the great dramatists always knew, "Trouble is interesting."

And at least on earth, the converse is also true. Given the annual crop of films and TV programs documenting World War II (see The Hitler Channel), it's worth wondering: Why aren't there more peace movies? Why are there no films about international crises that were successfully resolved without resort to arms—like the Fashoda Incident in 1898, which almost sparked a war between England and France over some godforsaken acres of sand in Sudan? Because the parties sat down together, argued out their differences, were amenable to compromise, and treated open warfare as the last resort. In other words, they followed just-war teaching, and the outcome should have been obvious: dull, dull, dull. I'm yawning already. The only decent film I can think of about an avoided war is *13 Days*, which pictured the Kennedy brothers' face-off with Nikita Khrushchev and warmongering U.S. generals during the Cuban missile crisis. I recommend the movie, if not the Kennedys.

As a fan of "alternative history" novels, I've often thought about writing one myself. Since our species' story is full of what-ifs, there are infinite opportunities. Most of the obvious ones have already been written: What if Germany had won World War II? What if Hitler had died in the trenches? What if the South had won the Civil War? What if the South Africans had used a time machine to furnish AK-47s to the Confederacy? Ho-hum. The one thing about all these books is that they echo the message of Professor Pangloss in Voltaire's timeless, worthless novel *Candide*: we live in the best of all possible worlds. Go back in history and change the course of events, and the outcome is sure to be either (a) exactly the same or (b) far worse than what really happened.

I'm not sure why novelists feel compelled to make these points, unless they're simply captives of the Whig theory of history: the notion that progress, while fitful,

Inspirational photo courtesy of Urban Mobility, GmbH.

is inevitable, and every hiccup, every genocide, is an unavoidable part of the providential march toward universal democracy, human rights, and consumerism. All of which, as Jeremy Bentham once observed, is "nonsense on a Segway."

Of course, there *were* events that could have turned out differently—and better. I could fill this book, and launch an entire series, listing them. Just for starters, well, the Spanish Armada could have landed.

But that was not the book I wanted to write. No, I've bent my agent's ear about the following lurid scenario: imagine how history would have turned out differently if . . . man hadn't fallen. The Bible and Church history would read quite differently. Wouldn't you love to hear about

- Cain and Abel shaking hands and making up;
- Isaac and Esau splitting the difference;
- the Pharaoh telling Moses, "*Mazel tov*";
- the Maccabees trading land for peace;
- Herod kneeling with the Magi at the manger;
- gladiators fighting it out in the coliseum with Nerf bats, and Christians tied up with bungee cords forced to play with cute little kittens?

(P.S. To publishers out there, *that* manuscript is still available, but the bidding war will soon put my expected advance out of your price range. So act now!)

Without "man's first disobedience," there isn't much of a story, and in light of that, I decided to start with sin. After working through the Seven Deadlies, I briefly considered other categories from the Catechism, like the "Sins that Cry Out to Heaven for Vengeance." Here they are with the relevant biblical verses, and the state and party affiliation of the U.S. senators most likely to promote them:

- Voluntary murder, Genesis 4:10 (D-NY)
- Sodomy, Genesis 18:20–21 (D-CA)
- Affliction of widows and orphans, Exodus 21–23 (R-MS)
- Cheating a laborer of his just wage, Deuteronomy 24–25 (R-SC)

Try as I might, I can't find much that's entertaining in any of these. This explains why I failed in my brief foray into writing speeches for politicians and why I turned next to thoughts of quite a different catalog: the Seven Corporal and the Seven Spiritual Works of Mercy. Together, they make up a fairly exhaustive list of the good deeds a Christian is expected to perform and will have to answer for, come the Day of Judgment. (Think of them as CliffsNotes for the exam.)

When faithful women found the empty tomb and came back to the apostles[7] to report the Resurrection, they also brought the following "to-do" list, which they'd found pinned to the the Shroud of Turin. Here it is, helpfully annotated:

The Seven Spiritual Works of Mercy

1. *Convert the sinner.* Make sure she doesn't convert you.
2. *Instruct the ignorant.* No evangelizing over the top of the bathroom stall.
3. *Counsel the doubtful.* But don't use phrases like, "Trust me."
4. *Comfort the sorrowful.* You think you got troubles? Check out this bunion!
5. *Bear wrongs patiently.* Count to very high numbers before you explode.
6. *Forgive injuries.* But insist on perfect contrition.
7. *Pray for the living and the dead.* "I'll pray for you . . . Bless your heart!"

The Seven Corporal Works of Mercy

1. *Feed the hungry.* Send Harry and David baskets.
2. *Give drink to the thirsty.* Buy kegs for college freshmen.
3. *Clothe the naked.* . . . with those Speedos you have no business wearing.
4. *Shelter the homeless.* Probably not in your guestroom.
5. *Visit the sick.* But leave your hand puppets at home.
6. *Visit those in prison.* But steer clear of the "conjugal trailer."
7. *Bury the dead.* Except not secretively, all around your property.

---

7. The men mostly hung back at the sight of this stunning miracle, except for Peter, who blundered right in, picked up the winding sheet ("First-class relic!"), and broke up the stones for sale at the Vatican gift shop.

But that's pretty much all I can find to say about them. And anyway, it seems a tad unbalanced to offer a catalog of evils without an offer of antidotes. So, at last, I decided to counterbalance each Deadly Sin with what theologians call its Contrary Virtue. Given the norms of our society, we might as well dub them the "Contrarian Virtues," since they cut straight across the grain of the way we live and even of our aspirations.

The flippant amoralism that made Oscar Wilde's plays so piquantly outrageous was once the province of isolated indi-

viduals—flamboyant aesthetes wearing green carnations, cynical statesmen who wrapped realpolitik in velvet platitudes, and sociopaths hammering rocks on chain gangs. The history of the twentieth century amounted, in one sense, to the mass marketing of such morals. This happened most obviously in sexual ethics. As Maggie Gallagher observed in her neglected classic of social criticism *Enemies of Eros*,[8] attitudes once reserved to corrupt elites and the underclass became common property in the 1960s, when bohemianism and egalitarianism met and had an affair. Their love child, the sexual revolution, was popularized in magazines like *Playboy* that encouraged the Everyman to adopt the mating behavior of decadent aristocrats seducing the likes of Eliza Doolittle. Both sexes of every age were taught to emulate the randomized randiness of the stereotypical sixteen-year-old boy.

The Elizas found their revenge, of course, in the form of modern feminism—a medley of toxic ideological elements patched together in service of righteous anger at the beastliness of men. Men like Hugh Hefner[9] really did deserve to have to listen

---

8. Maggie Gallagher, *Enemies of Eros* (Chicago: Bonus Books, 1989).
9. According to former Playmate Sandy Bentley (who served Hefner along with her sister), by the 1990s, "The heterosexual icon [Hugh Hefner] . . . had trouble finding satisfaction through inter-

to women like Betty Friedan, who famously compared her comfy suburban home to a concentration camp. But did the rest of us?

The fallout hit hardest the millions of women who were encouraged to forgo childbearing into late middle age so they could work alongside "organization men"—in the same tedious jobs those men tried to put out of their minds by reading . . . *Playboy*. How much more meaningful and serious is a life spent selling paper supplies in Scranton than one engaged in shaping human souls that were formed inside one's body? What a classic swindle—which served at once the Marxists who sought to apply the dialectic of class struggle to the family and the capitalists who wished to double the labor supply and abolish the family wage. (It's no accident, as Allan Carlson points out in *The American Way*,[10] that the sole moneyed sponsor of the Equal Rights Amendment, back in the 1920s, was the National Association of Manufacturers.) The "family wage"—a goal the Church had supported for over a century, which had been offered voluntarily by millions of employers—was outlawed as part of the Civil Rights Act. This, to my mind, outweighs the good done by the act in repressing racism.

Combine these new economic realities with the universal embrace of contraception, and none of us should be surprised at the plummeting birth rate in the West. As a wag (okay, it was me) once said, "If feminism were a plot to wipe out Europeans from the earth, how exactly would it look any different?" (Margaret Sanger developed birth control in the hope of weeding out everyone else, which leads me to believe that somehow, somewhere, her Screwtape is snickering; see Chapter 1.) But it wasn't the Eliza Doolittles who started the fight, even if they will finish it. In the form of aborted children, feminism worldwide has racked up a higher death toll than Nazism

and competes now with Communism. So pardon me if I'm reluctant to call Pope John Paul II's profound reflections on the dignity of women "new feminism," any more than I'll dub monasticism "Old Communism" or the German social market economy "Catholic National Socialism." It leaves a bad taste in my mouth.

---

course; instead, he liked the girls to pleasure each other while he masturbated and watched gay porn." See Benjamin Wallace, "The Prodigy and the Playmate," *Philadelphia*, June 2001, cited in Mercer Schuchardt, "Hugh Hefner's Hollow Victory," *Christianity Today*, November 1, 2003.

10. Allan Carlson, *The American Way* (Wilmington, DE: Intercollegiate Studies Institute, 2003).

Aware that such thoughts are countercultural—and not in the fun, friendly, "hippie-girl-who-smells-of-patchouli" way—I decided to plunge into the Seven Contrary Virtues that were listed alongside the sins in the funky, proto–sci-fi Christian epic *The Psychomachia* (or *War for the Soul*) by the fifth-century poet Prudentius. I'm reading a literal translation of this work, and it certainly ain't *The Aeneid*. In fact, it would read much better if it came as a graphic novel. But who can resist a poem that describes the battle for purity as follows?

> The next person to step out on the grassy field is Chastity, the virgin, shining in armor. Lust, who has come from Sodom, is armed with torches. The vice thrusts a burning pine knot dipped in sulfur and tar into the maiden's eyes. But without fear she strikes the hand with a stone and the blazing torch is knocked away. With only one thrust of her sword, she pierces the throat of the whore and stinking fumes with clots of blood are spat out; the foul breath poisons the nearby air.

That's enough to purify my own thoughts of hippie girls for some time to come. So I looked to Prudentius for my first guide to the virtues—keenly aware that more people read Dante's *Inferno* than his *Paradiso*. It's hard to see the fun, on the face of it, of reading in depth about the virtues. Done poorly, it could read like the lives of the saints, minus the fun stuff like bleeding relics and talking bears.

But have no fear! Just as for those of us who need them, there will be beagles in heaven, I tell you with the surety of Faith that in the virtues we can find snark—for those of us who need it.

The chapters that follow are paired, listing one of the systemic character flaws, or habitual vices, that Christian moralists (drawing on Jewish and Hellenistic sources) over the centuries came to call the Seven Deadly Sins, then the Contrary Virtue we're meant to cultivate instead. I list each poison along with the antidote.

Now here's where it gets a little complicated. Tracing the spectrum from Virtue to Vice requires a delicate moral calculus, and as Barbie said, math is hard! As all good Thomists know—which means that nowadays, it's practically a secret—you can't just take a Vice and look for the opposite extreme, then tag that as a Virtue. Otherwise, the Contrary Virtue to Lust would be Frigidity, and the cure for Wrath would be a steady course of cringing, fawning Servility. In trying to resist a Deadly Sin, we take the crooked timber of our humanity and try to train it the other way—countering Lust with ascetical practices that remind the flesh who is boss or Wrath with slow, deliberate actions meant to school our will in Patience. Aristotle described this as like bending back a stick to get it straight. However, it's possible to bend the stick too far—for instance, leaping from Sloth to Fanaticism, without ever stopping at healthy Diligence, passing Go, or collecting $200. For instance, someone countering Sloth shouldn't do so by becoming a workaholic. Nor should Lustful people try to rip out their sexuality, root and branch. We're not meant to binge and purge. Our Lord really doesn't want us to cut off our nose to spite our face.

A healthy conscience avoids the extreme of laissez-faire laxity on the left, and self-destructive scrupulosity on the right. Likewise, each Contrary Virtue lives somewhere between a Deadly Sin and what we moderns might call a neurosis:

Vice	Virtue	Neurosis
Lust	Chastity	Frigidity
Wrath	Patience	Servility
Gluttony	Temperance	Insensibility
Greed	Generosity	Prodigality
Sloth	Diligence	Fanaticism
Vainglory	Humility	Scrupulosity
Envy	Magnanimity	Pusillanimity

In each case, we seek what Aristotelians call the Golden Mean. Each Contrary Virtue stands not just between two extreme modes of behavior but *above* them—reconciling the partial truths they exaggerate in a higher synthesis that points to Truth. To determine where the pursuit of a Contrary Virtue shades off into a Neurosis, we lean on the Church's wisdom, remembering that, if some interpretation of Scripture we've come upon sounds too extreme, to the point of lunacy, it usually is.

Before doing violence to yourself, get advice from a trusted priest. Indeed, the Church insists we get permission for something as simple as fasting, to prevent us from harming ourselves through misguided, shortsighted zeal. (Some saints, like Ignatius Loyola, did permanent damage to their health this way and came to bitterly repent their penances.)

Throughout this book, with each pair of opposing Vices and Virtues, the reader will face a quiz—not on the names, dates, and concepts gleaned while skimming the text in the rest room, but rather on where he[11] lands on the spectrum of Virtue/Vice/ Neurosis. If you find yourself on the Golden Mean that hangs in tension between the two, you're safely marching the "straight and narrow" path that leads to Heaven. Or else you're lying on the quiz. But that's between you and your confessor. If this book accomplishes nothing else, I hope it sends people trooping off to those curious wooden booths that are open for approximately fifteen minutes every Saturday

---

11. The author is aware that the generic "he" is considered offensive by many and also that women buy most books that don't somehow involve World War II or motorcycle repair. He employs it throughout simply to irritate people.

afternoon at local Catholic parishes to talk to the well-educated celibates who sit in them, playing Sudoku. These men dedicate their whole lives—and several chunks of each weekend—to the service of souls. As it stands, most of the folks who stir themselves every Saturday come to confess the sins of their grandchildren, by which I mean you. Why not show up sometime and give your side of the story? Sure, it isn't exactly therapy. For one thing, it's free. For another, you climb out with absolution, not a prescription—and much better side effects, in my experience.

Now the emphasis placed throughout on keeping to the Golden Mean might strike some readers as surprising. Is it really as dangerous to engage in misguided zeal as to indulge in a Deadly Sin? Usually not, in the short run. The man who represses Lust by suppressing every trace of his sexuality is surely better off than the guy who "lets off steam" in some stranger's Jacuzzi. But Frigidity doesn't wear well; it's typically brittle, and when a sinner's resolve snaps in half, the results are rarely pretty. In James Joyce's *A Portrait of the Artist as a Young Man*, the hero, Stephen Dedalus, was scared out of his habit of visiting whorehouses by a hellfire sermon he heard on retreat. To fight temptation, he squelched all sexual feelings (not easy for a teenager), channeling them into endlessly repeated, (Adrian) monklike religious practices. He kept himself pure for a while by means of theological OCD,[12] but the effort so strained his spirit that he grabbed the first chance he could to flee the Faith. Even vowed celibates are not meant to quash every trace of eros from the soul but rather to sublimate it and offer it up to God. Likewise, Martin Luther's violent scruples about his unworthiness to celebrate Mass were the fuel for his final rejection of the Eucharist.

St. Thomas Aquinas himself warned of the danger of overreacting to the Deadly Sins—or needlessly cutting off one's hand or plucking out one's eye instead of soberly learning to use it properly:

Whatever is contrary to a natural inclination is a sin, because it is contrary to a law of nature. Now everything has a natural inclination to

___

12. In this context, I refer to obsessive-compulsive disorder rather than Order of Carmelites Discalced.

accomplish an action that is commensurate with its power: as is evident in all natural things, whether animate or inanimate. Now just as presumption makes a man exceed what is proportionate to his power, by striving to do more than he can, so pusillanimity makes a man fall short of what is proportionate to his power, by refusing to tend to that which is commensurate thereto. Wherefore as presumption is a sin, so is pusillanimity. Hence it is that the servant who buried in the earth the money he had received from his master, and did not trade with it through fainthearted fear, was punished by his master. (Mt 25; Lk 19; *Summa Theologica* II: 2, 133)

When we are talking about character Virtues—such as the seven that are opposed to the Deadly Sins—moderation and prudence are the keywords, and extremes are typically dangerous. But the theological virtues are a horse of a different feather. Faith, Hope, and Charity don't spring up out of our natures but are outright gifts of God, poured into the soul. While the practice of these virtues must be governed by reason, they often will call us to do things that seem—and are—extreme. Think of St. Francis standing naked before his bishop or Joan of Arc tied to the stake. The sanest man in Renaissance Europe, Sir Thomas More,  chose martyrdom over compromise and was widely condemned at the time as a reckless fanatic—mostly by those who'd preferred their skins to their souls.

Compared to Faith, Hope, and Charity, the Golden Mean is a fourteen-karat electroplate, a gaudy distraction from God's own mysterious gifts. The answer to a clash between fanatical faith and violent atheism isn't lukewarm religiosity—no matter what your RCIA[13] facilitator taught you during the puppet shows. Instead, we should take the portions we're given of Faith, Hope, or Charity and seek through prayer and study to purify rather than dilute them. A deeper Faith, grounded in Hope and infused with Charity, is the answer to fanaticism. A self-righteous Catholic Pharisee probably needs to spend more time ladling soup to beggars—instead of mincing off to join the Units at the Unitarian Church . . . you know, the one in the really posh neighborhood that sports a rainbow flag made out of hemp.

If our Lord's words on the "lukewarm" are to be believed—and given what happened to the Gadarene swine, I'm not inclined to argue with Him—those who

---

13. Repelling Converts In-Advertently.

follow Goldilocks's recipe for heating up their souls will end as Dante predicted, sloshing around unworthily outside the gates of Hell. Now it's true that this book is meant to help its readers stay out of Hell . . . but even bad Catholics should aim just a little bit higher than that.

Of course—just to make matters more complicated—our attempts at practicing Faith, Hope, and Charity can never violate the four "cardinal virtues." That list (another list!) of virtues, which St. Thomas Aquinas gleefully adopted from Aristotle, runs as follows: Temperance, Fortitude, Justice, and Prudence. I won't explain them all here (read Josef Pieper's *The Four Cardinal Virtues*—it's much more fun than it sounds). But just to get you started: Justice is what each of us owes the other in an unconditional debt. We cannot violate that Justice in pursuit of Faith, Hope, or Charity. When we contemplate any action that stokes in us the sentiment that we're being "more radically Christian" and really "living the gospel" by going beyond "merely natural" virtues, every alarm bell in our conscience should start going off. We can no more attain theological virtues by violating the natural ones than we can build the dome on a cathedral by pulling steel from its foundations. Whatever we achieve that way will amount to blind Faith, false Hope, or bankrupt Charity. While the genuine articles are infused directly by God, such counterfeits are cobbled together out of one-sided theology and our sentiments.

We cannot practice Charity toward the poor through confiscation from the rich; only if something is owed the poor in simple Justice should the state make sure they get it (as Pope Leo XIII taught in *Rerum Novarum*). At the height of the high Middle Ages, the Church never furthered the salvation of souls by confiscating non-Christian children, baptizing them, and rearing them in the Faith. At age eighteen I wondered why not, until a wise priest explained to me that the natural rights of pagan parents could not be torn away in such a "higher cause." As the Church learned during the sex abuse crisis, the natural rights of parents to defend their children from rape cannot be sacrificed on the altar of priestly solidarity, compassion for "troubled brother priests," or the need to avoid bad publicity for the Church.

I'm aware that, in the course of this book, I am liable to make the reader more or less uncomfortable at times, for instance, when you take one of my Trademark-Busting *Cosmo*-Style Quizzes™ and it turns out that your favorite unexamined habit is a symptom of one of the Deadly Sins. Sorry about that. But it really is better to find out such things on this side of the grave—or so says every apparition of the Holy Souls from Purgatory. At other times, the reader will cringe at my recital of the crimes racked up by one of the role models for a Deadly Sin. (One colleague told me, tactfully, that my account of famous Gluttons made him lose his appetite for ortolans.) Again, that comes with the territory.

I hope the sensitive reader will pardon me if sometimes he encounters illustrations that seem offensive. Tromping through the seven sorts of sin that bedevil the human race never promised to be pretty, and without comparing (see Vainglory) my literary significance in any way to Dante's, I'd like to point out in advance that readers of the *Inferno* will face the following:

- Gluttons stuck face down in mud, eating refuse
- Profligates running endlessly from packs of vicious, feral dogs
- Blasphemers, sodomites, and usurers cowering under fire that rains from heaven
- Pimps and seducers on an unending death march, led by devils
- Flatterers sloshing around in a sea of human waste
- Crooked politicians in a vat of boiling tar
- The prophet Mohammed torn bodily into pieces
- A treacherous count gnawing forever on the skull of the traitorous bishop who starved the count and his children to death
- The apostle Judas being chewed in the mouth of Satan, while his back is perpetually skinned by the devil's claws

Next to that, my illustrative stories of sinners and scandals are a game of Chutes and Ladders played by Pollyanna, Tintin, and Little Lord Fauntleroy in Eloise's suite at the Plaza.

Nevertheless, to any reader who takes offense at one of my illustrations or whose feelings are hurt by my gallows humor, let me offer this preemptive apology and suggest a way for you to get your money's worth out of this book.

Think of the person who most gets on your nerves with the scruples he likes to share, who spams you with email sob stories, or sniffs disgustedly at your jokes. You know, the person who makes you bite your tongue for fear of piercing his preternaturally thin skin. . . . *Put this book down right away, find some really tasteful wrapping paper, wrap the book up, and give it to him.*

1

Lusting for the Suburbs

Of the seven areas of life where fallen man might say Jesus spoils our fun, the subject of sex is one where He intervenes the least. Wistful, liberal Catholics like to point out that Christ spent much more time on earth denouncing the rich than the randy. Such people are missing the point: when it came to sexuality, Christ didn't need to make matters much worse for us poor, fallen primates. It's true that the light of the Resurrection—a high beam it seems the Church doesn't know how to switch off—shows up the shabbiness of man's very best sexual shortcuts, like divorce, polygamy, and fantasy. We squint a bit, zip up, and stare down at our shoes.

But Creation was already painful enough; Redemption simply tightened a couple of screws, so we couldn't squirm out of the fundamental dilemma posed by sex's very nature: we want it to serve our day-to-day personal happiness, and it wants to do something else entirely. In the "fallen" state that we received this hand-me-down, the sex instinct is less like a tool we use to build our home than the tectonic plate that rumbles underneath it.

The standard account of what moralists have always, through clenched teeth, described as Lust is that it's the inordinate, excessive, or misdirected desire for sexual pleasure. Okay, whatever. That sounds like it only applies to "home wreckers" angling to be trophy wives, or the kind of guy who spends his days downloading videos of Japanese girls in Catholic school uniforms. If those were the only people whose cravings were "inordinate," the rest of us could kick back and find happiness doing what comes naturally.

Yeah, that works real well. See you in family court. I can't wait for the long-delayed launch of EWTN-2, its entertainment channel. I've applied to produce their first reality show, *Annulment Court.* "Live from the Roman Rota. . . ."

What's more, the old, moralistic account understates what we seek from sex. If what you want is short-term pleasure, ecstatic moments of seamy bliss—hey, it's out there. But not even teenage boys are long satisfied with that. "Catholic feminist" chastity advocates are fooling themselves when they claim that women look for love, but their quest for lifelong tenderness is frustrated by men (who, by the way, are beasts). If that were true, then the sexes really would be natural enemies, doomed to mate—cobras and mongooses who called an occasional truce so they could "hook up."

No, we are each looking for something much more elusive than pleasure. What we want is happiness—day-to-day satisfaction, order and quiet, leisure time, regular bouts of pleasure, and peaceful companionship. That's what we "lust" for—and battle nature, tooth and claw, trying to get.

Now, those of you who are happily married, with a sexual relationship that's satisfying and untroubled, who find no difficulty balancing the fleshly cravings and fathomless feelings of two human beings . . . well, I'm not talking to you.

Y'all who put the *Theology of the Body* into practice, who cheerfully welcome the gift of new life whenever it explodes into your home—or who find it painless, for "just and rational reasons," to practice natural family planning . . . well, why don't you just skip this chapter, m'kay? Just go on back to your houseful of little von Trapps and teach the kids to sing another Mozart opera or build a miniature Chartres in the yard out of Popsicle sticks. Go on, scoot!

For some of us—for instance, a goodly slice of unmarried males—when we hear chipper sermons that call sexuality "one of God's greatest gifts," we smile thinly and try not to snark back, "Where's the counter where I can go exchange it? Like, for a sweater?"

I don't think I'm lapsing into Gnosticism when I say that, for much of mankind, sexuality is less like a big, shiny present left for us by a loving Father than a dose of poison ivy that lasts for decades—which it's a mortal sin to scratch. In the modern West, most of us mature so slowly that marriage before the age of thirty seems almost suicidally rash. You can't support a family on one income, and children need decades and decades of expensive education before they can move briefly out of your home—then return to live on your couch while they "figure things out."

Things weren't always so impossible. Some of the problems here are the side effects of technology—by which I mean machines that help us do what we want. Doing so frequently blows up in our face, since *what we want*—and let me emphasize this point, which seems essential to understanding Creation—*is entirely beside the point.*

The natural order is blithely unconcerned with our happiness; our bodies are built with the family's and hence the species' best interest in mind. So, by nature, we barrel bedward with all the zest of salmon swimming upstream to spawn—with the same results. Have you ever seen the battered state of those fish at the end of their selfless, frantic fight against the current, over rocks, up hills, and over dams—their tattered skin, broken fins, and glassy stares? They look like parents emerging, drained and dazed, from Chuck E. Cheese.

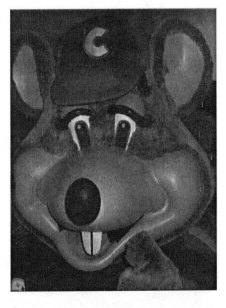

No wonder modern man, having figured out biological means to skip that whole, exhausting slog, prefers to live in a fish farm. We'd rather subsist like those shiny, bloated salmon that slurp around in corporate hatcheries, chowing down on niblets of corn, staying "healthy" with regular doses of hormones and antibiotics, and using Red Dye No. 2 to keep our flesh nice and pink. Our offspring are fewer but fatter. We may not build up all those healthy omega nutrients that the authorities say would make us "better fish." So what? We might not turn out as complex or courageous—but our "effort to pleasure" ratio is a whole lot better.

In the "old days"—and still today in countries that don't have air-conditioning or bear examining—we didn't face this tempting choice. Nor was unassuageable sexual frustration the normal state for men and women, for decades running. People's sexual maturity pretty much launched them into a state historians refer to as

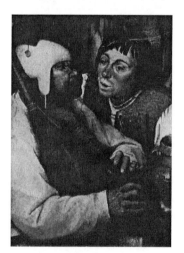

"adulthood." People got randy, so they got married. Children worked from a young age at tasks on the farm or in family shops and learned skills that put them in good stead to feed and house the little ones they would soon enough be producing. Parents saw in additional offspring extra hands to help around the household, whose labor would more than compensate the cost of their upkeep. What is more, the children they raised would be their mainstay and support when they grew too old to work. Sure, sometimes boys and girls would get into mischief before they were married—but that's why God made shotguns.

Men were still disposed by their fallen nature toward polygamy—but most of them could barely support a single wife, so the point was moot. Divorce entailed disgrace, but men and women alike knew that a wife's chance of dying in childbirth was high—so each had some reason for hope. Fertility was pretty much out of our hands, but it was kept in balance by the old-school method of natural family planning: infant mortality.

It's true that the women aged pretty quickly. (In the blue-collar neighborhood where I come from, brides still seem to gain fifty pounds at the reception.) But on a diet of turnips and potatoes, spiced with the occasional slow-moving weasel and washed down by vodka, the men didn't exactly mellow like Paul Newman, either. Indeed, by age twenty-five, pretty much everyone looked like something out of a Brueghel painting, and by thirty, they became a lot of Bosch. Five years later, most of them died. So it all worked pretty well.

At least, there was a certain harmony between the desires of the average man, the culture in which he lived, and the needs of the species. The whole structure of things—from regular famines to periodic invasions by Asiatic hordes—made clear to nearly everyone just how low in the cosmic hierarchy his own desires ranked.

It's not surprising that, as soon as we could figure out how to rebel against such an arrangement, we would. And, as usual, we didn't know where to stop.

As late as 1920, most users of contraception were prostitutes. By 1968, contraception was the norm among married Catholics. This wasn't so much an explosion of unfathomable evil as a giddy attempt to tame biology and make it "play nice" with our desires. And now we're finding out that, as usual, nature wins—if only by default, as wild salmon outbreed us farm-fed fish. In fifty years, demographers predict, Europe will be largely populated by Muslims—who by then will have a birth rate of 1.2 children per couple, I predict.

There are plenty of cultural conservatives and many Catholics who'd like to see us return to a more natural way of life. They urge us back to the land, to renounce not just contraceptives but also Botox, iPads, and maybe Novocain. But most of us won't go willingly. If it turns out that the geniuses in charge of our banks, bureaucracies, and borders really have plunged our continent back to the status quo of, say, 1492, I will make a final pilgrimage back to the Holy City. I'll climb the stairs of the Chrysler Building, bring along my laptop, and I'll keep on watching YouTube till the Wi-Fi flickers out.

News Flash: Women Incapable of Sin!

When the subject of Lust pops up, men typically bear the blame. Male sexuality is more outgoing and (ahem) external than female and, to careless Christians, can seem somehow more deeply fallen. The fact of sexual difference—which God created and judged as "good," and He's entitled to His opinion—leads some addled Catholic moralists to try reanimating the corpse of Queen Victoria. The zombie they revive is the late Romantic stereotype of men as lustful predators and women as hapless victims—a notion that would have puzzled such biblical figures as Samson and John the Baptist. (St. Augustine would just have laughed.) But guilt-soaked modern Catholic men who've misread their Mariology can fall victim to the self-styled "New Feminists" who peddle such twaddle, typically by appealing to their chivalry. I saw this botched experiment performed before my eyes in the course of a single dinner.

There we were, the four of us: myself; an academic colleague of mine; a sixty-something, salt o' the earth, sarcastic Yankee pastor; and a smart Midwestern seminarian on the brink of ordination. The beer was flowing freely—into my glass, anyway—and we were having the kind of conversation laymen have with priests these days—which means that topics arose that I'm confident never came up between clergy and laity in previous centuries. In contexts like this, I feel a little uncomfortable, constrained to somehow convey the following points:

- I know you're not one of the "bad ones." Isn't it a shame how a few pervy priests and a lot of feckless bishops put good men like you under a shadow?
- I know you don't say the traditional liturgy, but I hope you'll consider it, since it really is a superior expression of the meaning of the sacrament to the Novus Ordo, which is all you've ever said. Not that there's anything wrong with that.
- I've got a pretty good idea how thankless, lonely, and tough your job really is. We really do appreciate you guys. Here, let me pick up the check.
- No, I don't have a vocation. If we talked for another half an hour, you wouldn't ask.

In the course of the evening, a topic came up that rang certain alarm bells and almost got me pounding on the table. It was nothing doctrinal; the "heresy computer" that Rev. John Hardon, S.J., soldered into my head didn't register anything dangerous. (By contrast, when I went to the campus ministry in college, the dang thing kept going off like a Geiger counter at Chernobyl.)

Instead, the issue at hand was something pastoral and subtle. Normally, that's the kind of thing I'd miss. Indeed, as I've always said of my taste in art and apologetics, "Hulk no *like* subtlety. It confuse him. Then it make him MAD."

Perhaps because it's an intellectual mistake I've made myself—and paid for in tears and treasure—this error upset and alarmed me, like finding the head of a rat floating in my soup. It's hard to just eat around it.

We were talking about the prevalence of abortion and its root causes in modern sexual behavior. We'd already agreed on quite a bit: that women got a raw deal in the sexual revolution, which touted the horn-dog fantasies of adolescent boys as the model of "liberated" behavior. We agreed that feminism was, in a sense, the bloody revenge—insisting on legal abortion so young women could equal the field with men and minimize the consequences of promiscuity. We agreed that many of the women who have abortions pay a terrible psychological price.

So far, so good. But then the seminarian offered this theory, which I'm paraphrasing as closely as I can:

"Women who have premarital sex and abortions are only looking for love. Most of them had poor relationships with their fathers, and they're seeking substitutes for the paternal love they never had. And men take advantage of that. That's why if we're going to change the abortion culture, it's going to have to be men whose attitudes we change. Men have to take responsibility for this, and they have to be the ones who learn how to say 'no' to premarital sex."

This earnest, orthodox gentleman who studied in Rome and who's willingly embracing lifelong celibacy and practical poverty to serve the Church—which is more than I'd ever do—had clearly been doing his reading. Indeed, he sounded like he was reading off a script from some pious text or other he'd been assigned at a pastoral seminar by well-meaning "pro-life feminists."

To this, I responded, "What planet are you from?"

Which kind of stopped the conversation cold. It's a good thing I was prepared with a two-minute monologue, detailing all the many shades and colors of utter nonsense he'd just uttered. In sum, I said (less eloquently, I bet), "Granted, there are women who blunder into premarital sex because they're exploited by older or more sophisticated men who lie to them, who promise a lifelong commitment in return for a one-night stand. And some of those girls get pregnant, feel abandoned, and have abortions.

"But is that really the average profile of a woman who has premarital sex—a clueless, damaged damsel who isn't driven by any sexual desires of her own but instead is searching for pure and perfect love, dragged down by the grubby cravings of filthy men? Is the average unmarried American woman—who is, by all accounts, 'sexually active'—an emotional basket case whose father left her wounded, vulnerable to exploitation by heartless, Y-chromosomed hedonists? If so, she is barely culpable for any sexual sins—and hardly to be blamed for having an abortion. We should treat her purely as a victim and not as a rational adult with free will who committed a sin. Why bother to absolve her—much less excommunicate her?[1] Is this the outcome of the pro-life insistence that we never foresee any legal penalty for women who have abortions, only the doctors? If so, the price is too high."

Then I asked the seminarian, "Have you ever dated? In fact, have you *met* any women? The ones I've known don't fit that description—including the ones who don't practice perfect Chastity.

---

1. Excommunication is the automatic, ipso facto punishment for anyone who procures, performs, or directly enables an abortion.

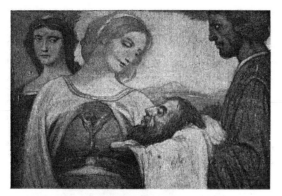

BLESS
YOUR HEART,
Tramp!
and Other Southern Endearments

CELIA RIVENBARK
AUTHOR OF We're Just Like You, Only Prettier

"In my limited experience, women have sexual desires, too. They are capable of making rational decisions and should be held responsible for them—just like men. Why do they go out and have sex when they know they shouldn't? Here's a theory: Original Sin. And about your idea of making men the gatekeepers, expecting that (since women are pretty much helpless) it's going to fall to guys to be the new enforcers of Chastity. . . . Good luck with that one."

The pastor turned to the seminarian. "Just wait till you hear some confessions," he said and went back to his soup.

And now you can see why I don't get invited out to dinner very often. But at least I picked up the check.

By the way, the title of this section isn't original. It comes from a priceless book by Celia Rivenbark, who, because she is Southern, would have treated the seminarian much more tactfully than I did. She would have said, "Sweetie, you need to watch yourself some *soaps.*"

Role Model: Margaret Sanger

When we're thinking about the Deadly Sins, it helps to use examples. It's too easy for theological writers to sling around Abstractions with Capital Letters, as if with each stroke of the pen they're tapping into Plato's realm of changeless, ineffable Forms, or if they're writing in German, where all nouns start with capitals. A friend of mine used to write weekly for the estimable investigatory journal the *Wanderer*. Founded by German-Catholic immigrants, it was published *auf Deutsch* well into the twentieth century. As my friend recalled, "The editors were, I think, waiting for the rest of the country to catch up with them. At last they admitted that this was unlikely and agreed to translate the paper. But they kept on as their typesetter someone named Uncle Otto, who for years insisted on capitalizing every noun."

At least, that's the story. Such Teutonic stub-
bornness served the *Wanderer*'s editors well
in the wake of Vatican II, as the newspaper
became a snout-rapper—whose reports,
as Archbishop Rembert Weakland
whines in his memoirs,[2] were what
Joseph Cardinal Ratzinger used to
roll up and smack heretical bishops
on the nose. I urge all to subscribe.

But capitalizing your Concepts in
order to give them an Air of spurious
Authority will only take you so far
in this world—as far as "B-minus,"
which I learned back in freshman rhetoric class at a staunchly secular school.
So I've decided to give the Virtues and
Vices a little flesh, to fatten them up for
the reader, so he'll remember how they look,
sound, and even smell.

As a young pro-life polemicist, I made great hay
out of the scathingly elitist statements[3] made by the founder of Planned Parenthood,
Margaret Sanger, whose program of eugenics directly influenced Hitler and led to
laws in a dozen or so American states, forcibly sterilizing or even castrating thousands of the "unfit" who flunked primitive IQ tests. I hoped that such a rhetorical
attack might undermine liberal support for abortion.

It didn't. Sometimes it sowed doubt about the motives of my opponents, but I've
never seen it change anyone's mind—any more than someone who is solidly pro-
life would change his convictions if he came to believe in the spurious claim made
in that airport classic *Freakonomics* that abortion helps cut crime. Here's one problem with this tactic: attacking an organization that aborts hundreds of thousands of

2. Archbishop Rembert Weakland, *Pilgrim in a Pilgrim Church* (Grand Rapids, MI: Wm. B. Eerdmans
   Publishing, 2009).
3. Here's just one: "Our failure to segregate morons who are increasing and multiplying . . .
   demonstrates our foolhardy and extravagant sentimentalism. . . . [Philanthropists] encourage the
   healthier and more normal sections of the world to shoulder the burden of unthinking and indiscriminate fecundity of others; which brings with it, as I think the reader must agree, a dead weight of
   human waste. Instead of decreasing and aiming to eliminate the stocks that are most detrimental to
   the future of the race and the world, it tends to render them to a menacing degree dominant. . . . We
   are paying for, and even submitting to, the dictates of an ever-increasing, unceasingly spawning class
   of human beings who never should have been born at all"; Margaret Sanger, *The Pivot of Civilization*
   (New York: Brentano's Publishers, 1922), 116, 122, 189. For many more see Robert G. Marshall
   and Charles A. Donovan, *Blessed Are the Barren: The Social Policy of Planned Parenthood* (San
   Francisco: Ignatius, 1991).

children every year because it might, just *might*, be a little racist is a joke in very poor taste—like denouncing Hitler for destroying German typography.[4]

There's only a limited usefulness in focusing on Sanger's racist positions, and not only because a host of other Americans held onto crackpot eugenicist theories in her day. Indeed, she was one of the main figures helping to spread such ideas. Far being from a passive recipient of a tainted cultural commonplace, Sanger crusaded to inform American WASPs of the "genetic threat" posed by Southern Europeans, Jews, blacks, and other races.

No, the problem is that most people realize that racial eugenics aren't really at the heart of what Planned Parenthood does today—whatever grim racial anxieties might stir in the souls of Botoxed Republican hags who send that organization checks. As Robert G. Marshall and Charles A. Donovan document in their definitive history of the birth control movement, *Blessed Are the Barren*, Sanger began as a sexual radical and libertine, a close associate of early sexologist Havelock Ellis. A wife who abandoned her husband and young children to travel Europe and conduct a series of casual affairs, Sanger was an apostle of "free love" before the term was even invented. Her philosophical inspiration was not Houston Stuart Chamberlain but the Marquis de Sade.

Sanger had been campaigning for sexual license for years before she discovered the handy "wedge" issue of Anglo anxiety over the rise of other ethnic groups. A

savvy political activist, she trumped up a minor panic over "dysgenic" births and "hereditary" criminality in order to break down the social taboo against even discussing birth control. Such squeamishness prevailed among most Protestants before the Anglican Council of Lambeth broke the dam and, in 1930, offered the first tentative approval of contraception in the history of Christendom. As *Blessed Are the Barren* shows in exhausting detail, Sanger used the tribal fear of displacement on the part of Protestant elites to undermine their theological position—which they'd inherited from Luther, Calvin, and Augustine. Odd as it sounds today, Sanger *used racism to make birth control respectable*. Of course, given the numbers of men like my grandfather who were arriving every day, Anglo Protestants had good reason to fear displacement. Instead of antihuman measures like sterilization, they should have looked to immigration

---

4. Which he did. That cool Gothic typeface called "fraktur" that appeared in German books printed before the 1930s . . . Hitler eliminated it, as he did the medieval architecture of Rotterdam and Warsaw.

control—and so Congress did in 1926. Americans had a perfect right to enact such laws if they chose on whatever grounds seemed prudent to them. They had no right to neuter immigrants like pets.

Sanger abandoned the race issue pretty readily. As the Nazi crimes against humanity were exposed after World War II, Sanger dropped her Klan hood like last year's hat and donned the white coat of a futurist: she "discovered" that the reason birth control was so urgently important was not the swelling ranks of dusky Sicilians and blacks but rather the "population explosion." Without missing a beat, her organization shifted its rhetoric and provoked another panic—one that, ironically enough, has helped contracept the European peoples to the brink of extinction. Experts like Paul Erhlich appeared on the *Tonight Show* with Johnny Carson predicting mass famines throughout the 1970s and the collapse of civilization. Their warnings never came true, but what did it matter? The "meme" had taken root and pushed forward Planned Parenthood's agenda; indeed, it was the Rockefeller Commission's infamous report on population that helped sway Justice Blackmun to change his position on abortion and write the decision in *Roe v. Wade*.

All of this is not to say that there is no limit to human population or that no response was necessary to the happy collapse in infant mortality that marked the late nineteenth century. Ironically, the Catholic Church moved to accommodate this reality by the mid-twentieth century, approving the use of a method of family planning that worked with (instead of against) the Natural Law and relied on occasional self-denial rather than hormones and surgery. Doctrine often develops in response to heresies; we wouldn't have the Nicene Creed without the Arians who denied the divinity of Christ. What is more, the Church moved much more quickly to offer a measured, realistic response to this new development than it had on previous issues, such as usury. Sadly, too few Christians bother to think about the moral implications of technologically interfering with fertility—and in doing so, they align themselves with the likes of Sanger against the Fathers (and Reformers) of their own churches.

The fact is that Sanger and her followers cynically exploited racial anxieties for almost thirty years to promote their agenda of sexual liberation—before changing tactics. If we can cite those old disgraceful pamphlets to teach our contemporaries not to trust this organization, I don't see why we shouldn't. But we ought not to expect too much.

There's a deeper issue buried beneath all the filth of racism, lies, and promiscuity in which Planned Parenthood sank its roots, and it is this: the old Whig vision of an America that could do without Faith or even the Virtues was never more than a fantasy. The "invisible hand" of the free market can help generate wealth, but it does not produce "spontaneous order" in society; in fact, without the constraints of deep religious piety and common cultural codes, competitors in the market economy resemble less the Bees of Mandeville's "Fable" than the termites that eat away the load-bearing walls of your house. When Western elites began to apply the implications of their own individualist ideology to matters of the heart, the result was the near-total collapse of the family. As the decadence that infected coteries like Margaret Sanger's and Alfred Kinsey's filtered down into the middle classes and then into the poor, the results should have been predictable.

By the middle 1960s, reality began to kick down the door. Urban pathologies, funded and made possible by a judgment-free welfare state, began to make the best American cities unlivable. In embracing attitudes toward sex that erode any self-restraint and demean the sanctity of marriage, Western elites had unleashed social problems that would haunt their grandchildren: an epidemic of illegitimacy, a massive dependent underclass, and shattered families that bred children afraid of commitment, who in turn would fail to reproduce themselves.

The blithe rejection at once of biology and morality that underlay Sanger's call for "liberation" of "the sex instinct" was incompatible with a free society. On some level she knew this, which is why she was more than willing to use the coercive power of the state to neuter, control, and selectively breed the unruly poor. All this was in service of her squalid, upper-middle class dream, which was dramatized best by the dreary, wife-swapping couples of Ang Lee's *The Ice Storm*. Some libertarians profess puzzlement that prosperous leftists support at once social libertinism and a pervasive bureaucratic nanny state—seeing here a philosophical inconsistency. Maybe so. But in the real world, a state without the private virtues can only survive through the continual growth of an all-knowing, all-seeing state. If you want to live like the Marquis de Sade, you will end up (as he did) inside the Bastille.

Just one more thing: Some jaded dissident Catholics and bitter ultratraditionalists claim not to see much difference between Sanger's panacea, contraception, and the Church's approved means of spacing children, natural family planning. As I pointed out in *The Bad Catholic's Guide to Good Living*[5] (available on Amazon, and be sure not to waste your money on any of those tainted, "used" copies that may have been read in the *bathroom* by dozens of strangers), the contrast is stark. I'll use one of those analogies that were so much fun on the SATs:

Natural family planning is to contraception as dieting is to_____.

    a. skiing   O
    b. sushi   O
    c. Lithuania O
    d. bulimia   O

Be sure to use a No. 2 pencil and entirely fill in the oval for answer "d."

---

5. John Zmirak and Denise Matychowiak, *The Bad Catholic's Guide to Good Living* (New York: Crossroad, 2005).

Licensing Lust, Canonizing Kinsey

If Sanger provided the technical know-how to strip sexuality of its biological purpose, it took Dr. Alfred Kinsey to convince ordinary Americans that once-shunned acts of perversions are only "natural." If you're like me, you might have heard of Kinsey in passing and thought of him primarily as "some guy who got mentioned in a Cole Porter song." But millions of middlebrow Netflix junkies now know all about the good doctor, who was canonized, almost deified, in the 2005 biopic *Kinsey*. As one promo poster says of Kinsey, "Where there was darkness, he brought light." You know, like Christ (as is seen in John 1:5). The "light," it seems, is Lust.

The film pictures Kinsey as a redemptive figure who suffers at the hands of Pharisees, in pursuit of the simple truth that will set men free. It doesn't hurt that he's portrayed by the gifted Liam Neeson—already sainted in the public mind as the guy who saved Ben Kingsley from that Nazi, Ralph Fiennes. Neeson competes with Tom Hanks and Jim Cavaziel for the Oscar in the category "Most Messianic Face."

Kinsey's passion begins with a brutal upbringing by a puritanical father, who preached a stern fundamentalism to a church full of Indiana bluenoses and sadists. Kinsey grows into a solitary, emotionally repressed researcher, the classic "man in the white jacket," heroically devoted to knowledge instead of personal advancement. The work of the first half of his life is collecting gall wasps on pins and classifying them in dusty tomes. When he meets his young and extremely understanding wife, they encounter a sexual difficulty that gets Kinsey thinking. After two young newlyweds come to him for advice and display their astounding erotic naiveté, Kinsey awakens to the fact that human sexual behavior had never been studied as

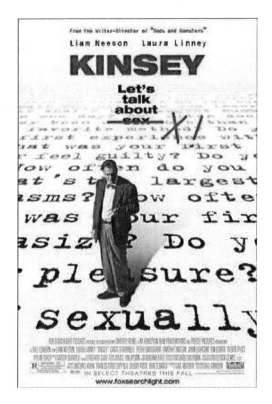

comprehensively and dispassionately as gall wasps. And he conceives a research project to peel back this veil of ignorance.

At around the same time, another student of human nature was investigating eros. The young bishop of Krakow, Karol Wojtyla—the future Pope John Paul II—spent much of the 1950s drawing on his extensive experience counseling married couples to write *Love and Responsibility*, a philosophical attempt to ground sexual morality in human dignity, mutual respect, and other themes emphasized by personalist thinkers such as Gabriel Marcel and Dietrich von Hildebrand. The insights Wojtyla pursued have flowered into what we now call the *Theology of the Body*, which explores, without squeamishness or false modesty, the physical and psychological intricacies of love. The pendulum has swung away from the excesses Catholics might have gone to in the past to protect modesty and preserve innocence. Now the Church is exploring the realities of erotic life, without sacrificing its moral and interpersonal dimensions.[6] Kinsey might have been intrigued to know that Wojtyla explicitly wrote about the different sexual responses of men and women and counseled men to "slow down the rhythm of their arousal" to accommodate and ensure the sexual gratification of their wives.

Then again, maybe Kinsey wouldn't have cared. It seems that he had by age seventeen rejected Christianity as so much fear-mongering mumbo jumbo, which perhaps his father's version was. But his childhood experience became a lifelong prejudice, one that could hide quite comfortably behind the mask of biological science, employed to downplay or erase the differences between human beings and other, lower animals.

In the film, Kinsey collects a band of idealistic young followers who form his research team on a mammoth project: to compile and document a representative sample of the sexual habits of American men and women. To Kinsey, these "subjects" were nothing more than sources for statistics. As they talked to him and his

---

6. And this new eros-friendly Church uses such upbeat and chipper-happy language that some of us single folks are left to sit and sulk, but never mind.

team about the most intimate, traumatic, or wondrous moments of their lives, they appeared to the Kinsey team as interchangeable, and as significant, as gall wasps.

The studies, when they appeared, seemed to document an enormous, appalling hypocrisy among Americans; in a nation where pornography, sodomy, and even adultery were still illegal, half of men and 40 percent of women admitted to cheating on their spouses, and 10 percent of men were actually homosexual or bisexual. Pedophilia, bestiality, you name it—each was dispassionately recounted and proved surprisingly widespread. These explosive findings confirmed thousands of Americans in their secret vices—and spurred millions more to "experiment," preparing the ground for the sexual revolution, all under the rubric of cool, unassailable "modern science." This proved a more enduring rationalization for Lust than Sanger's "racial hygiene."

Check out Craigslist some time and see how many married men are seeking another woman to join their wife in bed, how many normal-looking girls from Iowa and Indiana are looking for "bondage," "threesomes," and "voyeurism" to fulfill desires they might never have even conceived but for the prurience of media, from *Cosmopolitan* magazine to sitcoms on the "conservative" Fox Network. As scientists now realize, to observe something is to change it, and Kinsey's successful attempt to normalize each and every sexual activity sparked in many a morbid curiosity. It rendered others jaded, in need of ever more intricate perversions to reignite erotic desire. If, as Cole Porter put it, "in olden days a glimpse of stocking was looked on as some-

thing shocking,"[7] nowadays five seconds with Google will yield the "Top 10 Animal Sex Sites on the Net." To those men susceptible to pornography (i.e., the ones who can see), the Internet can serve as a spigot for hot and cold running heroin. Meanwhile, ever more men under fifty are resorting to Viagra and Levitra to counter the effects of too much information, too many varieties, and too little love, all of which have calloused the soul. In the long run, Lust isn't even sexy.

We now know what to think about Kinsey's science. As Dr. Judith Reisman has documented in *Kinsey, Sex,*

---

7. Lyrics to *"Anything Goes."*

and Fraud, somewhere between 25 and 33 percent of the "ordinary" American men surveyed by Kinsey for his study of male sexuality were in fact prison inmates, including sex offenders—hardly a representative slice of Americana. He networked extensively in the gay subcultures of major cities, recruiting men to skew his sample. In his female survey, Kinsey blithely reclassified prostitutes and any woman who'd lived with a man for at least a year as "married"—rendering his conclusions about the "average" American wife completely invalid.

Kinsey and his researchers engaged in a series of sexual liaisons with each other and with subjects they'd met in the course of their studies. The movie accurately portrays Kinsey having sex with a young male assistant—who then sleeps with Mrs. Kinsey so that she can even the score. (This sequence, which begins with an honest exploration of the devastating effects of adultery, quickly descends into a bedroom farce.) The film shows how Kinsey's researchers destroyed their marriages by swapping spouses, having sex with strangers, and turning their cocktail conversation into crass, depressing cross-talk about orifices. Oh yes, and they *filmed* their exploits as part of Kinsey's "research." (These stag films still sit in locked vaults at Kinsey's Institute for Sex Research in Indiana, unavailable to researchers; so much for "science.") Both Dr. and Mrs. Kinsey became serial adulterers, using their image as a happily married couple as little more than a public relations ploy to help Kinsey's conclusions gain broader acceptance. The film also omits Kinsey's lifelong obsession with erotic self-torture—which he carried out for decades by sticking a toothbrush into . . . one of those places where you wouldn't think it could ever fit. But the film in fact hints at Kinsey's bizarre stunt of circumcising himself at home in the bathtub. (Did I mention that it's not an ideal date movie?)

Kinsey does include an encounter between Kinsey and a particularly creepy sex addict and pedophile, who relates with lip-smacking glee his molestation of babies—and provides Kinsey with information about infantile ejaculation that the researcher duly publishes. Other researchers might have refused to use data collected by a criminal on unwitting victims—as they even today leave untouched the results of grisly Nazi experiments. But not the intrepid Kinsey. Kinsey corresponded with this pedophile for more than a decade, derived large portions of his data from the sex criminal's confessions, and never troubled to report the deviant's ongoing crimes to the authorities. (Doctor-patient confidentiality does not cover child abuse.) All of which is to say that Kinsey was at best an enabler of pedophilia—even more culpable than reckless bishops such as Roger Cardinal Mahony and Bernard Cardinal Law. As the Kinsey movie opened, so did a Broadway play depicting Law's negligent handling of pedophile priests. Try to imagine things the other way around—an exposé of Dr. Kinsey and a soft-focus, inspirational biopic about Cardinal Law. Kind of hard to picture, isn't it?

But *Kinsey* reaches its sterile climax when Kinsey confronts his aged father, now a miserable shell of a man, and convinces him to take part in one of Kinsey's sexual interviews. In its course, the old man confesses that he had by age ten developed a habit of compulsive masturbation—which his parents "cured" by locking him in a primitive chastity belt. At this, Kinsey quails for the first time and finally reveals some compassion for the man he has always hated; the wicked father is revealed at last as one more victim of sexual repression. "Oh Dad, I'm sorry. I'm so sorry," he whispers.

The story ends with Kinsey and his wife amid the majestic sequoia trees of California. The scientist confessing that he has always envied the trees—who live without feeling, consciousness, or doubt. The scientist who has tried to remain abstracted from life's realities—standing above moral, emotional, and spiritual concerns like a bloodless, observing angel—finds himself jealous of the beasts, bugs, and plants of the field. The one condition he could not abide, and could not accurately record, was the human.

Kinsey and *Kinsey* remind me of pop singer Madonna's old picture book *Sex*, which might more accurately have been called *Gynecology*. Attempting to strip the erotic of all its mystery, modesty, emotional content—even its shame—is self-defeating, in the end. Lust renders human flesh finally meat and replaces the tender touch of one lover's hand upon another with the scalpel of a doctor doing the autopsy on Cupid's cadaver.

A Sex Film for Your Pre-Cana Class: Unscrewed

In contrast to the happy-clappy Photoshop job that *Kinsey* performed on modern sexual misery, the low-budget comedy *Unscrewed* is cruel enough to be truthful. I recommend that engaged couples rent it—indeed, I think it ought to be shown as part of parish Pre-Cana classes—since it tells more about the *Theology of the Body* than a dozen well-meaning lectures. (When I first wrote about it, a conservative seminary invited the bemused, secular filmmaker to screen the film for future priests. I wish I'd been a fly on that particular wall.)

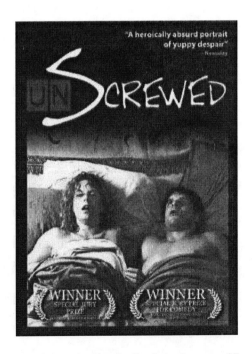

The film concerns the absence of sex. Made in the style of *Spinal Tap* and *Best in Show*, *Unscrewed* tells the story of a couple named Joseph and Mary St. John who love each other dearly, still find each other attractive, and are devoted to saving their marriage. They just can't seem to have sex. After six years of wedded bliss, the two have completely lost interest in intercourse—and they don't know why. In fact, it's driving them crazy. Each one still craves sex, but for some reason they can't get it together. So the couple embarks on a quest to find out what has gone wrong in their marriage—and brings us along for the ride, as empathetic voyeurs. The actors mostly improvise the script, to painfully plausible effect.

The pair is exquisitely thorough, exploring the material, psychological, and spiritual realms for the source of the problem. The movie intercuts among the various authorities whom the hapless couple consults:

- A pretty, grimly reductionist urologist with a Soviet accent played by the film's director, Leslie Shearing. She informs Mary and Joseph that "sex is nothing more than chemicals and clockwork. You get machinery right—you make the happy sex!" She subjects each of the partners to grimly invasive physical exams; plies them with wires and goggles; and sells them thousands of dollars worth of hormones, lubricants and latex toys—as if they were opening a sex-research lab in their bedroom. Oddly, none of this helps.

- An insightful, well-meaning sex therapist, who interviews the couple repeatedly, asking probing questions about their mutual feelings, prodding them into painful revelations, and convincing them to mime their foreplay for him on his office's Murphy bed while he hovers nearby to critique them. He finally goads them into explosive anger at each other, expressed as they pound on pillows with cushioned bats, hurling curses at each other while he stands safely to the side in a hockey mask. After many months of expensive sessions, he discovers that each of them is sexually frustrated and pretty ticked off about it. *Eureka!*

- A band of nebbishy self-trained specialists in tantric yoga who dress in exotic Indian getups and lounge on saffron-colored pillows. These for-profit spiritualists ("We do pretty well. It's a good business," the yogi explains) try to create an atmosphere of sacred eroticism, tinkling little bells and spritzing the couple with incense. They make Mary sit naked on top of a mirror and learn to appreciate her "yoni."[8] These mystics teach Joseph the esoteric pleasures of prostate massage (don't ask). At the end, the couple come away with a list of contortionist sex positions from the

---

8. This is helpfully defined by yoni.com as "a woman's sacred circle"; http://www.yoni.com.

Kama Sutra—which, when tried at home, resulted in pulled muscles and damaged furniture.

Like other mockumentaries, such as the brilliant hip-hop saga *Fear of a Black Hat, Unscrewed* is sharply satirical. But it is also moving. You quickly learn to empathize with Joseph's impotent rage and Mary's ongoing humiliation, made worse by all the rituals, interrogations, and exams they undergo. These two people really love each other, and all they want is faithful eros—nothing adulterous, nothing degrading, just the sexual connection that brought them together in the first place. They are tender and exquisitely consider- ate of each other, which makes it all the more painful to watch their futile attempts to reconnect. We wonder along with them: if these people can't keep up the flame, is there hope for anyone?

By the movie's end, the couple have burned through most of their savings, worn out their bodies, and run out of patience, while audience members are weary from blushing and squirming in their seats. Attempting to escape from all the science, psychobabble, and spiritual flim- flam, Joseph and Mary jump in their car for a weekend in a charming bed and break- fast, out in the countryside. The natural solitude, silence, and stillness exert their charms—and to everyone's surprise, the spouses fall upon each other with hungry affection, achieving at last the ecstatic union they'd sought all along.

Happy ending, right?

The sex is good, and it stays good for months, the epilogue informs us, but the couple decides to separate. We see each one alone, attempting to explain what finally went wrong. They admit, in the end, that the quest for healthy sex had become the focus of their marriage—"And once we achieved that, there didn't seem to be any further point in staying together. Our relationship wasn't *about* anything anymore," Joseph explains.

This brings the thoughtful viewer back to one of the very first scenes in the film—a moment that passes so quickly it's easy to miss. At the movie's outset, Mary opens her medicine cabinet, takes out a dispenser, and casually pops a birth control pill. It seems a piece of bitter irony at the time, since the couple is miserably celi- bate. But perhaps there's something deeper going on. At no point in the film does either partner mention the notion of having children; in fact, none of the experts they consult show any awareness that the sex act might have some underlying biological purpose, apart from intimacy and ecstasy. It's as if all the characters lived in one of the mythical, primitive societies that had never learned the connection between sex and reproduction.

Which brings us back to the reason the partners decide to separate. As they admit, there is no higher purpose to their marriage, no third dimension to give their (hard-won) sexuality any reason for continuing, no focus or future to their intimacy. The two have lived in an endless, pointless present, exploring their sexual selves like a pair of fumbling teenagers—and unsurprisingly, they found that this wasn't enough. In perhaps the single sharpest irony of the film, it never occurs to either one of them that perhaps their relationship was barren *because it was sterile.* When flowers wither, they turn to seed or fruit, which is the reason the plant bothered to grow them in the first place. The one hopeful passage in Orwell's nightmarish *1984* consists of a meditation on this truth so poignant that it is worth quoting at length:

Tirelessly the woman marched to and fro, corking and uncorking herself, singing and falling silent, and pegging out more diapers, and more and yet more. He wondered whether she took in washing for a living or was merely the slave of twenty or thirty grandchildren. Julia had come across to his side; together they gazed down with a sort of fascination at the sturdy figure below. As he looked at the woman in her characteristic attitude, her thick arms reaching up for the line, her powerful mare-like buttocks protruded, it struck him for the first time that she was beautiful. It had never before occurred to him that the body of a woman of fifty, blown up to monstrous dimensions by childbearing, then hardened, roughened by work till it was coarse in the grain like an over-ripe turnip, could be beautiful. But it was so, and after all, he thought, why not? The solid, contourless body, like a block of granite, and the rasping red skin, bore the same relation to the body of a girl as the rose-hip to the rose. Why should the fruit be held inferior to the flower?

"She's beautiful," he murmured.

"She's a metre across the hips, easily," said Julia.

"That is her style of beauty," said Winston.

He held Julia's supple waist easily encircled by his arm. From the hip to the knee her flank was against his. Out of their bodies no child would ever come. That was the one thing they could never do. Only by word of mouth, from mind to mind, could they pass on the secret. The woman down there had no mind, she had only strong arms, a warm heart, and a fertile belly. He wondered how many children she had given birth to. It might easily be fifteen. She had had her momentary flowering, a year, perhaps, of wild-rose beauty and then she had suddenly swollen like a fertilized fruit and grown hard and red and coarse, and then her life had been laundering, scrubbing, darning, cooking, sweeping, polishing, mending, scrubbing, laundering, first for children, then for grandchildren, over thirty unbroken years. At the end of it she was still singing. The mystical reverence that he felt for her was somehow mixed up with the aspect of the pale, cloudless sky, stretching away behind the chimney-pots into interminable distance.[9]

I am tempted to call *Unscrewed* a feature-length explication of *Humanae Vitae*. On at least some level, the makers of this film understand precisely what Pope Paul VI was saying when he reluctantly issued the century's single more unpopular document: sex deprived of consequence, rendered harmless, is also useless and finally joyless. It transforms the act of sex into a two-dimensional shadow play with no third act and only an anticlimax. Binge, then purge.

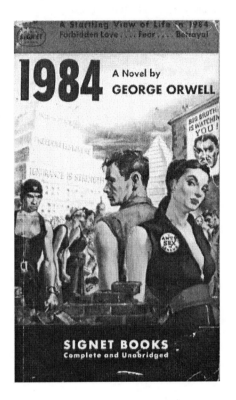

Unscrewed's protagonists aren't caught up in Lust. They're just trying to fix their marriage, but they find themselves flummoxed by a medical and marital establishment guided by Sanger's and Kinsey's shallow assumptions. Joseph and Mary are decent people, but their moral development has been stunted in a grimly familiar way. They have matured beyond the point of simple narcissism, where each seeks only his own pleasure, only to get stuck at the very next level— in the endless, finally hopeless quest to fulfill each other's needs. But sex is meant to do much more than gratify mutual narcissism. Beyond its biological function, sex is also a tool for building community, for socializing individuals into persons—that is, human beings with multiple dimensions who are connected to the fabric of society. By having a child, a couple looks beyond even each other's needs, to provide for the well being of a third person. But even this is not enough; we all know about parents who turn their kids into extensions of their egos, seeing them as science projects (or cultural or even religious projects), looking no further than the confines of their own home in gated subdivisions. Parenthood is meant to do more than that. It should draw us into concern for

---

9. George Orwell, *1984* (London: Secker & Warburg, 1949), chap. 10.

the whole community, from playgrounds and schools to crime and ecology, as we apply the virtue of prudence to our duties as voting citizens. The sexual instinct, as the most powerful one that extricates us from ourselves, finally weaves us into the fabric of the world.

These characters get a glimpse of these truths, if only by negation, through the course of this film. It would surely have ended differently (though perhaps still not happily) if Mary and Joseph had found themselves with a newborn on their hands— even if he wasn't named Jesus.

Chastity: Silk Vestments and Fishnet Stockings

Despite the evidence of my implausible last name—customer service staff refuse to believe it, force me to repeat it two and three times, and sometimes even argue, "It can't be spelled like that!"—the provenance of my Catholic faith is Irish-American, courtesy of my catechetical mom. Whatever specifically Croatian quirks dad had going into the marriage were quickly worn away. Indeed, since he'd learned the "Our Father" as a boy from Irish Christian brothers, my father always said the prayer with a notable brogue. Somehow, over the decades, he even began to look Irish, to the point where I started describing him as a convert. Indeed, I've come to think that being Irish-American is a religion unto itself—particularly after attending the wedding of a friend. She and the groom were both third generation, and neither had traveled extensively in Ireland. I doubt either could quote more than a poem or two by Yeats. And yet, their nuptials were accompanied by a kilted bagpiper, conducted in a church named for an Irish saint, by a priest from the Old Country, whose sermon was all about . . . Ireland.

I can't speak for everyone with an Irish-American mom—not that they're used to getting a word in edgewise—but I really did grow up thinking that sexual sins weren't merely the worst forms of evil but, aside from foul language, the only ones. I'll never forget my mother sitting with her box of Entenmann's, happily munching away to a video of *A Nightmare on Elm Street 4* as some psychopath opened a teenager's head with a coroner's saw. When the dying teenager spluttered the F-bomb, mom sighed and wondered aloud, "Now why'd they have to ruin a perfectly nice movie with that kind of filth?" This incident made me wonder how many IRA terrorists walked away from their bombs with clear consciences—then trooped off to confession for impure thoughts.

Which leads me to a revealing conversation I had with some old college friends a few years after graduation as we sat around over gin and tonics talking sex. The topic not far from my mind—since one of them, Monica, was the loveliest woman I'd ever seen. Her green eyes flashed under jet-black hair, which she coiled thoughtlessly

around a finger, its skin the stark white of Xerox paper. Think Jennifer Connelly. Think Morticia Addams. It's a wonder I could think at all.

Monica hailed from Manhattan's Upper West Side, where her father worked as a classical Freudian analyst—a dinosaur, practicing not far from the Museum of Natural History. Across from her sat Eric, an affable, articulate law student from Long Island who reminded everyone of Richard Dreyfus—all of which is a tortuously PC way of saying that they were Jewish.

I forget how the subject came up, but we were discussing how we first learned "the facts of life." Their stories were typically modern. Eric had taken careful notes during a thorough fifth-grade sex-ed class, while Monica's doctor father had briefed her well before puberty and loaded her down with homework. They shared the details without embarrassment, as if we'd been recalling how each had prepped for the SATs. Then my turn came around. I finished my drink and called for another.

"When I was twelve, I asked my parents where babies came from, and they claimed not to know. I almost believed them. I had a vague notion about sperm and eggs, but I couldn't figure out how one got anywhere near the other. How did the sperm jump bodies? I hypothesized about hypodermic needles—but why were some pregnancies called 'accidents'? Were people being careless with those needles? Anyway, what did the cave men do? Scratch that theory. So I studied some medical books, but the charts and graphs were cross-sections, and the language was so technical I couldn't figure it out. It took one of my friends getting hold of a dirty magazine for me to get a graphic notion of how things worked. I wish I'd grown up on a farm. . . ."

"Didn't you have *sisters*?" Monica wondered.

"Two. A lot older. I remember watching ads for feminine hygiene products on TV. I figured out that women seemed to need these things—whatever they were. But I never saw any in the house. Anywhere. So I theorized that there was either something wrong with my sisters or something special about them. I couldn't guess which."

"Didn't you ask anyone?" asked Monica, her bright eyes now wide.

"Once I asked my father, 'What's menstruation?'—a word I'd come across somewhere. He said, 'Woman stuff. None of your business.' Sometimes my mother would yell at my sister for going out of the house without a bra. I asked my sister why, and she told me it was illegal. That frightened me. So whenever my mother tried to buy a halter dress—no shoulders, so I couldn't see how she'd wear a bra—I'd throw a tantrum, to keep her out of prison."

Eric shook his head. "Irish, right?"

"Half," I said, tipping back the drink. "The dominant half."

Monica was briefly speechless. At length she said, in a kind of awe, "You're like one of Freud's original patients. There hasn't been a case of primal repression like this since 1918. My father would love to meet you. . . . He could get a *journal article* out of this!"

"Any time," I said, flirtatiously.

And that, I would like to say, is how I met my wife.

But that isn't true. I haven't seen Monica since, and whatever insights her father might have extracted from my corseted formation must remain a loss to science.

But I drew from this a hypothesis of my own—that Irish-American sex guilt can only be matched by Jewish race guilt. There are two basic forces driving fallen human history: sheer Lust and rank inequality. If you feel compelled to suppress one, then (unless you're a saint) you'll give yourself a pass on the other. Historically, such differing attitudes have helped shape American culture. They gave us lots of Irish cops and plenty of Jewish shrinks. (Not too many Irish shrinks; Freud famously said that the Irish were the one race "for whom psychoanalysis seems to be useless. It simply has no effect on them.") Jews formed the American Civil Liberties Union; Irish formed the Legion of Decency. Jews went on freedom rides; Irish held draft riots. Think of Fr. Coughlin. And Woody Allen.

All kidding aside, in a poignant moment, my mother once admitted concerning marital sex, "I mean, I've always enjoyed it, but I've never stopped feeling guilty about it." To which I muttered silently, "Poor dad."

In the course of the doctrinal crack-up that occupied the 1970s, mom had much less trouble with most bruited "reforms" than the idea of married priests. "I don't want to take Holy Communion from a married man," she said with a puckered face. "That's *disgusting.*" What can one say to that, apart from, "Mom, I think they probably wash their hands"?

But the lady was on to something. Friends at a Melkite parish I attend (whose excellent pastor is married) have reminded me that clergy in that rite are expected to abstain from marital acts on the eve of singing the liturgy, which nicely explains why Eastern rite churches don't offer daily Mass. There's something deeply . . . anthropological going on in the attempt to separate the rites of sacrifice from the acts that transmit life. Perhaps it's akin to the explanation I once heard for keeping milk separate from meat: "You don't want to mix up the principle of life with that of death," my Jewish friend explained between bites of a cheeseburger. And that seemed to make sense.

While we know that the Mass is a source of eternal life, the priest's role is still a sacrificial one. He stands in the person of Christ and offers in unbloody form the corpse of Christ in atonement for sin, which we duly troop up and consume. Perhaps the reason most of us like our liturgies brief and banal is because it helps us forget how (on some level) *creepy* all of it is. Even Romans whose amphitheaters were full of orgies and snuff productions were authentically appalled to learn about the Eucharist. No wonder that the first time people got the chance to reinvent Christianity, almost every branch of Protestantism reduced the Eucharist to some sort of gray, symbolic ritual. They also did away with clerical celibacy; it was no longer needed.

There's a deep tension inbuilt between the aspirations of a Faith whose highest clergy imitate the virginity of Jesus and the ordinary, life-affirming desires that motivate marriage. The Church has fought over the centuries to uphold the special perfections of the celibate state without lapsing into world-despising Gnosticism. It helped that, historically, Gnostics tend to set really deranged ideals—like universal celibacy, sometimes crowned by suicide—then throw up their hands and allow the laity to engage in every kind of perversity.

In recent decades, we have heard far more than we used to about the Virtue of Chastity as practiced within a marriage—faithfulness to the spouse, openness to life, and self-sacrificing love between the spouses. Pope John Paul II made a point of canonizing thousands of married laymen—even those who weren't martyrs or Catholic monarchs. And this is all to the good. We need more role models of Chastity than monks who tamed their flesh by wearing hair shirts and refusing to bathe.

Still, I know that I'm not the only person who feels a little . . . squeamish when speakers wax eloquent about the Theology of the Body. I'm perfectly comfortable with the Church's traditional discussion of Chastity—that it's connected to Temperance, designed to restrain a biological drive within the bounds of reason and charity. Couples owe each other a marital "debt," which if refused can put one or both parties into the occasion of mortal sin. (And the Church managed to say all this long before the invention of the Internet.) The marital act of love is not "merely" the method for generating new human souls but also the ordinary means of grace within the sacrament; in other words, sexual intercourse is to being married what saying Mass is to being a priest.

In the stricter form of Chastity, the clergy and religious are called to a sterner discipline, inspired by Christ's example to wed themselves not to a single person but to Christ and His Church. Hence, their calling is in some sense truly higher—and their falls all the more abysmal, in case you don't read the news.

What makes me squirm in my seat is when Catholic writers try to compensate for sexual attitudes like those I imbibed as a kid by laying really heavy emphasis on the theological realities of marriage—more emphasis than ordinary human experience will bear. It may well be true, as one Theology of the Body writer likes to emphasize, that in some sense marital intercourse helps both partners to enter into the "inner life

of the Holy Trinity." But is that kind of thinking . . . sexy? I'm single, so readers can correct me here, but the last thing I'll want to hear about on my wedding night is Trinitarian theology. If the Sorrowful Mysteries make lousy foreplay— sorry, mom—the Joyful ones won't do much better.

It may be that we can't use much New Testament material here—since its protagonists trended celibate. The Old Testament, with its overriding concern for producing more healthy Jewish babies, might make better grist for marital meditations. Fatherly Abraham; lusty, penitent David; exquisite Esther; "my beloved" of the Song of Songs—perhaps

these saints are the ones we need to invoke as we enter the marital bed. Let's think of the saintly celibates in the morning, as we change muddy diapers, soothe deranged teenagers, and schlep off to work at ridiculous jobs to pay all those bills. At such times, living on a pillar in the desert might not sound all that bad.

Beagle-Related Digression #1: Openness to Life

My girlfriend and I are getting serious. We already have a family in common—two manic little beagles named Susie and Franz Josef, of whom we have joint custody, and whom we call "the babies." With every relationship that inches toward the sacramental, it's critical that the two parties establish common ground on the central issues that arise in any marriage. We've spent the past few years hashing out healthy compromises on most of the subjects over which we'd disagreed. (Okay, which frightened her.) In consultation with each of our spiritual directors, we have established at last that I'll no longer

- help ex-girlfriends with their rent. Especially the really cute ones.
- spend hours in earnest conversations with commies, neo-Nazis, or racists of any color in the hope of "reforming" them and luring them into the Church.
- give work to BUCLs (brilliant, unemployable Catholic losers) of whom I'm fond—then dash about at the last minute cleaning up the mess so they can get paid.
- let sociopaths sleep on my couch. For months.
- run up debt buying overpriced "crunchy" groceries and cases of imported monastic beer with the excuse that I'm "researching my next Catholic cookbook."
- pay only utility bills that have already been disconnected.
- respond to my beloved's rare, hormonally driven binges by hiding every carbohydrate in the house.
- pretend that letters from the IRS demanding payment are "junk mail."

On the positive side, my lady friend has no problem with my policy that any and all dogs we acquire will sleep in the family bed. And in return for all these binding resolutions, she undertakes not to keep bringing up past instances of any and all occurrences of the aforementioned phenomena. So now I think we're golden.

Aware that more marriages founder on financial rather than sexual disagreements, we've spent a lot of time talking through our different monetary habits and expectations—most of which we inherited. She hails from prosperous, skinflint German surgeons and Southern aristocrats; my family tree is full of Irish cabbies who knew it was time to go home when they fell off the barstool. We've worked through all this and come to an arrangement: I'll earn the money, and she'll refuse to spend it.

We have agreed to be open to life. We have two beagles together already and will prayerfully welcome any other hounds whom God sees fit to send our way.

That leaves just the issue of progeny. We're neither of us young, and we're both pretty high strung. A houseful of homeschooled Patricks and Philomenas is biologically unlikely—and would anyway land both of us in the sanatorium and the kids in foster care. On the other hand, the Church teaches that child-rearing is the primary purpose of marriage. (All that love and companionship is crucial for happiness, but it's icing. The kids are the cake.) What is more, we have private reasons for wanting a decent-sized family. My beloved finds children as cute and funny as puppies, while I feel responsible for spreading my genes around the planet—if only as a form of posthumous sabotage.

Most importantly, though—and I hope that some of you will take these considerations into account—we have decided that having some children would be very good for our beagles. Veterinary psychologists have established the character-building benefits that children can bring to family pets. The following are some examples:

- They teach a dog responsibility. Whenever a toddler drops a binky on the street near Susie, she already knows that it's her job to pick it up and chew it.
- They train a dog in unconditional love. There's nothing quite like a baby's face smeared in Gerber franks n' beans to draw out a hound's affectionate soul.
- They teach a dog that the world isn't "all about them." The presence of children can help to mitigate canine narcissism and train your dog to "play well with others."
- They help to socialize a dog. If you've given up on public or private obedience schools and exercised your right as your animal's "primary educator" (*Familiaris Consortio*, 36) by schooling your dogs at home, having children will offer the dogs the social interaction they otherwise might not get.

We've heard the Malthusian arguments against bringing more human children into the world. We've worried together over the environmental, political, and economic situation our offspring might inherit. We have even noted with alarm the research that shows the common thread linking Adolf Hitler, Josef Stalin, Margaret Sanger, and Adam Sandler: *Each was at some point a child.*

But one can't dwell on dark thoughts like that. They are not of God. We're commanded by Christ to live in hope, in the hope that a loving Father will provide for our children and beagles a livable world—or at least a really smokin' and satisfying Apocalypse. As the song says, "Be not afraid."

GEORGE SIMMONS

His second chance
is his only hope.

RE-DO

THIS CHRISTMAS

The Chastity of Queen Catherine

Much as I love St. Maria Goretti, the traditional patroness of Chastity, I'm not sure how useful her story is nowadays for illuminating this Virtue. Having long been  importuned by a lustful young man who offered her a lucrative niche as his mistress, Maria steadfastly said, "No," until at some point he flew into a rage and started to rape her. She resisted, and he stabbed her to death. She is quoted as having chosen "death before sin," and in another context, that's surely a worthy maxim. But it's worth pointing out, over and over again, that *rape victims who don't fight back are not committing a sin.* A woman I knew, the victim of a violent rape, said that tales of Maria Goretti (which she'd learned as a girl) fed into the crippling, inappropriate guilt that haunted her after the attack. What's edifying about Gorretti's tale, I think, is how she forgave her attacker before she died, and how he converted afterward— even attending her canonization Mass. That part is enough to break your heart, but its matter is Mercy, not Chastity.

So let's move on to another story, a longer and sadder one, of Chastity lived over decades and under duress in its most common context: marriage. I speak of someone well known to Showtime subscribers, Queen Catherine of Aragon. The beleaguered first wife of Henry VIII, she started life with every promise of pleasure and power— as the youngest daughter of Europe's richest monarchs, Ferdinand and Isabella. She learned Spanish, French, Latin, and Greek and all the liberal arts in an education infused with the Christian humanism that formed Erasmus and her future friend Thomas More. Obedient to her parents, she made a political marriage at age fifteen to the English Prince Arthur—a shy young man who died only six months later.

According to Catherine, Arthur carried shyness to quite an extreme, since she always claimed the marriage was never consummated. This may seem implausible now, but it pays to remember two things:

1. Arthur was sickly.
2. Arthur was English.

A few centuries down the line, it would take seven years for Louis XVI to look into the minor medical issue that kept him from consummating his bond with Marie Antoinette; perhaps the prospect of handing on royal genes can cause performance anxiety. Whatever the case, the pious Catherine swore repeatedly under oath that she'd never gone fully Arthurian, so it probably behooves us to believe her; otherwise, her actions in later years make no sense.

After Arthur's death, Catherine was left for seven years an impoverished widow living under something close to house arrest in damp and alien England. She escaped this fate when her parents arranged with Henry VII for her to marry Arthur's brother, the dashing and learned Prince Henry. Because of Leviticus 20:21, canon law forbade a widow's marrying her brother-in-law. But royal dispensations back then were as thick on the ground as Kennedy annulments, so Henry and Catherine married in 1509. A very different man from his brother, Henry made Catherine pregnant five times—in between long bouts with mistresses, a sport that historians think gave Henry syphilis. That disease contributes to infant mortality, which might explain why only one of Catherine's children, Mary, outlived infancy.

Lacking a legitimate male heir, with his own family's claim to the throne still legally tenuous, Henry began to doubt the validity of his marriage to Catherine. By sheer coincidence, he'd fallen in love with one of her teenaged ladies in waiting, Anne Boleyn. Thus began the well-known story of the English Reformation, whose sordid origins have given Irishmen ever after the chance to snipe at their English landlords (as poet Brendan Behan is said to have quipped):

Don't speak of the alien minister,
Nor his church without meaning or faith,
For the foundation stones of his temple
Are the bollocks of Henry VIII.

Some say that it was this text that finally moved John Henry Newman to abandon the Anglican Communion for the Church of Rome.[1]

A morals manual isn't the place to rehearse the tedious legal proceedings by which Henry VIII sought a divorce from Catherine or the violence he used on those who resisted him. His efforts were slowed, not stopped, by the fact that Catherine was the well-loved aunt of Charles V, whose armies held the pope a virtual

---

1. Alas, they are kidding.

prisoner. There was little honor on any side of this issue, most of whose protagonists (except for saints such as Thomas More and Bishop John Fisher) treated the sanctity of marriage as a pawn on Europe's chessboard. It all ended with butchered Carthusians; roofless abbeys; bare, ruined choirs; and the liltingly lovely language of the Book of Common Prayer, most of whose sacraments are invalid.

What matters to us is Catherine's unfailing commitment to her marriage. As the wheels of her persecution ground slowly and certainly, she found herself losing first her privileges, then her rights. In the end, she was banned from even visiting the disinherited Princess Mary and imprisoned in a crumbling castle far from court. At any point in time, Catherine could have freed herself, left England, and returned to Spain—to life as a pampered dowager. All it would have required for Henry to set her free was a simple letter, admitting that their marriage was invalid.

But Catherine wouldn't write it, not even long after she'd given up any prospect of the throne. To the end, she concerned herself with "my husband's" health and holiness—both in steep decline. She died in poverty and solitude but would never renounce the reality and the sanctity of her vocation as a wife. Deeply in love with her husband, affectionate and romantic, she was sentenced to decades of celibacy in the midst of the marital state. Abandoned, she never abandoned God. She never even gave up on Henry. She wrote him the following the year before she died:

> My most dear lord, King and husband,
>
> The hour of my death now drawing on, the tender love I owe up forces me, my case being such, to commend myself to you, and to put you in remembrance with a few words of the health and safeguard of your soul which you ought to perforce before all worldly matters, and before the care and pampering of your body, for the which you have cast me into many calamities and yourself into many troubles. For my part, I pardon you everything, and I desire to devoutly pray God that He will pardon you also. For the rest, I commend unto you our daughter Mary, beseeching you to be a good father unto her, as I have heretofore desired. I entreat you also, on behalf of my maids, to give them marriage portions, which is not much, they being but three. For all mine other servants I solicit the wages due them, and a year more, lest they be unprovided for. Lastly, I make this vow, that mine eyes desire you above all things.[2]

She died with dignity, as true to her vocation as any monk or martyr. I cannot think of a worthier model today for all the married.

---

2. Available at http://englishhistory.net/tudor/letter5.html.

Trademark-Busting Cosmo-Style Quiz™ #1: What's Your "Road-Whore Quotient"?

As I warned in this book's preface, there will be a quiz—seven of them, in fact, each inspired by Walker Percy's quizzes in his satirical work of philosophical linguistic apologetics,[3] *Lost in the Cosmos: The Last Self-Help Book*. It's a marvelous book; I only plagiarize the best.

As I treat the trio of Lust/Chastity/Frigidity, as always I'm in search of the fleeting Golden Mean. Before I dive in, however, I must make a stark admission: I write from the male point of view. Now, readers have sometimes complained about the testosterone content of my writing, which apparently leaches through the page even when I write of bloodless, neutral topics like the economy. It is no surprise, then, that when the subject is sex, my prose is even muskier. When I sent an early draft of

this chapter to my beloved for her feedback, her eyes rolled audibly. She sighed, "You are such a guy." Some of us take that as a compliment.

Rather than trying uselessly to approximate the feminine point of view by dressing my brain in drag, I'll just confess my bias right up front, and if I can't offer female readers direct insights, I can at least provide a bracing glimpse of how the other half lusts.

Let me preface the quiz with an insight I think is almost as important to the understanding of masculine sexuality in its fallen state as psychologist Barney Stinson's discursus on the relational significance of external erotic attraction and psychological dysfunction: "The Hot/Crazy Scale."

I have not yet submitted my own results to a peerreviewed journal, so it's best

---

3. This is more fun than it sounds. Of course, it could hardly be less.

not to cite my work in your own research, but I can't resist sharing with readers the abstract of my discovery: "The Orange Traffic Cone Hypothesis." It is drawn not only from personal experience but also from interviews with hundreds of other heterosexual men, many of them deeply chaste and extremely devout. Here goes:

From the age of eleven right up into Alzheimer's, your average straight male walking down the street doesn't see people in their various demographic categories (i.e., according to age, ethnicity, social class, etc.). Instead, he sees his fellow humans breaking into two categories:

1. Good-looking women
2. Orange traffic cones

I know what the kindly lady reader is saying, the one who has many men in her life whom she loves and respects as fellow Christians. "Well, that's not true of . . . Harvey! When he works with me at the soup kitchen, I know that he looks at each of those homeless men who come to us as human beings. In fact, he once said to me that he viewed each of them as an image of Christ."

Nope. Sorry, sister. That may be what he wants or tries to see, but when he looks over the bubbling kettle of hot dog soup in the dim church basement at that long line of "people-who-aren't-good-looking-women" (it's a broad and all too common category), what he really sees are orange traffic cones. Now, when he looks at you, on the other hand, notice how his face lights up. That's because you're literally the first person he's seen all morning. Try to take the compliment. He can't help it. None of us can.

Likewise, when one of us enters a room, the first thing our eyes scan for is someone attractive we can glance at, from time to time, just to keep our spirits up. It's the same thing with movie posters, magazine covers, and car calendars. That's the reason advertising types stick pretty women almost at random into ads for all sorts of things. It's not so much to stimulate Lust as to keep us from feeling lonely. In the midst of this otherwise dismal, lengthy meeting, subway ride, or rosary cenacle, there will at least be a few real live human beings alongside all those cones. Those of us who aren't caught up in the deadly sin of Lust just take a flicker of pleasure from these moments, then look away. Want to spot a guy with a problem? He

wears dark sunglasses so he can stare as long as he wants without worrying about eye contact.

I have not embarked on the lengthy, Kinseyesque research that might be required to explicate Lust from the feminine perspective—and indeed, I think the very effort might constitute a near occasion of sin, so I'll leave that task to those who might find the task less of a "trigger."

Now that my biases have been accounted for, on to the quiz, which is meant to help you diagnose your soul. Do you suffer from the deadly sin of Lust? Have you attained the virtuous Golden Mean, treating with due respect the created good (eros) whose abuse would lead to this vice? Or have you done such a good job of "mortifying" this particular passion that you've actually lurched into Frigidity? (That probably can't land you in Hell, but it might make your earthly life a short-term substitute.) Answer these impertinent questions, and find out.

> **Important Note:** If you plan to write in the book, please think about the impression you'll make on the next dinner guest who finds it in your restroom or the children who dig it out of your secret stash, where you keep those pop-up Theology of the Body books and your guiltily unread copy of *The Secret of the Rosary*.

The Quiz

When you see an attractive, well-dressed member of the opposite sex, which of the following runs through your head?

a. The pleasing pattern those clothes would make spilled on your bedroom floor
b. A twitter of interest, followed by a quick prayer of gratitude for the goodness of Creation
c. The image of Miss Piggy, languorously swimming through a pool full of champagne—the only trick you've found to banish impure thoughts
d. A surge of anger at the torrents of filth to which decent people are subjected, followed by images of the souls of the impure, falling into Hell like leaves in the autumn, just as Our Lady said at Fatima

Here are the results:

- If you picked "a": Time to zip up your libido, and quick. Read up on the connection between promiscuity, unwanted pregnancy, and abortion—and remember that every "unplanned" pregnancy started out as a raunchy thought just like yours. It might also help to go home and Google some images—only this time, instead of "barely legal," try "herpes lesion."

- If you picked "b": A wholesome thought. Ramp it up a little by actually praying for the person you found so distracting. Wish him or her a happy marriage, and ask God to send you joy in your own vocation. Then, for heaven's sake, look away.

- If you picked "c": Whatever works for you, man. Careful that it doesn't start to backfire; once you start associating sexual arousal with Muppets, those kind of neural pathways are really hard to alter.

- If you picked "d": You're not a lone "decent person" surrounded by sinners. We're each of us fallen, and the first step is admitting it. Just make sure that's not also your last step. Find a Catholic therapist who accepts insurance (good luck with that one!) or a wise, compassionate priest. Schedule some serious time in front of the Blessed Sacrament, pleading for guidance and peace of mind.

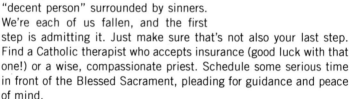

Activities

If you think you're in spitting distance of a serious problem with Lust, increase your prayer time and invoke the appropriate saints—for instance, St. Thomas Aquinas, whose libido was so robust that when his brothers tried to ruin his vocation by locking him up with a harlot, he had to chase her out of the room with a blazing poker. For his effort, God granted him a lifetime of uninterrupted Chastity after that. If you're having similar troubles with your blazing poker, chances are you'd benefit from the following:

- ❑ *Increasing your daily exercise.* Those old-time priests who drove their teenage charges into the boxing ring and the rugby fields knew a thing or two about human nature.
- ❑ *Engaging in little sacrifices that remind your reptilian brain just which quadrant is in charge.* Give up one tangible, sensory

pleasure every day—such as smoking that second cigar, putting whole milk into your coffee, or letting your dogs dump on the lawn of your least favorite neighbors. Keep doing this until temptation diminishes, or those people finally move away.

❑ *Spiritual reading.* Here your selection depends on your situation. If you're married or someday hope to be, you might start with Old Testament texts that celebrate sexuality in its good and holy context—faithful marriage. The Song of Songs and the book of Tobit are nice places to start. Move on to more hands-on works, such as psychologist Gregory Popcak's *Holy Sex! A Catholic Guide to Toe-Curling, Mind-Blowing, Infallible Loving.* (Yes, it's a practical guide. No, it isn't illustrated. Get your mind out of the gutter, young man!)

❑ *Finding peace with your situation.* If marriage is out of the question (for whatever depressing reason), it's best to shove aside all such happy talk. The Twelve-Step Serenity Prayer is remarkably powerful; if it can help aging rock stars stay off crystal meth, it's certainly worth trying. Regular Eucharistic adoration is enormously comforting, as is frequent Confession. (Find a priest who won't either berate you for falling yet again or shrug you off, explaining that the only sin is racism.) Finally, adopt a program of nightly spiritual reading, with classics like Brother Lawrence's *The Practice of the Presence of God*, Robert Benson's *The Friendship of Christ*, or the forgotten masterpiece *Gateway to Hope: An Exploration of Failure*, by Maria Boulding. This last book is one of the best I've ever read, so of course, it is out of print.

Wrath: Massive, Disproportionate Retaliation

That neglected Catholic poet of the 1970s, Kinky Friedman (lead singer of the Texas Jewboys), wrote movingly of the Resurrection in a tender Easter ballad, frequently used at suburban Texas parishes as a post-Communion hymn. "High on Jesus" concludes with this envoi:

Oh, let's get high on Jesus, high on Jesus,
They tried to put His body under ground.
Flashing high on Jesus, high on Jesus,
But friend, you just can't keep the good Man down.

Try as we might, and we've been making a noble effort since roughly 33 AD, there are moments in the life of any believer when he's still tempted to shoulder the stone and hermetically seal the tomb.

The unregenerate natural man—the seedy, potbellied homunculus each of us quietly treasures as our deepest and truest self—is far from thrilled at the prospect of safely buried Messiahs popping up out of the ground and giving us orders, then flying to Heaven. On the one hand, we feel a certain excitement at the prospect that each of our actions will have an eternal significance. There is just one problem with that.

It seems to imply that *each of our actions* will have an *eternal significance.*

As we think those actions over—especially that one and *that* one, sheesh—the silence of the grave and the infinite void sound better and better. The only part of the Last Judgment we might enjoy is the wholesale exposure of everyone else's sins. With the proper editing, that's a miniseries I want to see. Sounds like a violent, sexy soap opera that runs for thousands of years.

In the chapter on Lust, I covered Jesus's busybody meddling with our easygoing lives and His hobby of playing "spoiler" in the bedroom—like a big, smelly Labrador that insists on sleeping between us. But He's just too cute to kick out. And anyway, He's omnipotent.

Now we come to a passion that has a signal advantage over Lust: instead of spawning new relationships and sometimes (blech!) new people, this one typically snuffs them out—sometimes with a really big BANG and lots of shiny shrapnel.

I speak, of course, of Wrath. That's the best word the moralists could find for this phenomenon, but the term is slightly confusing. If we stick with the name, it sounds like the only "Deadly Sin" that the Bible attributes to God. Now I'm no Evangelical, so I don't spend all my spare time reading Semitic genealogies. But I'm pretty sure that none of the executive summaries of scripture I've heard each week at Mass ever mentioned the "Greed" or "Gluttony" of God. I suppose I could check for myself (see Sloth), but that would entail the danger of *private interpretation* of Scripture. And as the Church's documents on ecumenism point out, we all know what that leads to. . . .

That's right—*handling snakes.* So I'll leave the job of reading and explaining those puzzling Jewish books to expert celibates, thanks very much.

Still, I'm guessing that the human authors of the Old Testament didn't mean to suggest that God's anger was ever "inordinate," in the sense St. Thomas means when he distinguishes righteous anger from sinful Wrath. This helps when we come to "hard sayings" in Holy Scripture, for instance, "Fair Babylon, you destroyer, happy those who pay you back the evil you have done us! Happy those who seize your children and smash them against a rock" (Ps 137:8–9).

Sentimental liberals try to explain such verses away, but I'm guessing those little Babyls were *precocious.* Maybe somebody told them they were "gifted," hence the popular bumper sticker, which I put on my minivan right above the Jesus Fish, "My Psalmist Smashes Your Honor Student against a Rock."

No. Wrath, in the sense that won it a coveted place among the Seven Deadlies, must mean something different. In *The Seven Capital Sins,*[1] Archbishop Fulton Sheen writes,

1. Fulton J. Sheen, *The Seven Capital Sins* (New York: Alba House, 2001), 1–2.

MY PSALMIST SMASHES
YOUR HONOR STUDENT
AGAINST A ROCK

Not all anger is sinful, for there is such a thing as just anger. The most perfect expression of just anger we find in Our Blessed Lord cleansing the Temple. Passing through its shadowed doorways at the festival of the Pasch, He found greedy traders, victimizing at every turn the worshipers who needed lambs and doves for the Temple sacrifices. Making a scourge of little cords, He moved through their midst with a calm dignity and beautiful self-control even more compelling than the whip. The oxen and sheep He drove out with His scourge; with His hands He upset the tables of the money changers who scrambled on the floor after their rolling coins; with His finger He pointed to the venders of doves as He bade them leave the outer court; to all He said: "Get these things out of here, and do not make My Father's house a market place." Here was fulfilled the injunction of the Scriptures, "Be angry, and sin not"; for anger is no sin under three conditions:

- If the cause of anger be just, for instance, defense of God's honor;
- If it be no greater than the cause demands, that is, if it be kept under control; and
- If it be quickly subdued: "Let not the sun go down on your anger."

What is more, while anger is perceived as a passion, it also carries *information*. It tells us that we're not getting something we want—perhaps something we need and have a right to, like a just wage or decent treatment. Or it informs us that we're being sprayed with something we don't want, and perhaps that we're being abused. When counselors at domestic violence centers urge battered wives to get angry instead of depressed, they're employing a human passion, the better to protect the innocent. Anger is often the spur to rectify or end destructive relationships or find a better alternative to a futile, dead-end job.

St. Thomas Aquinas, following Aristotle, taught that anger at *actions* can be perfectly justified—depending on the cause—and even virtuous. But rage directed at *people* is off the menu: hate the sin, love the sinner. For us fallen types, this gets things exactly backward. It's hard to hate something as abstract as a "violation of justice" or "contravention of the positive law," especially if you're busy trying to spray the perpetrator with Christian love.

Anyway, in many cases, the sin is a whole lot sexier than the sinner. It's the part with which we can sympathize—it might even be an old friend. You needn't

Get a room!

hate Sloth in general to loathe the pudgy federal employee behind a wall of bulletproof glass who seems to go "on break" every thirty minutes thanks to "union rules." In fact, it might very well be Sloth on your own part that makes you so crotchety about standing in line. Likewise when we retch at other people's public displays of affection. "Get a room!" may be the fruit of sincere, offended modesty—or the envious growl of a dog whose nose is pressed at the butcher shop window.

I suppose it's possible, for exquisitely holy folks, to seal off in separate compartments the person who commits an evil from the action that he commits. But I'm not sure how it works in practice. The authorities don't arrest a "murder" and throw it in jail for forty years; they

lock up the guy who committed the crime (or, at least, someone who eyewitnesses think resembles him closely enough as not to make much difference). When we fight in self-defense, our instincts drive us not just to stop the assault but also to level the guy who started the fight—and leave him something to remember us by every time he looks in the mirror.

Now, it's true that when a country engages in war, the Church's just war teaching prescribes that we avoid needless destruction rained down on civilians. Happily, lay strategists who respect our Christian traditions have learned to work within its strictures, explaining that we will never employ more nuclear weapons than are *strictly necessary* to reduce our enemy's continent to an uninhabitable wasteland, just in case they get any ideas. So that's all right, then. This strategic doctrine is called mutually assured destruction (MAD). It inspired my own approach to conflict resolution, which I call massive, disproportionate retaliation (MDR).

This might surprise you, but I wasn't always such a mild, soft-spoken guy. Before my conversion to St. Francis of Assisi's gospel of peace, you might have called me . . . contentious. Provoked, I acted rather prickly—and I mean that as an adverb. Growing up bookish in a blue-collar neighborhood full of guys named Vito who thought my pointy head could be best used as a hood ornament on a Trans Am, I learned the fine art of verbal repartee and the means to deeply humiliate an iron-pumping guido in front of his *paisans*. I also learned (and this next step is critical) at the end of the school day to escape from the building intact and unobserved, no matter how many guys from the soccer team were pounding their fists in front of what they *thought* were all the exits.

In a similar way, the Zmirak family dynamics made of our cramped, rent-controlled apartment an elite dojo in the emotional martial arts—although our school of power play was less like the elegant aikido than the inelegant but highly effective technique of personal combat called *Krav Maga*. Developed by the Israeli Defense Force, the point of *Krav Maga*, as an instructor once explained to me, is "not so much Oriental philosophy or learning how to think like a lotus or that kind of *drek*," but rather to "make the *fershtinker* who attacked you cough his *beytzim* up out of his mouth!" (These remarks were addressed to the Catholic men's retreat I was attending, but that's another story.)

Serving as the only conservative at my college crazy enough to write regular pieces on abortion and other social issues helped sharpen my fangs and thicken my hide. The perks of my position—frequent insults, profane graffiti using my name, Amish-style shunning, and the occasional punch in the face—schooled me in the art of the vicious comeback, the anonymous parody, and the *preemptive conversational tirade*. These experiences, in synergy with ancient, grudge-nursing Gaelic and Croat chromosomes, helped me formulate MDR (pronounce it "madder").

After prayerful reflection on the Gospel, I concluded that "Turn the other cheek" is one of many biblical sayings whose meaning is so opaque that laymen cannot responsibly presume to interpret it. (What am I, a Lutheran?) Like the Book of Revelation, it is one of those impenetrable allegories best left to the professionals. And how had theologians interpreted it in the past? Against the vulgar, literalist reading of this text, I cited the Church's doctrine of just war; the multiple pontiffs and canonized saints who'd supported, even fought in, the Crusades; the military expeditions of Renaissance popes; and the example of Jesus cleansing the temple. How many times I dreamed of imitating Christ by charging into the "peace and justice" chapel run for Catholics on campus as I sat in my dorm room, patiently knotting cords. . . .

Reflecting on the almost univocal support of American Catholics for the bombing of Hiroshima and the role our nuclear doctrine of MAD had played in containing atheistic Communism, I personalized the political. I explained my strategic doctrine to a friend: "If somebody screws with you and you let him get away with it, what lesson are you teaching him?"

My friend just stared at me. A well-meaning but utterly harmless philosopher in training, he'd learned meekness the old fashioned way—from a deeply manipulative Irish mother. Instead, I tried to teach him MDR.

"The lesson you're teaching is that *crime really pays*," I explained. "You're encouraging him to go forth unto others and *do likewise*. Is that fair to his next victim?"

"I'm not sure it's our place. . . ."

"And if you don't retaliate, aren't you *tempting* the wrongdoer to do it again? Which means you're serving as a near occasion of sin. . . ."

"Well. . . ."

"I don't know about you, but I don't want that on my conscience." QED, hence, MDR.

This theory was not some new synthesis but a catechetical summary of the tacit creed that had kept me going for twenty years: *let no slight go unanswered, no insult unreturned.*

While I no longer hold to this axiom, over the decades, my practice of MDR did produce some edifying results. Here are just two of the more printable examples. There were many, many more, but those moulder now on the cutting room floor at the Crossroad Publishing Company.

Case Study #1. Edgar, a stuffy, insufferable pipe-smoking Hegelian invited me out to lunch—and I wondered why, since our mutual dislike was open. I soon discovered that he wanted someone on whom to try out his favorite anti-Catholic zingers. He recited one in particular with such relish that I could tell he'd been waiting for years to use it: "What I don't

understand about you Catholics is how you can worship a God who tells you, 'Eat me.'" I smiled and offered the mild answer that turneth aside Wrath: "What I don't get is how you Jews can worship a God who forbids lobster to the only folks who can afford it." Turning purple, he stamped his little Rumpelstiltskin foot and accused me of making fun of his religion.

Case Study #2. At a cocktail party organized for Manhattan Republicans—hey, the drinks were free—I was trapped between a neoconservative pundit (let's call him "Ganesh") and a flamboyantly gay libertarian ("Willy"). Now, I have no interest in other men's personal lives, but Willy and I were alums of the same conservative group in college, and every time I ran into him, he made a special point of reminding me about his sexuality and dropping some snarky comment about the Church. Usually, I'd just shrug it off (did he expect me to run into the ladies' room and cry?), but this occasion was special. Ganesh was waving his hands and gibbering like a speed freak, describing his spiritual search: *"I've-I've-I've fl-flirted with be-becoming a Baptist, and I've fl-flirted with becoming a Catholic, but I just can't m-make up my mind!"* Willy leaned back and

drawled, "Well, sweetie, you just make sure it stays a flirtation. You don't go all the way with any of those nasty old religions." Ganesh laughed appreciatively, and I guess this was my cue to break down sobbing. Instead, I offered some solid advice: "Actually, Ganesh, I think you should have anonymous encounters with hundreds of strange religions in public restrooms." The two men ran for the exits as if I'd pulled the pin on a grenade.

From these and many, many other attempts to morally educate my neighbor, I've drawn life lessons myself. You might have heard the French expression, *"L'esprit d'escalier"* (the wit of the stairs), for the witty comeback to a humiliating quip that comes to you on the stairs, after you've slunk out of a party. I've always had the opposite problem, which a Francophone friend helpfully terms *"La finesse d'escalier*" (tact of the stairs), for the bland and harmless remark you could have made—instead of an enemy for life.

I later learned from a spiritual director that the best way to deal with Wrath is to liberate yourself from it. To break its hold over you by invoking a Higher Power. Or as he liked to put it, "Pray for the jackass. It won't necessarily make him less of a jackass. But it might make you less of one." With God, all things are possible.

Other tactics for diluting and diffusing the sin of Wrath appear in Solomon Schimmel's *The Seven Deadly Sins*—a fascinating, accessible scholarly work, marred only by its paucity of self-referential anecdotes and dog photos. Schimmel draws on Stoic authors such as Seneca and Plutarch, who recommend a dogged internal resistance to anger in any form—even justified indignation at abuse you suffer firsthand. Of course, I cannot agree, for reasons I'll explain. But since most of the times when we justify getting rip-roaring mad at people, we are *at least partly fooling ourselves*, it's certainly safe to err on the side of caution. The Stoics recommend we diffuse our anger by thinking, long and hard, "Might I have done something to *provoke* this?" For instance, if someone has hit me in the face, might it have something to do with the "harmless" ethnic joke I made, or my "helpful" suggestions on how his wife could lose the weight she'd been putting on? ("I'm just saying. . . .") More subtly, have I been unconsciously treating someone with contempt, abusing power, or otherwise acting unjustly?

If you can't find any proportionate reason for all those curled-up, frozen hamsters the local Methodist minister has arranged in a swastika pattern on your lawn, you might follow Seneca in trying to analyze whether the offense committed against you was intentional, accidental, or the fruit of weakness or even madness. As Seneca says, "Whatever works." He suggests you try to make excuses for your enemies, at least until your temper cools and you've disassembled that (shoddily assembled and unreliable) pipe bomb. Everything works better when it's undertaken with clear eyes and a cool head.

The Weak Shall Inherit the Smurfs

Ten thousand difficulties do not make one doubt, as Newman wrote. So I feel safe exposing a difficulty that troubles me and many well-meaning Christians. I encountered it while attending a daily Mass—a habit I can't manage to acquire, partly because I find the liturgy so moving that it is enormously draining, and partly because I can't quit thinking that Mass on a Tuesday morning is meant for black-veiled old Italian ladies named Rosaria.

The problem was the Gospel. I know that Our Lord quite regularly said things that sent His fellow Jews stalking off, indignant. Some of the sayings were meant for universal application, while others were aimed primarily at the sinner He was addressing. ("Sell all you have, and give it to the poor" is for most of us meant as a "counsel," not a command.)

Some statements Christ meant in a terribly literal sense, while others were partly or wholly allegorical. For instance, the promise to tear down the Jewish temple and rebuild it in three days was pure allegory, since the temple He meant was His body. Perhaps to onlookers He pointed at His chest with both His thumbs; otherwise, we can forgive them for misunderstanding. He was likewise using allegory, thank God, when He brought up that unnerving business about becoming a "eunuch for the kingdom of Heaven." Poor Origen, the greatest Christian theologian of his day, took that injunction with bloody-minded literalness, and the Church refused to ordain him because he was no longer "intact." When Christ spoke of the Eucharist, He was almost, but not quite, speaking with absolute literalness; Eucharistic Presence is different in some mysterious sense from His earthly form, and Jesus didn't expect the apostles to butcher and eat His crucified corpse. What is more, at the Last Supper, He confected and distributed Communion, with an earthly body still breathing and unbloody. These waters are too deep for me, but the point is that He wasn't calling for flat-out cannibalism.

The Gospel that day at Mass was one I've always found challenging. Okay, that's not quite candid. I find it appalling:

> But I say to you who hear: Love your enemies, do good to those who hate you, bless those who curse you, and pray for those who spitefully use you. To him who strikes you on the one cheek, offer the other also. And from him who takes away your cloak, do not withhold your tunic either. Give to everyone who asks of you. And from him who takes away your goods do not ask them back. And just as you want men to do to you, you also do to them likewise.
>
> But if you love those who love you, what credit is that to you? For even sinners love those who love them. And if you do good to those who do good to you, what credit is that to you? For even sinners do the same. And if you lend to those from whom you hope to receive back, what credit is that to you? For even sinners lend to sinners to receive as much back. But love your enemies, do good, and lend, hoping for nothing in return; and your reward will be great, and you will be sons of the Most High. For He is kind to the unthankful and evil. Therefore be merciful, just as your Father also is merciful.
>
> Judge not, and you shall not be judged. Condemn not, and you shall not be condemned. Forgive, and you will be forgiven. Give, and it will be given to you: good measure, pressed down, shaken together, and running over will be put into your bosom. For with the same measure that you use, it will be measured back to you. (Lk 6:27–38)

Compared to such injunctions, mysteries like the Incarnation, Christ's warnings of "the worm that dieth not," and all the phantasmagoria of St. John's Apocalypse are easy to swallow. Taken literally, and applied universally, such commands would result in a world where

- Christians never called the cops. Thieves could walk right in their homes and take all their stuff—and the Christians would offer their ATM cards and PIN numbers as parting gifts.
- Christians had nothing to do with banks. Even credit unions (invented by the Church—I bank at the oldest one in America, St. Mary's Bank, founded by a French-Canadian priest) couldn't charge a fee to cover their costs. All loans would be interest-free and unsecured—and soon utterly impossible, since compulsive gamblers and crack addicts would have bankrupted all believers, including the bishops. We'd worship in tents. Until they took our tents.
- Christian wives of abusive husbands would meekly take their beatings.

Too many priests over the centuries have encouraged exactly that, it shames us to admit.

- Christians couldn't vote against taxes that bankrupted them, transferring their hard-won wealth to the lazy and the envious.
- Christian Indians whose land had been stolen by conquistadors couldn't demand it back.
- Christians wouldn't serve in the army, or if they did, they wouldn't shoot back. Christian countries would soon be overrun by conquering Communists, Muslims, or Huns. No Crusaders (St. Louis IX) could really be seen as saintly, nor soldiers (St. Joan of Arc), nor kings (St. Edward the Confessor).

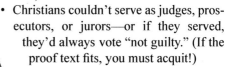

- Christians couldn't serve as judges, prosecutors, or jurors—or if they served, they'd always vote "not guilty." (If the proof text fits, you must acquit!)
- Christian citizens couldn't resist the acts of tyrannical governments but meekly would have to accept the dictates of "lawful authority," as Russian serfs, Irish peasants, and American slaves were often taught by captive clergy. At best, they could resist assaults on the clergy and the Church but not on their own rights or their human dignity. So give Big Brother your guns and act like a good Uncle Tom.
- Christians whose children were abused would never contact the authorities but would meekly ask their bishops to send the poor abuser off to counseling.

- Trying to live as lambs, we would leave the world to be run by the wolves.

See what I mean about the dangers of literal interpretation? This is why we needed a Church in the first place. Indeed, when the Church climbed gratefully out of the catacombs and resolved to sanctify the Roman world, she had to struggle with how to interpret such radical—and, on the face of it, antisocial—commands. Could New York City be run on such principles? Even the Amish, who come the closest to living literally by this Gospel, are sticklers for property rights. If you don't believe me, go down to one of their puppy mills some time and haggle over the price of a shorthaired pointer.

After Mass, I grabbed our college chaplain by the cassock and asked him to help me make sense out of this. Okay, at first I wanted him just to explain the whole thing away. "It's all just a metaphor, right, Father? I mean, the Papal States had an army. The Vatican owns a bank. . . ."

He calmed the layman down, as good Irish clergymen know how to do, and soberly laid out the Gospel's extent and its proper limits. "We are meant to strive heroically not to hate those who wrong us, in fact to forgive them even before they repent," he said. "While we can and should strive for justice, we must not dwell on personal slights, such as a slap in the face. We should give voluntarily to the needy and resist the urge to calculate our own best interest at every turn. Leave that to God, who looks after us far better than we ever can."

"But what about. . . ." I insisted, and laid out all the previous bullet points in the kind of quick staccato fashion only native New Yorkers can manage.

The good father nodded. "The Church teaches that we must show mercy, *except when it enables or encourages others to sin*. When we do that, we are complicit in their sin. Often, we must insist on strict justice for ourselves or for innocent others. That means we maintain a police force; we engage in just, defensive wars; and we administer the law. We push back against tyrannical acts by the government and stand up for our human dignity—in part because not doing so would tempt evildoers to go right on sinning and lead them to Hell."

And that, my friends, is why Christ gave us poor lambs pastors. Would that all were as wise as mine.

Role Model for Wrath: Josef Stalin

Some readers cringe when I flesh out the Deadly Sins with examples, instead of sticking to abstractions. Then again, people winced after Dante published his *Inferno*, which was full of the names of real people whom he'd known personally and included in hell the pope who was reigning when it was written (Boniface VIII).

To some, it seems uncharitable to dig up the bodies of infamous sinners and put them posthumously on trial. That's what Pope Stephen VI did to the corpse of a preceding vicar of Christ. In the course of the festively named "Cadaver Synod," Pope Stephen had the rotting form of Pope Formosus disinterred, stripped of the three fingers used for papal blessings, vested in papal robes, propped up in a chair, and charged before a court of bishops with a long list of crimes. These ranged from perjury and simony to an attempt at seizing the papacy by force—but all were merely pretexts for the new pope to vent his rage on his predecessor, a longtime enemy. The reigning pope (surprise!) won a guilty verdict against the dead one, and the court declared that even the priestly ordinations Formosus

Pope Formosus, before they buried him and dug him up again.

performed had been invalid. Formosus's body was thrown in a potters' field, then dug up again and tossed into the Tiber.

Legend tells that Formosus's body bobbed back up in the Tiber and began performing miracles.[2] This comeback so impressed the Roman mob that they rose up and deposed Stephen, who was promptly strangled in prison. This sordid, Dark Age prequel to *Godfather III* was mitigated only by the absence of actress Sofia Coppola.

I'm tempted to cite Stephen VI as the role model here for Wrath, except that the backstory behind this pope's "hermeneutic of discontinuity" is too tortuous to unfold. For a scholar's attempt to untwist the writhing viper's nest of ninth-century papal politics, see the *Catholic Encyclopedia* article on Formosus. Go on, I dare you. Any reader who slogs through that concatenation of Agiltrudes and Arnulfs and recalls a single fact of the case faces a lucrative career as an annulment attorney.

Instead, I'll tell the story of a very different sort of man who won't stay buried: Josef Stalin. In the bittersweet Soviet film satire *Repentance,* the body of a small-town tyrant clearly modeled on Stalin insists on popping up out of the ground, to the embarrassment of everyone. It seems that the earth itself is offended and keeps on rejecting the corpse. The film proved, alas, prophetic; Stalin has risen back to prominence in post-Communist Russia as an icon of the nation's vanished greatness. If that surprises us, it shouldn't; many of the great men whose names crowd the history books are there because of the body counts they racked up pursuing power and glory. Alexander the Great, Attila the Hun, Tamerlane, Genghis Khan, and Napoleon aren't familiar names today because of all the pediatric cancer hospitals they endowed. Likewise, history dwells on the crimes of tyrants against civilians: Ivan the Terrible, Pol Pot, Adolf Hitler, and Josef Stalin.

Of all these names, Stalin's seems the most fitting to illustrate pure Wrath. A slow-witted ex-seminarian with an excellent memory for insults and injuries, Josef Jughashvili was won over early to Lenin's program for force-feeding Marx's utopia. He joined the Bolshevik wing of the socialist revolutionaries, where he quickly made a name robbing banks and kidnapping local notables for ransom. Unlike his rivals for prominence Leon Trotsky and Nicolai Bukharin, Stalin never really grasped the nuances of Marxist theory. He didn't need to; Stalin's genius was organizational. He mastered early the art of counting votes in

---

2. None of these has been evaluated by the Congregation for the Causes of Saints, I hasten to add.

back rooms and squeezing cadres for support in taking over key committees. Nowadays, he'd be the majority whip in the House.

A gray man devoid of cultural or intellectual interests, Stalin volunteered for tedious bookkeeping work that was shunned by intellectuals. This allowed Stalin to gather dirt on people, pile up institutional power, and harness the support of his fellow mediocrities against evil geniuses like Trotsky. By 1929, Stalin had engineered the removal of most of the other "old Bolsheviks" who'd played key roles in winning the Russian Civil War. Stalin then crushed potential resistance in the captive nation Ukraine by hunting down its independent farmers—seizing their land, their grain, and finally all their farm animals in an artificial famine that killed an estimated 10 million farmers from 1932 to 1933.

Stalin spent most of a decade avenging the petty wrongs his party rivals had done him, searching out potential rivals for power and engineering their murder, then purging the Soviet party and army of anyone who might challenge his power. Instead of simply butchering them, as Hitler did his enemies on the "night of the

Stalinist paranoia depicted in a propaganda poster from the era of the Purge trials.

long knives," Stalin took morbid pleasure in forcing his rivals to confess to outrageous, impossible crimes. Sometimes after weeks of torture, these broken men would appear before a courtroom in a blatantly rigged trial and admit that they had served simultaneously as agents of England, Hitler, and the Vatican—and had single-handedly caused factories to malfunction or entire crops to fail. At party congresses, Stalin would deliver speeches that ran several hours to crowds of terrified apparatchiks who'd bloody their hands applauding. Indeed, on at least one occasion, Stalin dispatched his secret police to watch for the first man who stopped clapping—who died in jail with a bullet to the skull.

Whole nations that seemed to Stalin potentially disloyal were uprooted from their lands and deported to distant deserts, while the "progressive" Soviet Union undid the work of Tsar Alexander I—who'd abolished serfdom—by creating in Siberia a vast industrial network based entirely on slave labor. We call it the Gulag.

Not everyone reading this will think I'm entirely fair to Comrade Stalin. For instance, the civil rights leader W. E. B. DuBois penned a famous obituary for Stalin, which reads, in part, as follows:

> Joseph Stalin was a great man; few other men of the 20th century approach his stature. He was simple, calm and courageous. He seldom lost his poise; pondered his problems slowly, made his decisions clearly and firmly; never yielded to ostentation nor coyly refrained from holding his rightful place with dignity. He was the son of a serf but stood calmly before the great without hesitation or nerves. But also—and this was the highest proof of his greatness—he knew the common man, felt his problems, followed his fate.
>
> Stalin was not a man of conventional learning; he was much more than that: he was a man who thought deeply, read understandingly and listened to wisdom, no matter whence it came. He was attacked and slandered as few men of power have been; yet he seldom lost his courtesy and balance; nor did he let attack drive him from his convictions nor induce him to surrender positions which he knew were correct. As one of the despised minorities of man, he first set Russia on the road to conquer race prejudice and make one nation out of its 140 groups without destroying their individuality. . . .
>
> The poor Russian peasant was the lowest victim of tsarism, capitalism and the Orthodox Church. He

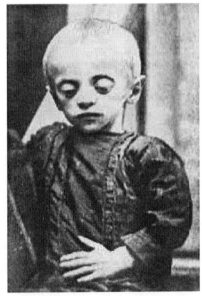

One of the "rural bloodsuckers" driven out by Stalin.

surrendered the Little White Father easily; he turned less readily but perceptibly from his ikons; but his kulaks clung tenaciously to capitalism and were near wrecking the revolution when Stalin risked a second revolution and drove out the rural bloodsuckers.[3]

Intellectuals who may have conquered other vices, who would sneer at leaders clearly consumed by Greed or Lust or Sloth, can find themselves transfixed by the godlike power of men who are masters of Wrath. The list is long and squalid of the brilliant and the clever who tossed aside their principles to grovel gleefully for tyrants. Perhaps it's early exposure to the *Iliad* ("Sing O Goddess, the Wrath[4] of Achilles") or some inborn primate instinct to venerate the leader of the troop, but few of us easily pass by a bloody throne without fighting the urge to kneel.

---

3. W. E. B. DuBois, "On Stalin," *National Guardian,* March 16, 1953.
4. Imagine Homer had written "Sloth" instead. The whole story would have turned out rather differently.

Patience, for Christ's Sake

When it comes to Patience, my readers might well complain that I'm preaching to the choir: surely they of all people have grown in this Virtue, if only by working their way through my labyrinthine digressions, historical vignettes, and autobiographical dog anecdotes. And of course, I'm happy to help.

But there's much more to the Virtue of Patience than the eye-rolling, finger-tapping resistance to abandoning an experience (e.g., closing a book, walking out of a movie, dumping your two-year-old in foster care) in the hope that the "good parts" will turn up pretty soon. By itself, that's not so much a Virtue as a life skill we all pick up along the way, unless we plan to live in an isolated cult compound surrounded by razor wire. Which is always an option.

We could call the basic, postadolescent ability to delay gratification and see things through to the end simple "forbearance." As in, "My friend made me watch *Borat*, and I put up with it *for the bear*." And indeed, the scene where Oksana, Borat's bear, leans out of the back of the ice cream truck Borat is driving past a park and causes a

flock of terrified school kids to flee for their lives is one of the funniest things ever filmed. But it doesn't make the movie an edifying experience, so waiting around for it doesn't rank as a practice of virtuous Patience. (How's that for a digression? Now pat yourself on the back.)

Patience as a Virtue involves rather more than the old "wince and wait" that we learn while counting the

long, long seconds it takes traffic lights to change or other people's lips to finish moving so we can speak. There's much more to it than simply realizing that life is in fact not TiVo and you can't fast-forward through the laxative commercials. Trust me, I've tried.

Preachers have classically called us to look to Christ—specifically, to His monumental patience during His Passion. The Creator of the universe, Who really did have absolute command over legions of angels, endured long hours of mockery, spitting,

55

betrayal, abandonment, torture, and finally execution at the hands of His wretched creations. On a purely natural level, this is completely incomprehensible, like an old lady calmly allowing herself to be slowly eaten by her Persian cats—all the while explaining, "But it does the poor dears good."

But then, on a purely natural level, life itself is a nasty practical joke, a trick played on us by selfish DNA that uses our frail, dying frames to replicate itself indefinitely like some interminable Hollywood franchise entailing Nicholas Cage, until the sun sputters out, the planets stop moving, and the galaxies dissipate into a tepid, homogenous gruel. (Call it "cosmic sprawl.")

Perhaps the image of Christ enduring His passion is at once too emotional and too mysterious to invoke for everyday use. For instance, when I got in my cramped Lufthansa coach seat after a meal entailing white asparagus (*Spargel*) smothered in far too much drawn butter and realized I'd be spending the next seven hours climbing in and out of the coffinlike airplane bathroom, it really didn't seem the time to tell myself, "Think of what Jesus endured." Anyway, my snarky self would have answered, "The bible said, 'blows and *spitting*.'"

At times like those, when pathos foxtrots with bathos, it's much more helpful to think of the lesser trials Jesus suffered throughout His life. For instance, all that time He had to spend shuffling through crowds of cantankerous Middle Easterners, asking Him leading questions, questioning His authority, and showing Him their pustulent, suppurating wounds. Keep in mind that He could also read their souls, which, for Him (as for priests like Padre Pio), must have been as grueling and dispiriting as we would find a trip through an "all-ages" nudist camp.

I'm sure our Lord felt at once like a weary eighth-grade religion teacher, an overworked law associate, and a medical intern working triple shifts at Bellevue. Surely, there must have been times, long before the Passion, when Our Lord was tempted to reach out a hand, press Control-Alt-Delete, and uncreate the universe. But He didn't. And most of the time, we're grateful.

Our Lord was able to put up with ordinary life as the Messiah and His atrociously cruel death only because He knew of its redemptive purpose. We can suffer with many indignities if our eyes stay on the prize; He made us that way. This holds true at every stage of life, from the mastery of difficult but necessary skills—such as making roux for gumbo or writing formal verse—right up through the bouts of infant colic, phonics homework, school talent shows, staff meetings, performance reviews, marital squabbles, teenage tantrums, and occasional genuine tragedies that fill up our earthly lives. Even gleefully atheistic scientists admit that religious faith serves a purpose—keeping us going, day to day, by giving *us* a sense of purpose.

As Christians, we know that our Purpose also has senses—five of them. Our Lord slogged through most of the same quagmires we do. He shambled through squalidly crowded city streets in search of decent falafel, and He put up with tedious questions from learned idiots about the minutiae of legal disputes. (Did He ever change diapers? With all those cousins, I bet He did.) And amid it all, He made wine, cured the sick, multiplied loaves and fishes, and saved the world. He may not have always suffered with a smile—but then, that would have been creepy. The Patience of Christ was fully human, which meant that it had limits. For instance, He had no time at all for liturgical abuses.

But I digress.

Beagle-Related Digression #2: Pets as a School for Patience

When we call God's gifts to us "grace," we aren't typically thinking of the same quality we mean when we say someone is a "gracious" host or hostess. But etymology rarely lies, and in fact, we find throughout life that the analogy holds precisely: most of the time, when we haven't thrown up impregnable earthworks of pride He needs to blast away through suffering, God leads us to Himself through gentle means, attracting us to the one Good we cannot see through the many that we can. We can, if our heart is open, find signs of His kindness everywhere. It's part of the Virtue of Patience to step back from our passions, look for His fingerprints, and discern His still, small voice—which I've learned to hear in the incessant howls of hunting dogs.

The last time we had a thunderstorm, the crackling of the clouds sent the wimpier of my two beagles into a full-bore panic attack. Little Franzi cowered against my leg, buzzing like those massagers they use at old-fashioned barbershops, until I scooped up all forty pounds of the quivering hound and laid him next to me in the bed. I actually had to cradle him like a child—albeit a bowlegged, pigeon-toed, stinky, fur-covered child with an IQ of under twenty-five whom you have trained to defecate outdoors.[1] At first glance, Franzi seems like a cuddly, pokey, Dog Lebowski who yawns through most of the day.

Susie is my meth head. During storms, she dashes back and forth across the house, as if to chase the lightning and barks back at the sky. She crouches at the

---

1. It's best not to admit this when social services comes knocking, FYI.

window seat like Lee Harvey Oswald, daring little old ladies to walk past my apartment. Then she unloads a series of sharp, staccato barks that could cause a cardiac arrest.

Susie is the lean and elegant huntress who grew from the whirring puppy someone brought me in a shoe box, and she has spent most of her waking moments chasing critters, chewing bloody butcher's bones on the couch, and howling. I love the sound and have always encouraged it, so that now when I say, "Sing!" she lets out a long and poignant "*A-r-r-r-r-r-o-o-o-o-o!*" and then goes on doing it, sometimes for thirty minutes. Too bad it never occurred to me, back when she was a puppy, to invent a command for "Quit it!" Her breath reminds me of that summer in New

Susie, with the fruits of her labor.

Orleans when a friend spilled Vietnamese fish sauce in the car. But the look of fanatical love—pure, absolute, and indiscriminate—in those sharp brown eyes makes her impossible to resist: like the angels gazing on the face of God, in one of Giotto's frescoes. You learn to hold your breath.

I adopted Susie on the advice of a spiritual director, a Catholic shrink who hoped to banish my Jansenist image of God. "You wanna know pure and unconditional love, the kinda love God has for every human soul?" he asked between mouthfuls of pasta. (The doc looked and dressed alarmingly like Joe Pesci and scarfed down Italian take-out during our sessions.) "Get a dog." At least that's what I think he said. His mouth was full. . . .

His counsel proved wise. I actually found it easier to pray while Susie was singing, and she'd help me to ruminate by thoughtfully chewing the cud on the legs of my table. My productivity soared. And then I got cocky.

I decided that Susie needed a playmate. I looked into getting a basenji, one of those little African hounds that yodel. I downloaded some yodels and played them back—until a nosy old bat who lived nearby came pounding on my window, demanding, "Why are you torturing that poor dog?" The next time she walked past my window, Susie defibrillated her. *Good girl!*

The search went on, until I found the perfect writer's companion: a sweet and playful Dalmatian, with icy blue eyes, whom my neighbor owned but couldn't housetrain. So I took him temporarily. I discovered that crate training really works—if you can stand three days of continuous whimpering. Apart from that, I applied to Koto the Zmirak Method: no matter what the dog does, praise him—for eating, for scratching, for stretching, for barking at birds, whatever. It makes the dog feel

happy and secure, and as long as what he's doing isn't dangerous or illegal, it's usually pretty cute. So why not act like the God imagined, vaguely, by liberal Christians—C. S. Lewis's "senile grandfather in heaven"? It isn't like you'll be called to answer for the dog's soul (at least I hope not).

The first time I woke up with Koto laying on top of me, running and barking fran-

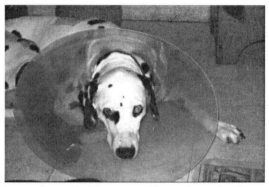

Koto, in his space dog costume.

tically in his sleep and shooting a two-foot stream of urine, I'll admit I was disconcerted. Okay, my inner Slavic peasant thought the dog might be possessed. Shaking him didn't wake him, and the St. Michael prayer didn't work, so I turned in desperation to science and learned that dog was stone deaf and suffered from epilepsy. Then I came across Ratzinger.

That wasn't his baptismal name. I later learned that "Homer" was the birth name of the abandoned beagle I found at 3 AM in front of my building, tied to a parking meter. At the pound, his life span would have been measured in days, since few folks are willing to adopt an overweight, aging dog with bleeding sores and infected ears who is missing half his fur.

Of course, I brought him home and named him for my favorite German theologian (now pope) whom the old dog closely resembled. Now I had three hounds in a two-bedroom apartment, two with serious medical issues, and a third with a singing career. Koto's original owner decided to take him back, and

Ratzinger, silent but deadly.

I spent about $1,500 at the vet nursing old Ratzi to health. I was back down to just two beagles, who I hoped would cavort, hunt, and howl as a happy team. (Susie is partial to squirrels and skateboarders—whom she'll pursue for blocks if you don't stop her. The one time I wasn't looking and a skater whizzed suddenly by, she took him down like a deer.)

The marriage didn't last. Susie tried to play, but Ratzinger mostly moped, stole her food, farted, and (whatever house-training methods I applied) peed in the same spot on the kitchen floor until my place stank like a subway tunnel. (Kiss that last month's rent good-bye.) In despair, I found a no-kill shelter that was willing to take

the incontinent cardinal, housetrain him, and place him—if I took one of their dogs instead. Which is how I ended up with Greystoke, a solemn but loving mix of German short-haired pointer and ghetto pit bull, who was found roaming the platform of the F train in Brooklyn—no doubt trying to transfer to the V. There was nothing much wrong with this dog, apart from the raging, uncontrollable diarrhea.

Which, you know, the folks at the shelter forgot to mention. They were later closed down for animal neglect but not before a miraculously housebroken Ratzinger had found a loving home. A friend of mine sighted him at a yuppie dog run in Park Slope, trying to hump some art consultant's hapless basenji.

Greystoke, menacing untrustworthy dinner guests.

Some pills fixed Greystoke's bowels, and I was finally able to get that . . . elemental scent out of the house. The parties I threw to celebrate the feasts of the Catholic liturgical year went off much better now that the guests could smell their food.

His fur the color of a blueberry, Greystoke was like those grumpy New York cops in 1930s movies who walked the beat shouting "Scram!" at the East Side Kids. At the dog run, he'd stand around looking officious, watching for other dogs who were playing a little too rough. Then he'd rush over to break up the "fight" with a hearty growl that scared all the dogs and owners alike. Affectionate and protective, he made me feel really safe walking at night, like having Mayor Giuliani on a leash. Apart from biting the occasional dinner guest, Greystoke was the perfect pet, and it broke my heart when he came down with terminal cancer. I sat on the floor of the vet's office to stroke him as they put him to sleep and took Greystoke (curled up in a ball, wrapped in a towel, frozen stiff) to a farm in Connecticut for burial.

Osama Franz Laden plans future attacks by his insurgent group, Al-Canine.

Like a seasoned HR manager, Susie took most of this turnover in stride. Each time a new stray arrived, she'd sulk for a few days, then promptly

start to fiddle and flirt with him, until at last they were cordial, if distant, friends. But when I lost Greystoke, she seemed confused. She'd walk around sniffing, then come back to me and stare. I could almost hear her wail, in the voice of Sally Field, "What have you done with my husband?" Then she went off to chew the scenery.

It took weeks of checking shelters and beagle rescue groups before I found my Franzi. When I drove up to the shelter in Westchester, Franz Josef broke from the pack of motley labs and terriers and waddled straight up to me. "Rowf!" he averred, like an indignant elephant seal. "Rowf! Where's your car?"

I gave Franz Josef the name I had been saving for a son . . . until my beloved demanded of me, "Do you want him to get the tar beat out of him on the playground every *single* day? Why don't you just call him Sue?" So the beagle got the name.

Thinking him a slow and compliant middle-aged dog, I unhooked the leash just outside my apartment door. Franzi raced off like a greyhound down the street. Who knew that a pudgy, sleepy dog could run so long, so far, so *fast*? I tracked him on foot for more than two hours, got close as he stopped to smell the garbage, sneaked up on him, and pounced.

If you've never fallen face first, flat, on a New York City sidewalk at 4 AM, then you haven't met Franzi. As I climbed to my feet, I watched him disappearing down Twenty-first Avenue—sure that he would meet a quick and ugly fate beneath the wheels of some guy's Camaro.

It took two days of my roaming the streets and posting flyers before a kind soul turned the rascal in. Two hours into his newfound freedom, it seemed that Franzi had gotten bored and followed some woman home. He'd trotted along behind her, walked in as if he owned the place, and looked up expecting breakfast. I happily forked over the reward. Who could stand to lose such a dog?

In the time since his return, Franzi has worked hard and achieved a lot. He has, on various occasions

- clipped my girlfriend at the knees like a seasoned linebacker;
- escaped through narrowly opened doors and under fences;
- climbed rocks and forded streams as I ran behind in frenzied pursuit, clad only in flip flops and boxer shorts;
- chewed the heel of said girlfriend's Manolo Blahnik;
- eaten the silk headband she had handmade from her favorite Pucci scarf;
- ransacked her Fendi bag, then trotted up to her thoughtfully, holding the bag in his teeth;
- shredded ninety-six rolls of toilet paper to make a feathered mattress, then went to sleep.

This reign of terribleness has led me to believe I might have misnamed this dog. He only appears as sleepy, peaceful, and benevolent as the long reign (1848–1917) of good Kaiser Franz Josef. Leave him alone for just a few minutes, and the dog morphs into "Osama Franz Laden." And in our War on Terribleness, it's always yellow alert.

Sometimes I envy those people who copped out and had a bunch of children, because they couldn't face the responsibility of beagles.

Icon of Patience: Alexander Solzhenitsyn

When somebody says "poetic justice," what that really means is the kind of justice dished out by poets. In which case, you'd better hope the poet's a man like Dante

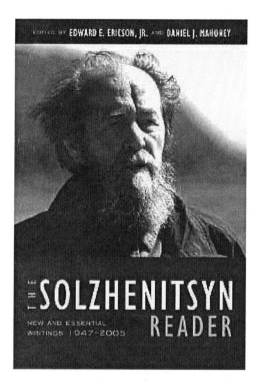

and not some maniac like Marinetti (who wanted to burn Italy's libraries and museums, then start culture from scratch) or a nattering pedophile like "Howl" author Allen Ginsberg (who held, essentially, that one's sex life begins at conception).

In the *Inferno*, Dante placed two men who betrayed their benefactors frozen side by side in the ice—the bloody-minded Archbishop Ruggieri and the equally treacherous soldier Count Ugolino. Since Ruggieri tricked Ugolino into surrendering, then imprisoned and starved him to death, Ugolino spends eternity chewing his enemy's neck. Now that, my friends, is justice.

It's a little dicier dealing out such rough justice when pairing off sinners and saints, since a holy soul isn't likely to spend his eternity slumming in hell, dishing out fitting punishments to the monsters who tortured him on earth. One shouldn't picture Thomas More sitting at a blazing fire, where King Henry VIII turns on a spit with an apple in his mouth, basting the king with honey mustard sauce (although now, of course, you're going to). Not even St. Lawrence, who kidded the Romans as they roasted him alive, seems likely to take up such a pastime—although, let's be fair, he is the patron saint of chefs.

The saints have better things to do, and we probably shouldn't listen to rigorists such as Tertullian, who gloated that the Christians who died in the Coliseum would chuckle up in Heaven at the endless torments of their persecutors. Tertullian died a heretic, by the way—but I won't gloat.

Still, it is right and just to counterpoise Josef Stalin, exemplar of Wrath, with his victim Alexander Solzhenitsyn as a paragon of the opposite virtue, Patience. Born to a prosperous farmer, Solzhenitsyn studied math and philosophy before enlisting in the Red Army that beat back Hitler's genocidal invasion of Russia. Although he won medals for valor, Solzhenitsyn ran afoul of the Soviet tyrant by writing a letter to a friend in which he criticized Stalin's moustache.

Henry VIII.

Okay, Solzhenitsyn also said a thing or two about Stalin's conduct of World War II, which the Russians nearly lost thanks to Uncle Joe's secret crush on Adolf Hitler, who would never, ever *think* of invading the Soviet Union—despite those hundreds of public statements where Hitler promised

- to wipe out Bolshevism,
- to ethnically cleanse the whole of Russia west of the Urals,
- to colonize the country with blond German warlords who'd "breed" with entire harems to repopulate the countryside with Aryans.

All those statements were meant ironically, Stalin insisted. There was no reason whatsoever in 1939 to prepare for the German blitzkrieg, which Soviet spies and ordinary journalists constantly warned was coming. (Stalin actually executed Russian agents for reporting on German troop buildups.) The Germans captured most of European Russia in just a few weeks.

Having seen his friends butchered in combat or taken prisoner by the Germans and then, at war's end, sent to labor camps in Siberia for "treason," Solzhenitsyn sent a single imprudent letter—and for that he was tortured, then sentenced to eight years in a labor camp and "internal exile" for life. During

that exile, he contracted cancer and nearly died in a third-rate Soviet hospital. But along the way, in the years he spent chopping wood barefoot in the snow, living on fish head soup, and witnessing brutal beatings of helpless prisoners by soldiers of

"progress" and "liberation," Solzhenitsyn rediscovered his childhood Christian Faith.

In the major works he composed on scraps of paper while still in prison or secretly after his release (he was constantly under surveillance), Solzhenitsyn depicts in stark and shocking prose the brutalities that attend upon Utopia. More importantly, he pictures the simple acts of Faith, Hope, and Charity that ordinary *zeks* (political prisoners) performed for one another, to affirm their human dignity in the midst of a man-made hell. Nor does Solzhenitsyn give vent to righteous anger; he figures forth the guards and even commanders as fully human, with admixed motives, driven in part by ideology, partly by hunger for power, but most of the time by fear. They were, in their own way, victims of the terror by which they reigned. Solzhenitsyn even reflects on his own part in advancing Stalin's power: "I remember myself in my captain's shoulder boards and the

forward march of my battery through East Prussia, enshrouded in fire, and I say: 'So were we any better?'"

Despite, or in part because of, all his suffering, Solzhenitsyn crafted novels that will endure as literary masterworks. *The First Circle* sketches a milder part of the Gulag, which the Soviets ran to exploit the talents of convicts with scientific training. It includes a brilliant foray into the mind of an aging Stalin, who wonders foggily what became of the "Old Russia" of his youth. What happened to all the peasants and the priests, the dying tyrant mutters. Why is everyone around me such a sniveling, cringing

coward? Solzhenitsyn has too much artistic restraint to offer the answer: because all the bravest people have been locked away in camps.

Cancer Ward sketches out Solzhenitsyn's tentative gropings back toward Faith. The unjustly neglected novel *Lenin in Zurich* explores in clinical detail the soul of one aspiring tyrant, while in his massive, multivolume historical novel of Russia, *The Red Wheel*, Solzhenitsyn seeks to explain how "Holy Russia" could fall into the hands of deluded ideologues. His answer is stark: the cynical stupidity of tsarist bureaucrats, fueled by and feeding into the reckless fantasies of intellectuals.

But Solzhenitsyn will always be best remembered for *The Gulag Archipelago*, which documents the lives and deaths of the millions who suffered in slave camps and whose very existence was doubted for decades by "fellow travelers" in the West. Its appearance in 1973 made Solzhenitsyn's life in Russia almost impossible, and he was forced into exile in 1974.

It was in the West that Solzhenitsyn had to learn another side of Patience. First hailed by liberal anti- and ex-Communists, Solzhenitsyn soon became the target of their barbs. He sought for Russia a rebirth of Christian Faith and traditional patriotism and didn't look to the secular, childless West as a moral model. This made him a dangerous reactionary in the eyes of recent converts from Marxism. His books began to fall out of print; one volume of *The Red Wheel*, last time I checked, had still not been translated into English. But Solzhenitsyn's reputation really began to darken in Western eyes when he made his prophetic commencement speech at Harvard in 1978.[2]

Trying to make friends with the media, he said,

> Destructive and irresponsible freedom has been granted boundless space. Society appears to have little defense against the abyss of human decadence, such as, for example, misuse of liberty for moral violence against young people, motion pictures full of pornography, crime and horror. It is considered to be part of freedom. . . .
>
> Hastiness and superficiality are the psychic disease of the 20th century and more than anywhere else this disease is reflected in the press. . . . Without any censorship, in the West fashionable trends of thought and ideas are carefully separated from those which are not fashionable; nothing is forbidden, but what is not fashionable will hardly ever find its way into periodicals or books or be heard in colleges.

Next, he celebrated Western consumerism:

> The majority of people have been granted well-being to an extent their fathers and grandfathers could not even dream about; it has become possible to raise young people according to these ideals, leading them to

---

2. Find the whole text online at http://www.columbia.edu/cu/augustine/arch/solzhenitsyn/harvard1978
.html.

physical splendor, happiness, possession of material goods, money and leisure, to an almost unlimited freedom of enjoyment.

So who should now renounce all this, why and for what should one risk one's precious life in defense of common values, and particularly in such nebulous cases when the security of one's nation must be defended in a distant country? . . . Even biology knows that habitual extreme safety and well-being are not advantageous for a living organism.

To those who believed that Russia didn't need to recover its ancient faith, but simply to emulate America's free markets and politics,[3] Solzhenitsyn offered the following:

In American democracy at the time of its birth, all individual human rights were granted because man is God's creature. That is, freedom was given to the individual conditionally, in the assumption of his constant religious responsibility. Such was the heritage of the preceding thousand years. Two hundred or even fifty years ago, it would have seemed quite impossible, in America, that an individual could be granted boundless freedom simply for the satisfaction of his instincts or whims.

He suggested instead this answer, which ought to be familiar to readers of Dostoevsky—or the Gospels:

If humanism were right in declaring that man is born to be happy, he would not be born to die. Since his body is doomed to die, his task on earth evidently must be of a more spiritual nature. It cannot be unrestrained enjoyment of everyday life. It cannot be the search for the best ways to obtain material goods and then cheerfully get the most out of them. It has to be the fulfillment of a permanent, earnest duty so that one's life journey may become an experience of moral growth, so that one may leave life a better human being than one started it.

It wasn't bitterness or hunger for vengeance that Solzhenitsyn took away from his decades of suffering, but the simple lesson, given earlier, which a Russian *babushka* might have taught her toddlers as they prayed before an icon. It's the wisdom he wrung from the grapes of Wrath that makes Solzhenitsyn an icon of Patience worth emulating. You can call on that Virtue as you work your way through the thousands of pages the great man has written. Every word is worth it.

---

3. What happened instead in the 1990s was that a kleptocracy seized most of the country's wealth, while Boris Yeltsin curled up in a vodka bottle.

Trademark-Busting Cosmo-Style Quiz™ #2: Score Yourself on the Scale that Runs from "Sociopath" to "Garden Slug"

Patience is the Virtue most conducive to social peace. At the opposite extreme, Servility only gives aid and comfort to tyrants and sociopaths. (As Fr. Benedict Groeschel likes to say, "The Gospel doesn't read 'Blessed are the doormats.'") Holy Patience resides somewhere between the two. The following hypothetical should help you place yourself on the continuum.

The Quiz

Imagine you're the owner of two delightful, spirited hunting dogs. In search of cheaper rent and better architecture, you've moved from the Legoland suburbs into an old city neighborhood. One house on the corner of your block is a precious, froufrou Victorian, done up like a birthday party cake with plaster cherubs and twee little fairies. Its garden spills out and merges with the sidewalk, so you practically trip over the topiary.

Its owners, under the mistaken impression that they have by restoring a house become the feudal lords of all they can survey, get angry that you walk your delightful, spirited hunting dogs past their property. It seems that sometimes the hounds sniff the topiary. Now, your pockets are always stuffed with biodegradable doggie bags, and you're conscientious about picking up after your critters. But the very fact that you walk the dogs past their garlanded angel sculptures three times a day—on the way to your own apartment, three doors down—outrages the owners of the Crystal Palace. They shout at you from the window and sometimes come out and get in your face, demanding that you avoid their corner. They follow you to your apartment and write down the number, eyeing your car and muttering threats. In response, you react as follows:

a. Create a list of all the harm these people could conceivably do to you—from vandalizing your car to hurting your dogs—and develop a contingency list of escalated acts of retribution. For instance, if they slash your tires, you'll spray weed killer on their rosebushes. Should they actually harm your dogs, remember one key fact about Molotov cocktails: flames don't *necessarily* wipe out fingerprints.

b. Make a point of walking your dogs past their house more often than necessary. Investigate whether their expansionist horticulture violates zoning laws, and find out whether their gardeners live here legally.

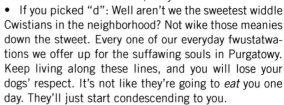

c. Walk your dogs wherever you normally would but don't go out of your way to pass the Crystal Palace. The next time they accost you, greet its owners with a confident smile. Force yourself to pray for these people's eternal salvation but take no guff from them. Go about your business with a spring in your step.

d. Avoid trouble at all costs. Leave an apologetic note under their door, and walk blocks out of your way to avoid bothering these people—who are clearly high-strung and overly materialistic. Think about their problems, focusing on their weaknesses and vices, and quietly congratulate yourself on how much more Christlike you're being.

Here are the results:

- If you picked "a": You are one of those few people in America who should *not* be allowed to own a handgun. You might want to consider keeping duller kitchen knives. You've got a lot more Stalin in you than you really need, and it is time to consider anger management counseling. Really, no kidding. Hey, buddy, don't kill the messenger. . . .

- If you picked "b": You're clearly from New York City, so you probably can't help it. But you really must do better than this. You can turn the other cheek here and avoid wasting time courting needless trouble. No, the neighbors don't need to be "taught a lesson," and it's really not worth the *agita*. Besides, all this confrontation is probably upsetting your dogs.

- If you picked "c": You've attained the proper balance of confrontation and compliance. But don't wear out your back from patting yourself on it, and keep those "Virtue End-Zone Dances" you do in the mirror to a minimum, okay?

- If you picked "d": Well aren't we the sweetest widdle Cwistians in the neighborhood? Not wike those meanies down the stweet. Every one of our everyday fwustatwations we offer up for the suffawing souls in Purgatowy. Keep living along these lines, and you will lose your dogs' respect. It's not like they're going to *eat* you one day. They'll just start condescending to you.

Activities

If you have an ongoing problem with Wrath, there's probably already some evidence of it: the many short-term gigs that clog your resume, that growing list of restraining orders, and your thinning Rolodex. (Writing those Bleep-You letters is fun, isn't it?) If your Facebook page has more "enemies" than "friends," that's another dead giveaway. Here are a few ideas for moving yourself from ball breaker to peacemaker:

- ❑ If you aren't involved in some serious, regular exercise, it's time to take that up—something high-impact, like jai alai or rugby. The experience of people stronger than you regularly knocking you on your butt should prove . . . instructive.
- ❑ You'd also benefit from more time spent with the scriptures—only this time, leave off the Old Testament battle narratives you've always used for *lectio divina*. Concentrate on the Beatitudes and the narrative of the Passion.
- ❑ Pick up the profound, and profoundly practical, spiritual book by Fr. Lawrence Lovasik, *The Hidden Power of Kindness*. Once you've read a few chapters, you'll realize why its real, secret title is *How Not to be Such a Jackass*.
- ❑ Also get hold of Jean Pierre de Caussade's classic *Complete Abandonment to Divine Providence*, which puts forth an interesting notion: that every piece of abuse God allows us to suffer at the hands of others is punishment for some sin we've committed but gotten away with. Now, this isn't true for everyone (think of kids in abusive households), but it is in your case. Isn't it?

Gluttony: God in the Belly

From the tenor of my reflections on the Deadly Sins, the careless reader might think I'm playing devil's advocate—or, even worse, that I've pumped up my ego to the point where I think I can compete with C. S. Lewis. In fact, the only Lewis I'm hoping to emulate is Jerry. (Watch Amazon.com for my hagiography of St. Jerome titled *The Nutty Confessor.*)

No, I'm not channeling Screwtape. In admitting to a certain wistfulness about each of the Deadly Sins, I speak on behalf of natural man—let's call him Mr. Natural—who chafes at the burden of grace, who learns that his moral choices have eternal repercussions, and who mutters about it into his Michelob. And who can blame him?

Consider the Four Last Things: Death, Judgment, Hell, and Heaven. Three out of four are appalling, and the fourth is unimaginable—so your mind tends to linger on the others. I mean, we've all seen horror movies and can picture those kinds of things happening to our souls and then to our resurrected bodies . . . forever. On the other hand, I've seen just a few Beatitude movies, and most of those involved Robin Williams in some capacity.

The first time the truth about Hell and Judgment sank into my mind, I remember exactly how I felt: like a tourist at Vegas, who'd sat in on what he thought was a "friendly game" of poker—then it dawned on him he was playing at the high-stakes table against a bunch of hit men for the mob. He started out in the hole and wasn't sure of the rules. Those "free" shrimp cocktails the waitresses bring this poor guy during the game? It turns out they're going right on his tab.

Which brings us to Gluttony, a universal human trait that transcends political category, crosses ethnic and ecclesiastical boundaries, and knits together the whole human family in a vast feeding frenzy and drinking game. From the pudgiest

telemarketer scarfing down his third plate of bacon at Shoney's to the daintiest gourmet losing her kids in the aisles at Whole Foods as she scrutinizes the labels in search of heresy—no one's left out. We have all heard the elegant cliché, "Less is more." And we all know it's bunk. *More is more.* As in, "Pour me one more for the road."[1]

At first glance, it might seem that Christian strictures on Gluttony are fairly light. According to the usually hard-line St. Thomas Aquinas, we aren't supposed to eat or drink so much that we make ourselves unhealthy or crazy. To which we might say, "Er, okay." It sounds more like straightforward advice we could get from a family doctor—or a loving request from a longtime spouse

THO AQVINVS

---

1. Few places take this saying as literally as Catholic Louisiana, home of the world's only drive-through daiquiri stores.

who has wearied of peeling a husband off a barstool or prying a wife with grease and a crowbar out of the tub.

But the Faith is not so simple, nor the good news so pleasant to hear. The Angelic Doctor was himself such a hearty eater that St. Francis Xavier, the apostle of Asia, once quipped that Aquinas's magnum opus should be called the *Sumo Theologica*.[2] No wonder St. Thomas looked past simple quantity when he considered the sorts of sins one might commit with a knife and fork. As the old *Catholic Encyclopedia* sums up his teaching, St. Thomas warned against eating or drinking

- too soon,
- too expensively,
- too eagerly,
- too much,
- too daintily.

"Too soon" probably made the list out of deference to harried medieval mothers who were tired of the little ones ripping chunks of half-cooked meat from the roasting boar or digging prematurely into the pot of fretted badger. Translated for modern Christians, this item of Thomist PowerPoint calls to mind the point at which, during

a drawn-out, forty-five-minute liturgy, your meditation on the Eucharistic meal gives way to fantasies of brunch. *Behold the Eggs of Benedict. . . .*

"Too expensively" requires a more complex moral calculus. There's no Church law that sets what percentage of your budget you should spend on food. Irritatingly, this question is left to our best judgment, which frequently fails—for instance, when we spend most of our after-tax income eating out or ordering in. I'm fond of how Starbucks treats its employees—offering health insurance and help with tuition. But I can't help thinking that most of us are spending a little bit more than we should when we pay five bucks for a cup of low-caf, demi-soy foppacino—whose paper cup is printed with socialist agitprop.

"Too eagerly" seems less an issue of morals than of manners. There are inbuilt, biomechanical constraints to how fast human hands can safely wield sharp pieces of cutlery, and the palate ingest pieces of food, without someone losing an eye—or

---

2. All documentation for this claim has, sadly, been lost.

talking with his mouth full. A blatant disregard of this Thomist injunction, if pursued with Kantian rigor, would lead to a nation of blind and fingerless citizens groping with nubby palms for scraps and conversing in staccato bursts of "Urmph," "Kmmmtrrimmle," and "Yerrtz." I know whereof I speak: the Zmirak family in 1999 laid out and gobbled up an eight-course Thanksgiving dinner in seventeen minutes. (Yes, I timed it. I'm just that kind of guy.)

"Too much" is more than obvious. It's patriotic. If you look at our nation's obesity statistics, there's nothing more American than a middle-aged spread, acquired some time during middle school. This form of individual expansion—let's call it "personal growth"—can be seen less as a sign of sedentary consumption than a citizen's quest to attain his Manifest Destiny, to claim your share of space in that elevator and burst forth from the constraints of a thirty-four waistband or coach seat on an airplane. If you notice in the mirror that you have become a tad too . . . Chestertonian, it pays to remember this: it isn't your fault. Your body was built to store up reserves of energy to provide for time of famine. Is it your fault our country isn't starving? Unless you're a farmer, the answer is no.

"Too daintily" tends to cluster around the upper-upper middle class, although it's increasingly open to upper middles—they'll let in just anybody nowadays, won't they? If it's solidly Red State and blue-collar to let your waistline go to pot, it's deeply Blue to spend more time avoiding calories than consuming them. Leave aside personal vanity and the hunger for a vampirelike earthly immortality. There are thousands of Americans who crave to climb the ladder of social class by developing sensitive palates, who think that by learning to smell the difference between Breton Salt and Himalayan, they somehow make up for the fact that their student loans exceed their incomes. These folks are called Foodies, so named because the rest of us would gladly use them as food for alligators.

Even if we avoid all the pitfalls laid out here, we are still not off the hook. According to common tradition, it is actually a sin to eat for pleasure. That's right. The Encyclopedists I cited earlier explain, in the following sobering passage:

It is incontrovertible that to eat or drink for the mere pleasure of the experience, and for that exclusively, is likewise to commit the sin of gluttony. Such a temper of soul is equivalently the direct and positive shutting out of that reference to our last end which must be found, at least implicitly, in all our actions.[3]

---

3. All quotes here from *Catholic Encyclopedia* (New York: Encyclopedia Press, 1913), s.v. "Gluttony," available on CD-ROM or at http://www.newadvent.org/cathen.

But don't despair, because

at the same time it must be noted that there is no obligation to formally and explicitly have before one's mind a motive which will immediately relate our actions to God. It is enough that such an intention should be implied in the apprehension of the thing as lawful with a consequent virtual submission to Almighty God.

I'm glad we've got that clear. So just to sum up: Eating and drinking are simple, natural pleasures given us by the generosity of God. And we're free to enjoy them as we like, provided we don't consume them too soon, too expensively, too eagerly, too extensively, or too daintily—and as long as we don't enjoy them for their own sake but maintain at least the implicit apprehension that we're nourishing our bodies to glorify God.

Somehow, the Italians have managed to keep the Faith all these centuries, despite a countryside brimming with wine vats, jars of tomatoes, and lush spaghetti trees. If they can manage it, so can we. Pass the salt. No, the *other* salt. . . .

Leaving eros aside—a special case since it entails enjoying and sometimes producing other people—every fleshly pleasure could be analyzed with an eye on the danger of Gluttony. Food and drink are only the most obvious and common forms that this sin takes. An unbalanced art collector might be gluttonous for beauty (although nowadays he's more likely hungry for the "interesting" or the "edgy"—see Andy Warhol, Chapter 9), while an iTunes addict might treat music as an all-suffusing replacement for silence and introspection. I'll confess that I have a family member who can only be described as a glutton for Hummels.

Even the intellect can get mired in this vice. The intellectual sin medievals called simply "curiosity" (Bet you didn't know there was anything wrong with that, did you?) entails a similar craving for data that don't relate to our vocation or deepening our love of God but rather keep the mind munching away on little tidbits of intellectual junk food. (New from Google: Crunchy DataNuts™—99 percent Gluten Free!) The sin of Adam and Eve itself was called by Scholastic theologians one of Gluttony, a hunger for "knowledge of good and evil" that expressed itself, ironically, through eating. Dr. Faustus likewise sold his soul to Satan in return for secret knowledge.

Once I look at the question this way, my own debilitating addiction to "all-encompassing theories of human behavior" kicks in, and I'm tempted to start grabbing evermore examples like peanuts on a long Southwest flight. But I'll exercise Temperance here and bring the issue back to food and drink.

While the temptation to drink too much alcohol has been widespread since the first Egyptian noticed that old spoiled grain turned into something . . . wonderful and miraculous, it hasn't always been possible for most people to exercise Gluttony at the table. Food was expensive, and a large portion of most peasants' or workers' incomes went to simply getting enough. Most work was manual, and the ethnic cuisines we're familiar with from our families, neighborhoods, or church potlucks reflect the need to maximize calories before, for instance, clambering up a nearly vertical hillside in the Rhineland to spend the day bent over picking grapes or going out to help a sickly ox plow the frozen earth in Ruthenia. Do that kind of work for a living and you need all the *knödel* or pierogi you can afford.

It was only in the twentieth century, in peacetime, in highly industrialized societies like ours, that food became so cheap that it was easy to overeat—and hard for farmers to make a decent living. After World War II, as the chemical industry turned its attention from killing Germans to fattening up Americans,[4] the shelves of our supermarkets filled up with an ever more lavish supply of cheap and easy calories. But the people shopping there remained the same old hunter-gatherer hominids whom God kicked out of Eden—driven by their instincts to fill their bellies every chance they got, since they never knew when a famine might come. But it never did. Instead, we got a tsunami of obesity, Type 2 diabetes, heart disease, cancers probably[5] triggered by a chemistry set of food additives, and stores like Casual Male XL. We go to stores like Costco and Sam's Club and stand agape like émigrés from 1970s Bulgaria before the sheer array of

---

4. As noted in Michael Pollan, *The Omnivore's Dilemma* (New York: Penguin, 2007), the first chemical fertilizers used in the United States were created to use up the gunpowder left over after V-J Day.

5. Who the heck really knows? Maybe cancer is just God's way of saying you're turning sixty. The fact is that we're conducting a mass experiment in artificial feeding, using the whole population as lab rats.

bonus-sized supersaver jumbo paks, and our hardwired instincts drive us to hoard the stuff in either our freezers or our abdomens. This wave of cheap food is easy for us to zap in the microwave and eat quickly, abundantly and inattentively—in other words, like Gluttons. What's more, it entails a set of evils that affect third parties to our scarfing.

The losers in the mass-consumption game are easy to overlook. Here's an example: I got an inspirational e-mail just before Thanksgiving from a solidly profamily, Christian educational institute, staffed by smart and learned people I'd even trust with my beagles. By way of reminding me of the things for which Americans should give thanks, the e-mail effused that "turkey prices offered at Thanksgiving are sometimes as low 58 cents a pound or less and are near what it costs to grow a turkey." Which is another way of saying, "Your farmers work in a sweatshop." It almost ruined my appetite.

Indeed, a long list of foods are produced in America in such abundance, using so much high-tech equipment and chemicals, that farmers can barely make a living anymore—which is why the farm population is now down to less than 2 percent of U.S. residents. Farm communities have been hollowed out, and farm regions offer so few economic opportunities that urban plagues like crystal meth addiction now rage across the heartland, and public officials have spoken of giving South Dakota back to the buffalo.

Nor are our animals thriving. You needn't join the lunatics like Peter Singer to be sickened by modern, high-tech farming practices:

- Beef cows (whom God made grass eaters) kept alive for less than a year before they're slaughtered, forced to eat cheap, federally subsidized corn grown with petroleum fertilizers, which makes them sick, then antibiotics to keep them from dying of indigestion—when they

aren't being turned into cannibals with rendered cow meal, a practice (supposedly banned) that gave rise to mad cow disease.

- Pigs (who are smarter than dogs) who never see the light of day but spend their few months of life in steel pens just inches over a sea of excrement, so overpopulated and inbred that they generate superviruses like . . . the aptly titled swine flu. The waste from these farms poisons whole counties downwind or down river.

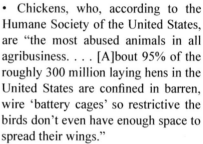

- Chickens, who, according to the Humane Society of the United States, are "the most abused animals in all agribusiness. . . . [A]bout 95% of the roughly 300 million laying hens in the United States are confined in barren, wire 'battery cages' so restrictive the birds don't even have enough space to spread their wings."

All of this so we can eat too cheaply, too quickly, and too abundantly.

We have ceased to be stewards of the earth and started acting more like irresponsible, short-term renters. Indeed, this hugely elaborate, technological attempt to thwart and dominate God's creation is eerily similar to modern reproductive technology. In the decades when our bodies ache to breed, we dose them into sterility, then as we reach the age when our DNA gives up trying, we call in the B-52s to bomb our bodies into conceiving. If liberals could learn to look at contraception the way they do at agriculture, they'd understand the Church's teaching. Conversely, if Catholics applied the same respect for Natural Law to Gluttony as to Lust, they'd find themselves shopping at farmers' markets.

Now this provokes the kind of ideological confusion for which people have no patience in our goofily polarized country—where droppin' final consonants is somehow necessary if you're agin killin' unborn babies, but if you care about the rain forest,

World's Greatest Packing Center

you're obliged to embrace homosexual marriage. Er, yeah, that all makes sense. . . .

In its modern context, I have grown impatient with the left-right distinction. It's not just the obvious abuse of language by the media, as when reporters call hard-line Communist generals in China "conservatives." It's more than that; there's something almost insane about attempting to use a one-dimensional spectrum to describe something as complex as political philosophy. It's like trying to build a house using only chopsticks and a hammer. You can see this more clearly by trying to apply a left-right distinction to something much simpler, such as cooking.

Let me propose that food writing—a topic near to my heart, which, in fact, dwells just below it, in the stomach—be simplified and clarified by setting up a left-right spectrum for national cuisines.

Logically, the Japanese kitchen should be situated on the far left, for its Bauhaus simplicity, its grimly Soviet portions and militaristic cruelty: Japanese regularly consume live, writhing lobsters, shuddering oysters, or struggling crabs. The uniform, collectivist nature of traditional Japan has left us few names of innovators or beloved chefs. Then there are those sushi dishes containing large doses of poison, which—like left-wing social policies—demand to be administered by experts who hold the consumer's life in their hands. Finally, think of the Japanese kitchen's reliance on vastly overpriced, state-subsidized rice. All these considerations place Japanese cuisine as the leftmost extreme of the culinary continuum.

What cuisine epitomizes the right? Why, French, of course. Rich, creamy, aristocratic dishes, replete with historically derived inflections, baptized after kings and their queens (or mistresses), or more piously after saints, abbots, and monasteries. (Coquilles St. Jacques, Dom Pérignon, and Chartreuse come to mind.) The French kitchen is replete with great names of great individuals, men who toiled in the kitchens of the rich, whose achievements "trickled down" to the ordinary fare of lady cooks in the provinces. Conversely, inventions of the common folk arose—through a truly Western social mobility—to grace the tables of the great. Bouillabaisse was once a cheap seafood stew enjoyed by Breton fisherman; now it's $28 a bowl at the Grand Central Oyster Bar. French foods give life to the libertine's pursuit of happiness.

One then might try to place somewhere on the spectrum between these two extremes the cuisines that arose in Italy, Germany, Ethiopia, India, and China. Those that use some sauce, some spice, but a modicum of fresh ingredients would fall between the Japanese and French extremes, forming "center-left" or "moderate" cuisines. Purists would scorn such compromise, of course, and street fights inevitably erupt over minor factional differences dividing Cantonesians from Szechuanites.

Another area where politics intersect with questions of Gluttony and Temperance is the question of "animal rights," since activists of this movement claim that human consumption of meat amounts to needless cruelty[6] in service of our sensual appetites—in other words, that anyone who isn't a vegetarian is really a glutton.

Now, to assert that animals have "rights" (What are their responsibilities?) is very different from saying that it is sinful and sick to treat God's helpless creatures with needless cruelty. The Christian position is that we have a responsibility toward animals to treat them decently. Just as it would be a sin to fill in the Grand Canyon with Styrofoam peanuts, it's a sin to torture animals—not because either the canyon or the canines have "rights" in any sense comparable to humans' rights.

Indeed, granting animals moral and legal rights implies that they are indistinguishable from and interchangeable with people. Philosophers like to make the implicit explicit, and Pete Singer, the best-selling theorist of the animal rights movement, asserts that an adult chimpanzee has more "intrinsic worth" than a preborn baby or retarded adult. More recently, Singer has embraced "interspecies eros."

Singer, who teaches freshmen ethics at Princeton, sees no problem with sex between human beings and animals—so long as the latter "consent," presumably by wagging their tails. Professor Singer is only being logical: if like him, we reject "speciesism" as just another form of racism, then there's no reason not to . . . well, to become a whole lot closer to our pets.

As an escapee from a rival Ivy, let me hoist a gin and tonic: to Princeton—in one generation, from Albert Einstein to SexFarm.com. This should figure in football fight songs forevermore; wherever Princeton plays, we'll sing, "Baa, Baa, Pete's Sheep."

Flannery O'Connor famously observed that "tenderness leads to the gas chamber." By this, she meant that intellectuals who cannot accept the insoluble residue of suffering in the world are willing to embrace any extreme to abolish it—so ironically, they'll

---

6. We could, technically, survive on peanuts and soy—although some animal rights activists are looking for ways to "raise" meat in petri dishes. Yummy.

end up sacrificing the lives of their fellow men in pursuit of this heaven on Earth. In Holland, this "humanitarian" impulse has already led to widespread euthanasia of the sick; for animal rights extremists, I'll argue, its logical implications are rather worse—by which I mean, of course, cannibalism.

My favorite tale of animal rightists involves People for the Ethical Treatment of Animals (PETA), as I heard over BBC in 2000. It seems some radicals invaded a medical lab in England and "liberated" the research animals. I don't know whether the rabbits were being harmed to make safe cosmetics or to find a cure for AIDS; it's not essential to the story. The activists whisked off the rabbits to their headquarters, where they commenced, like rabbits, to breed. (Is neutering unethical? They must have thought so. And single-sex dorms are sexist.) It seems there was soon a great surplus of rabbits, more than PETA could feed. So . . . they slaughtered the rabbits.

A local homeless shelter heard about this and asked if they could have the euthanized rabbits for their soup kitchen. Absolutely not, the answer came back. As Ingrid Newkirk, leader of Britain's PETA, told the BBC, "They were given a dignified burial. Animals were not put here for human beings to use."

Now it's interesting to note that PETA did not even offer the rabbits to the local dog pound to nourish other animals in need. I can understand how misanthropes might object to feeding British tramps, but what's wrong with foxhounds and spaniels? Do the maggots of the earth have a higher claim than unwanted pets? I'd like to corner Ingrid in a pub sometime and ask her if it's unethical for animals to live as carnivores. Are foxes a pack of murderers? If so, then I know of some English aristocrats who'd be happy to chase them down. . . .

Presumably not. I've never read of efforts by animal rightists to convince polar bears and lions to switch from animal protein to soy— although I'd like to encourage PETA to get out there in the field and commence the dialogue. We could film this historic summit for broadcast on C-SPAN and Animal Planet. The Jimmy Carter Center could sponsor the peace talks.

But why is it wrong for human beings—who've eaten meat at least since Noah's flood—to act like animals? Dr. Singer and Ms. Newkirk agree that it's wrong to make stark distinctions between human beings and other beasts. So let's take them at their word: we are beasts, with canine teeth, and we hunger for meat. Why hold human animals to a sterner standard than wolves and eagles? If we're just part of the circle of life, why can't we grab a steak along our way to feeding the worms? I really don't get it.

But there is an argument that would justify the animal rights position—although I doubt they've troubled to think things out this far. It goes like this:

a. Predator animals, such as sharks and whales and dolphins, have no choice but to eat other creatures, since they lack the rational faculty. However many monographs you press on them, at best they'll piss on them.

b. Likewise, prey animals such as cows and chickens have no choice but to serve as prey. They never volunteered for the duty; it imposes itself upon them in the form of tooth and claw.

c. Men and women have the capacity to choose, and some choose to reject the role of predator. They identify with the prey.

This is fine so far. In this question, I'm pro-choice. But how can animal rightists justify imposing this choice upon me? No one has demonstrated that squirrels are morally superior to cats; it's hard to demonstrate it is wrong for animals to prey on other animals. Of course, if some ethicists out there care to make this case, I hope they will go forth personally and preach this gospel to the grizzly bears.

Ah, the animal rights crowd responds, but those animals didn't choose to be prey. You're choosing to be a predator. So logic grinds on another, inexorable step:

d. It's wrong for creatures with a capacity for choice to impose the role of prey on creatures that lack the capacity for choice.

That works. And it leads me to my own conclusion:

z. So it's wrong for men to eat dumb animals. We should eat vegetarians instead.

If men are free to choose—and I'm all about choice—then they must also be permitted to choose the role of predator or else (in Kant's terms) their choice is "heteronymous." Forcing tofu on a steak-and-potatoes man violates his religious liberty (see Vatican II, *Dignitatis Humanae*). But human beings who chose the role of prey by rejecting speciesism have essentially volunteered, and it's time we cooked them at their word.

I'm excited about this conclusion. I'm sure that the animal rightists will help me test it. I'm already winning disciples for this view, which will spare millions of innocent animals the horrible, senseless suffering of the slaughterhouse and the hunt. It's unthinkable to impose on helpless creatures the status of prey, when tens of thousands of freely choosing human beings have already volunteered in their stead. It's a perfect synergy. Here is the common ground on which the slavering meat eaters of the world can meet the doctrinaire vegetarians and dialogue. (But not with our mouths full.)

Don't call us "cannibals." We consider the "c-word" hate speech. Instead, we prefer to be known as "succulent humanists," or "philanthropists," since we really do love man—especially in a nice cream sauce.

Who said that philosophy was useless? In this case, we've solved a bitter dispute by bringing both sides to the table. I look forward to a positively ethical feeding frenzy, and just to be prepared, I'm working on recipes. You can guess my very first:

Pâté Singer on toast.

A Glutton for Power: Francois Mitterrand

At least since the lavish dinners of the decadent Roman Republic, rulers and those who aspired to rule have frequently made a point of conspicuous consumption. Now, this isn't always despicable; we expect those who represent legitimate authority on earth to express the dignity of their office. Even in the vigorous early days of our own Republic, Americans took pride in the fact that our White House maintained high standards of hospitality, entertaining visiting dignitaries in the style they expected. The dangerously populist Thomas Jefferson—safely across an ocean, he welcomed the French Revolution—made a point when he took office as president of hiring fine French chefs, who have set the tone for White House cooking ever since. A Catholic monarch I've praised here for Humility (see Chapter 12), Kaiser Franz Josef of Austria-Hungary, ate elaborate dinners with his guests off exquisite china. Court protocol dictated that whenever the emperor finished a course, the plate must be removed. Not wanting to leave anyone hungry, Kaiser Franz Josef made sure to eat slowly and never put down his fork until the last guest had finished.

And there was indeed something cringe-worthy about the canine eagerness with which former President Clinton took each opportunity to chow down on greasy fast food. As his impeachment trial famously recorded, White House aide Betty Currie introduced Miss Monica Lewinksy to the president thus: "The girl is here with the pizzas."

Throughout history, many more public figures have made a point of garishly consuming outlandishly costly items, in gorge-churning quantities, to vaunt their riches and impress, bribe, or bully their influential guests. The best example of such epicurean imperialism is Lucullus (118–57 BC), a Roman general who conquered much of Asia Minor—and brought back with him so much loot that his wealth became legendary. With the silver, gold, jewels, and slaves he'd taken from the hapless Minor Asians, Lucullus built ornate palaces, lavish gardens, and elaborate aquaria. He failed, however, to spread the wealth among the troops who'd done the fighting, and their resentment led to Lucullus's eventual failure in politics. Shorn of the leading role he'd hoped for in the Senate, Lucullus retired to enjoy his stupendous wealth and dazzle his old political rivals with the splendors of his table. According to the curmudgeonly historian Plutarch, with his "dyed coverlets, and beakers set with precious stones, and choruses and dramatic recitations, but also with his arrays of all sorts of meats and daintily prepared dishes, did [Lucullus] make himself the envy of the vulgar." Such meals included delicacies such as salted snails, raw clams, whole pigs stuffed with sausages that spilt out when they were cut, brightly colored fish served as they slowly died in the sauce, and unborn or newborn rabbits. Pass the salt . . . the smelling salts.

Another famously outlandish monarch was England's Henry VIII, who housed a diplomatic meeting with France's François I in huge pavilions the size of the city of Norwich, woven from silk and gold (the stuff of which vestments are made) and bejeweled by precious ornaments and pricey handblown glass. Two fountains flowed with forty thousand gallons of fine red wine. A BBC historian reports that the food for the team of diplomats and nobles included 9,100 plaice; 1,200 capons; 7,836 whiting; 5,554 soles; 2,800 crayfish; 700 conger eels; three porpoises; and a dolphin.

As we know, King Henry's outsized hunger also ran to monastic properties and wives. Such linked, disordered appetites recur in the lives of many rulers. Genghis Khan conquered most of the continent of Asia and all of Russia. A herdsman who scorned those who grew crops and lived indoors, Genghis poisoned millions of acres of farmland by sowing them with salt and massacred the populations of whole cities such as Baghdad, Samarkand, and Kiev. It is said that he only refrained from slaughtering every city-dweller in China when one of his aides pointed out that live Chinese paid more taxes than dead ones. We know Genghis dined on the national dish of steak tartar (bloody raw meat tenderized by riders who kept it under their saddles), though history doesn't tell in what quantities.[7] But we do have proof of another gargantuan Genghian appetite. According to *National Geographic*, "After a conquest, looting, pillaging, and rape were the spoils

---

7. He did impose the death penalty on commoners caught being gluttons; as a child when he caught an older brother stealing his fish, Genghis stabbed him to death.

of war for all soldiers, but that Khan got first pick of the beautiful women."[8] All that on top of some five hundred wives and concubines. Still, it boggles the mind a bit to learn what genetic markers tell us that the Khan today has some *16 million descendants.*

No one in our time, thankfully, can hope to match Genghis Khan, but in his own way, one Western leader did his best to keep up the trappings of Oriental despotism in a modern, democratic setting—longtime French President François Mitterrand.

Mitterrand began life in right-wing circles. In his youth, he joined ultranationalist groups that dabbled in terrorism and abortive coups d'état against the corrupt, anticlerical Third Republic. A man who knew how to follow a trend—and the trend in the mid-1930s was distinctly skewing "fascist"—Mitterrand mixed with militaristic and anti-Semitic groups, joining the *Volontaires Nationaux*, a xenophobic militia modeled on Italy's Blackshirts. After serving in the army in 1940, Mitterrand escaped a POW camp and took a post with the collaborationist Vichy government—which he seems to have faithfully served until, in 1942, it became unclear who'd win the war. At that point, Mitterrand began making contacts in the Resistance and played both sides of the fence until the Allied invasion in 1944 made the outcome obvious. Then he joined the Resistance fighters. While Mitterrand claimed later that he spent the whole war spying for the Free French, historians question this—citing his decades-

long friendship after the war with convicted war criminal René Bousquet, a Vichy official who oversaw the deportation of thousands of Jews. (Ironically, while in power, Mitterrand kept close ties to the Hutu government that conducted the genocide in Rwanda.)

After meeting and marrying a Socialist in 1944, Mitterrand reinvented himself as a man of the Left. (It didn't hurt that Charles de Gaulle, the center-right war hero who'd helped liberate France, detested Mitterrand and excluded him from leadership.) As early as 1965, Mitterrand ran for president, courting feminist voters by

---

8. Hillary Mayell, "The Genetic Legacy of Genghis Khan," *National Geographic News*, February 14, 2003.

calling for the legalization of abortion (which would pass ten years later, with Mitterrand's support). Women voters might have been a little less enthused had they known that Mitterrand kept two wives and two sets of children—spending weeknights with one family and weekends with the other.

Becoming president in 1981 (he would serve for fourteen years), Mitterrand legalized millions of illegal immigrants from North Africa, laying the groundwork for the radical Arab ghettos that surround most major French cities. Mitterrand fought for passage of the Maastricht Treaty, which traded French sovereignty for a share of the power that a small, unaccountable European Union oligarchy now wields all across Europe.

Despite his role in liquidating France's past and compromising its future, Mitterrand craved the dignities once proper to France's kings. He surrounded himself with sycophants and demanded the strictest deference protocol could require. He littered Paris with monuments to his ideology, including the ghastly glass pyramid of the Louvre, and the eerie, funereal Monument to the Rights of Man and the Citizen. But his ultimate stab at attaining ersatz royalty came with Mitterrand's last meal.

In late 1995, dying of prostate cancer—an illness he'd long lied about and hidden from voters—Mitterrand decided to end his life by dining like a king. In centuries past, French monarchs were privileged to one very special delicacy: a small songbird called the ortolan (pictured), which was drowned in Armagnac, then flambéed and eaten whole. Since the bird is now endangered, it's strictly illegal to eat them in modern France—but Mitterrand didn't wish to die in the modern France he had helped to make. So on New Year's Eve, he organized a select group of his friends and enjoyed a royal menu—complete with lavish supplies of foie gras, thirty oysters for each diner, and ortolans. Each guest was allotted one of the birds, but according to the *Independent* (January 11, 1997),

> After grabbing the last of 12 birds, the dying president disappeared for a second time behind the large, white napkin, which is ritually placed over the head of anyone about to indulge in the horrific act of eating a charred, but entire ortolan. "Those who had already been through the ordeal once, looked at each other in astonishment," wrote Mr Benamou [a witness]. The table listened in embarrassment as the former president masticated the little bird to a paste behind the napkin, in the approved manner, before swallowing it. Then Mitterrand lay back in his chair, his face beaming in "ecstasy."

Mitterrand refused to eat after that. He suspended all treatment for his cancer and died just eight days later. He'd had his reward.

Losing Your Temperance

Some virtues get a bad name because of the ways their names are used. For instance, Charity is the mighty, cosmic force that Dante said "moves the sun and other stars." Nowadays it calls to mind a hovercraft full of eels—a writhing mass of irrelevant mental images such as

- tax forms itemizing "charitable" contributions,
- nonprofit organizations that pay their executives six-figure salaries to churn out begging letters,
- the grim term we use for some people we grimly hang out with, hire, or date—a "charity case."

Likewise, the Virtue of Temperance has had its good name tarnished by the company it keeps. The American Temperance movement advocated nothing of the kind: in answer to the evils of alcoholism, its leaders called for total abstinence from strong drink and, finally, the imprisonment of bartenders and brewers. It's as if in pursuit of Chastity, one called for absolute celibacy and set up for its enforcement a "Chastity Police." (The cuckolded Empress Maria Theresa did found such a bureau to crack down on adulterous Austrian nobles; after peering through plenty of keyholes, it briefly arrested Casanova and recruited him as an informer. It went down in history as the foil in comic operas.) Our priorities are different now; outside the Islamic world, we have instead the health police, so smokers huddle outside in the rain like Victorian prostitutes and government agencies mull over punishing parents who light up around their children.

Courtesy of Creative Commons License.

The catastrophic futility of Prohibition turned Temperance into one of those terms we snicker at, like "good government" or "diversity." But the need for Temperance in food, drink, and other tactile pleasures is deadly serious—for both this life and

Joe Eszterhas as crucifer at Mass.

the next. Last year I read a memoir called *Crossbearer*[1] by Joe Eszterhas, the screenwriter of such classics of Catholic cinema as *Showgirls* and *Basic Instinct.* In it, he recalls with mostly rue (and a little wist) the days when he would smoke his way through several Cuban fields, put a tequila distributor in the black, contribute to the Bolivian coca industry, and paw his way through a team of Vegas strippers by way of "research." Then he came down with throat cancer. Leaving the doctor who gave him a probable diagnosis of "terminal," he collapsed on a sidewalk curb and sobbed like a baby—a baby with yellow teeth and smoker's breath. A powerhouse in Hollywood, Eszterhas was powerless to control the habits that were killing him. For the first time since boyhood, he found himself calling on God—like one of the "Jesus freaks" he'd always scorned. The path wasn't straight or pretty, but Eszterhas rediscovered the Catholic Faith in which he'd been raised, and through much prayer he saved his marriage, his family, and his life. It's a rawly honest, riveting tale of a soul crawling on its belly up the mount of Purgatory.

But you needn't see cancerous lesions in your throat or feel your liver trying to slip out in the bathtub to see how important Temperance can be. Disciplined athletes, I have read, sometimes succumb to inordinate passions, which manifest themselves in the use of dangerous steroids or groupies. Even movie actresses, whose ascetical mastery of the flesh is plain to the naked eye, have been known to engage in those illicit pleasures St. Thomas describes as "sins that aren't fattening."

Temperance starts with the body but reaches its tendrils into the soul. God peskily created us as amalgams of the two, and it's hard to abuse the one without injuring the other. I remember showing a first date an early draft of my first *Bad Catholic's* book where I made the argument that the difference between natural family planning and contraception was like that dividing dieting from bulimia: at the end of the day, you end up with fewer calories but the means used make a difference. She read it, sat for a moment, then pounded on the

---

1. Joe Eszterhas, *Crossbearer* (New York: St. Martin's Press, 2008).

table. "I'll have you know I'm a bulimic, and I don't appreciate being compared to a contraceptor. That's a sin!" Nice as her figure was, I called for the check.

Starved of Temperance, our soul will slacken and grow as flabby as a body over-fed and underused. In his essay, "The Virtue of Temperance,"[2] Thomist philosopher Doug McManaman explains the sharp distinction between a dull disdain for the pleasures proper to life (the neurosis of "Insensibility") and a virile mastery over the fleeting impulses shipped up to our frontal cortex by our coiled reptilian brain. Now, staying alive means answering basic needs of our mortal bodies: I feed my reptilian brain a rat every couple of days. But I don't want it climbing out of the tank and rewriting my resume or swallowing one of my pets. McManaman discusses the usefulness of fasting in free-ing the will from a purely Pavlovian response to stimuli; just because that pile of fries came "free" with the turkey burger you ordered doesn't mean you have to eat it. And I've found out it isn't true that a fifth of bourbon "goes flat" once you've opened it, so you "might as well finish the thing." And so on.

Da Vinci's scientific sketch of the reptilian brain.

McManaman goes further and cites the habit of Temperance as key to the lov-ing treatment of other people. Excessive indulgence of short-term, instant pleasures is a sure sign of overpowering self-love, which leaves little room for concern with other's needs. Or put another way, "Are you gonna eat that, son?"

Since we're all Americans now—and foreign readers know this better than anyone—it might help win the unconvinced over if I call Temperance a power: the power to master our fleeting urges and hard-earned addictions and tether them to the cart we want them to pull, in the direction our reason tells us we need to go. Let's go further and call it horsepower; if your willpower is scattered and frittered, you're basically driving a broken-down gas-guzzler from the 1970s. Of course, divine Grace (like AAA) is always a phone call away, but really, in the long run you ought to get yourself a car that actually runs, with enough horsepower to get you up the hill without a tow and brakes that actually stop the thing short of a school bus.

And stop fiddling with the GPS while you're driving over seventy miles per hour, lighting a cigar, and changing the radio station while placing a bet on the phone with your bookie. Yes, soccer moms, this means you.

---

2. Available at http://catholiceducation.org/articles/education/ed0281.html.

The Trouble with Self-Denial

Here's a slightly seedy confession for a Catholic writer: the very notion of self-denial and penance has always left me cold and tempted me to follow the Protestant poet Milton, who scorned such papist practices as the folly of literal "lunatics." Indeed, in *Paradise Lost* he populated the sterile, fickle moon with the folk who engaged in what he viewed as vain and futile penances:

> Embryo's and Idiots, Eremits and Friers
> White, Black and Grey, with all thir trumperie. (III, 475–76)

I feel quite small for saying this: it strikes me that life itself is rife enough with suffering that few of us need to seek out a moment's more grimness than is grinning for us around the bend.

But there's no getting past the stark facts of history: Christ Himself spent forty Lenten days in the desert fasting, atoning for sins not even His own, mortifying senses that had never been corrupted. Are we somehow exempt from picking up our own (balsa) crosses? St. Benedict didn't think so: the monk who launched the Promethean effort of reconstructing Western civilization from the rubble of Rome through "work and prayer" lived for months in a cell the size of a casket hollowed in a Roman wall. St. Francis, the troubadour whose canticles still spark happy tears in the eyes of children, laid his holy head on a pillow of stone in Rome. I saw the thing with my own eyes at San Benedetto in Piscinula in 2007 and was appalled all over again. To a spoiled scion of the 1970s like me, a gym membership seems barely to justify the exertion: I've always strongly suspected (are there studies on this?) that the hours you add to your life by exercise will in the end add up to . . . *precisely the number of hours you spent at the gym.* Those few extra months in the nursing home just don't seem worth the sweat.

A part of me has never ceased to whisper that perhaps those liberal nuns who taught me might be right, that in the midst of ascetical practice and renunciation hides a hatred of happiness. That a Church that endorses celibacy, fasting, abstinence, flagellation, and martyrdom—whose very emblem is the ancient equivalent of a gallows—may really be half in love with death. The great Nathaniel Hawthorne, in his novel of Americans in Rome, *The Marble Faun*, gives one of his most sympathetic characters the following remarks about monastics: "A monk—I judge from their sensual physiognomies, which meet me at every turn—is inevitably a beast. Their souls, if they have any to begin with, perish out of them before their sluggish, swinish existence is half done. . . . They serve neither God nor man, and themselves least of all, though their motives be utterly selfish." (How Hawthorne felt when his daughter converted to Rome and founded the group now called the Hawthorne Dominicans is a question left to eternity.)

Of course, the sort of religionist who turns away from mortification with a therapeutic shudder is the most likely to indulge in other forms of self-destruction: crassly pacifist fantasies; a masochistic loathing of one's own kith and kin, culture and cult; the promiscuous embrace of "otherness" that welcomes immigrant gangs and murderous imams. A culture that will not permit the nun's veil will soon enough be donning the *hijab*.

The best cure for the confusion that afflicts me is a daily dose of G. K. Chesterton. Any one of his books contains more nuggets of sanity than a medicine cabinet full of SSRIs, but *The Everlasting Man* was my companion on a three-month stint in the papal city—and I couldn't have picked a more appropriate piece of *lectio divina*. If there's one man who clearly embraced the good things of life, it was Gilbert Keith Chesterton. Smoker, drinker, wielder of a potent sarcastic pen, Chesterton is an English type who suggests the kind of saint Henry VIII might well have become—had he beheaded Thomas Cromwell and embraced good Thomas More. In *The Everlasting*

Man, Chesterton accomplishes a great many things. He redeems the good name of the "cave man," showing him as not so much the brute of Freud's "primal murder" as the wide-eyed, life-loving cave artist of Lascaux. But in this book, which he wrote to answer H. G. Wells's *An Outline of History*—that prim pastiche of Whiggery—Chesterton takes on an even greater act of vindication: he burnishes the good name of pagan Rome. Chesterton reveals the Punic wars, which court historians for centuries have depicted as an act of commercial vandalism, as a defensive religious war. He contrasts the fantastical ghosts of Rome's pantheon and their loveable if inert household gods with the fearsome deities of Carthage, who demanded infant sacrifice. As Chesterton wrote, contrasting the nations' cults:

> Can any man in his senses compare the great wooden doll, whom the children expected to eat a little bit of the dinner [i.e., the Roman household god], with the great idol who would have been expected to eat the children? . . . If the passage from heathenry to Christianity was a bridge as well as a breach, we owe it to those men who kept that heathenry human. If, after all these ages, we are in some sense at peace with paganism, and can think more kindly of our fathers, it is well to remember those things that were and the things that might have been. For this reason alone we can take lightly the load of antiquity and need not shudder at a nymph on a fountain or a cupid on a valentine.[3]

And this is what Chesterton teaches about penance and suffering: that the only man whose life was an answer to death was the self-proclaimed Son of Man who marched to the cross as to a city whose walls he meant to scale, whose gates he would compass with his arms, whose deepest treasuries he would break into and ransack. To a modern weakling like me, who endures a few hours without his Nicorette as an afternoon spent in Hell, this isn't puzzling. Puzzles have solutions. It's not a surprise, since no one could have expected it. The figure of the risen Christ doesn't leap out at us from behind a door. It falls on us like a blazing tower, then creeps back up with a terrible smile like a tiny yellow flower. Its echoes

3. G. K. Chesterton, *The Everlasting Man* (San Francisco: Ignatius, 1993), 150.

ring through the truncated lives of millions—remembered in this city's coliseum or nameless in the ash heaps of Dachau and Siberia. How strange, how fitting, and yet how hideous that we still call our children after torture victims like Lawrence, Agnes, Lucy, Agatha, and Ignatius. How odd that once we stopped handing on such names and ceased to teach our children the age-inappropriate story of the baby born to be crucified, we soon stop bothering to bear them. Could it be that once we no longer believe we are procreating souls born to eternity, the whole business hardly seems worth the trouble? How bizarre it is that in cities such as Rome—and Madrid and Dublin—the birthrate seems to rise and fall with the ratio of sworn celibates. What role in reproduction is played by the presence of young men in brutal tonsures and thwarted wombs wrapped in coarse woolen robes? I await the verdict of the scientists.

Temperance: Invent Your Own Rule of St. Benedict

Since Gluttony is such a protean phenomenon, it's hard to choose a single exemplar of Temperance. For one thing, the form modern food Gluttony takes is unprecedented, and in the United States, this has meant, as Texan Senator Phil Gramm drawled, "We're the only country in the world where our poor people are fat."[4] We lack Scholastic commentary on the proper use of Jiffy Pop. Ironically, one person who has written most wisely on the proper enjoyment of fleshly pleasures is G. K. Chesterton, who manifestly couldn't walk the talk. (Sadly, by the end, he could barely fit in the bathtub.)

So instead of taking a single figure and trying to stretch him to meet the need, let me make instead a mosaic of wise men and women whose contributions can help our heads better rule our bellies. Let's consider, in succession, the following:

---

4. EMERGENCY ANTI-ELITIST DISCLAIMER: This isn't because the lower orders are culpably guilty of Gluttony but because the least healthy calories are the cheapest and quickest, and working-class folks don't find the time to prepare fresh veggies and healthy fruit salads. They're too busy bringing in two incomes so they can keep their kids from getting stabbed in public schools.

• St. Benedict of Nursia, the founder of Western monasticism. Unsettled by the self-starvation, idleness, and hallucinations that afflicted many hermits, Benedict gathered his monks into tight-knit communities that combined regular hours of worship with useful work that he counted as prayer. As monks, they would mostly shun meat, but Benedict's brothers were commanded to eat at least twice daily of a healthy variety of foods and to drink at most one tankard of wine. Given that Benedict's brethren became the leading producers of wine and beer in Europe (see *The Bad Catholic's Guide to Wine, Whiskey and Song* for encyclopedic documentation I damaged my liver compiling), this rule must sometimes have been more difficult to keep than Chastity. At least the monasteries weren't manufacturing women.

• Dom Prosper Gueranger, author of the encyclopedia of Christian worship *The Liturgical Year*—which was bedside reading for countless saints, the most famous Therese of Lisieux. In that book, Gueranger lamented the decline of fasting in the Western Church. As those of you who are centuries old will remember, this used to entail abstaining from meat every Wednesday and Friday, fasting most of the days in Advent and Lent,[5] and abstaining even from water from midnight until the moment we took Communion—instead of skipping that bagel in the parish parking lot. In his chapter "The History of Lent," Gueranger quotes Pope Benedict XIV:

---

5. This means having just one light meal and two snacks—which we now do only on Ash Wednesday and Good Friday.

The observance of Lent is the very badge of the Christian warfare. By it we prove ourselves not to be enemies of the cross of Christ. By it we avert the scourges of divine justice. By it we gain strength against the princes of darkness, for it shields us with heavenly help. Should mankind grow remiss in their observance of Lent, it would be a detriment to God's glory, a disgrace to the Catholic religion, and a danger to Christian souls. Neither can it be doubted that such negligence would become the source of misery to the world, of public calamity, and of private woe.

- TV chef Julia Child. Decorated for her service in World War II, during which she spied for the Allies in Asia, Julia Child is even more of a hero to millions of Americans who grew up on ersatz casseroles, canned peas, mystery meat, and marshmallow aspic. The bland, prepared dishes promoted by the food industry[6] had by the 1950s largely displaced both the wholesome (if plain) recipes native to Anglo-Americans and, in many immigrant homes, the complex ethnic cuisines they'd brought over from the Old Country. In an era when advertising's Mad Men really had convinced the average American that formula was healthier than breast milk and tinned vegetables better than fresh (they're more "scientific"), Julia Child's 1961 *Mastering the Art of French Cooking* drew on a thousand-year heritage of loving attention to the nuances of God-given ingredients, patient technique, and preparation that shows love not just for the food but also for those who will eat it. To her budding chefs, Child advised, "Moderation. Small helpings. Sample a little bit

Courtesy of Creative Commons License.

---

6. For hilarious examples and stomach-churning pictures from 1950s cookbooks, see James Lilek's classic of snark *The Gallery of Regrettable Food* (New York: Random House, 2001).

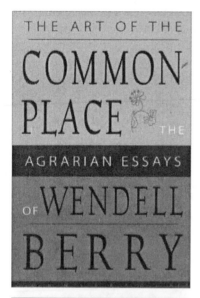

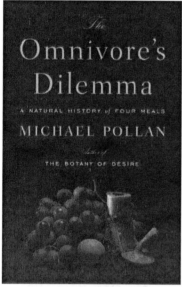

of everything. These are the secrets of happiness and good health."

• Technology critic, poet, and novelist Wendell Berry. In *The Art of the Commonplace: The Agrarian Essays of Wendell Berry*, this Protestant writer echoes the Thomist account of Temperance—a principle he applies to our technology addiction. Berry calls each of us to reflect on how many "labor-saving" devices actually end up adding to our burdens, making us at once dependent and insecure, and alienating us from God's natural creation. Instead of employing power tools to do our work, then autos and elevators to do our walking, we might try returning to the God-given order of things—really earning our daily bread in the sweat of our brows. That includes eschewing prepackaged "convenience" foods and spending the time and effort required to make things from scratch.

• Food philosopher Michael Pollan. His best-selling *Omnivore's Dilemma* explores the roots of America's farming and food dysfunction and looks for healthy alternatives that would at once shrink our waistlines and limit the damage our habits inflict on farm communities, animals, and the rest of Creation. Famously, Pollan explored the meaning of a meal by harvesting the veggies, picking the fruits, hunting and dressing the meat, then cooking the ingredients himself. On a more practical note, Pollan offers the following dictum for the kitchen: "Eat Food. Mostly plants. Not too much." By "food," he means "things our grandmothers would recognize as food," which rules out stuff like the dinosaur-shaped chicken nuggets that appeared on the Zmirak family Thanksgiving table in 2004.

Drawing on all these sources, one could come up with a personal program for cutting off gluttonous habits—adapted to one's state and station in life.

For instance, someone who enjoys several beers at a sitting might invoke St. Benedict and offer his thirsty liver the argument, "If one pint is enough for the monks who made this beer, it should be enough for me."

Someone with a serious weight problem might follow Dom Prosper, benefiting both body and soul through an old-fashioned Lent. (A nice, medieval Advent would be even more challenging and more useful, given the premature feasting that starts nowadays just a week after Halloween.)

Those with sedentary lifestyles can imitate Wendell Berry and swear off elevators, escalators, and power lawn mowers and chainsaws—and learn perhaps for the first time that their bodies are useful for something more than powering the hands that type on keyboards.

Those addicted to cheap, easy eats that are no sooner opened and nuked than they're coursing down to their buttocks might pick up Julia Child—and commit to eating elaborately only when they've done all the work entailed preparing it. No more fast food and no fancy meals in restaurants. If they want rich food, they'll need to spend several hours making it right. When they're too busy or lazy for that, they can gorge themselves on raw fruit and veggies.

Those who already care about healthy eating but who shy away from the sniffy, self-congratulatory cant of the NPR listeners they run into down at Whole Foods can follow Michael Pollan down to the local farmers' market—or join a Community Supported Agriculture (CSA) co-op, which pays the families who grow the stuff a fair price in advance. Then every week, members get wholesome produce. You don't always know what will come down the chute, and it's sometimes a puzzler trying to decide what to do with all those rutabagas. Doing this, taking what God's earth has given you and trying to make prudent use of it, is the opposite action to Gluttony. In fact, it's gratitude.

Trademark-Busting Cosmo-Style Quiz™ #3: Are You Gluttonous, Temperate, or Insensible?

Since Temperance is tied in so tightly to physical health, the Virtue takes different forms in various people, and its demands can change with age. A young person with a fast metabolism can healthily eat an amount that is for somebody else "too much," while a sedentary fifty-something-year-old may need to eat in a way that strikes his friends as "too daintily." People born with genetic predispositions to alcohol must be much more careful consuming it, and those who have been addicted must practice total abstinence. It's inspiring to think of the Irish-founded organization the Pioneer Total Abstinence Association, which, fifty years before Alcoholics Anonymous, gathered men who weren't problem drinkers to swear off the stuff—as a witness and an act of sacrificial reparation to the Sacred Heart of Jesus. As the organization says on its Web page (http://www.pioneerassociation.ie), "The Pioneer

by abstaining from alcohol, which like all of God's gifts should not be abused, is forgoing one of life's pleasures and therefore dying to self for the greater good." This amounts to what I can only call heroic Temperance—two words nobody expects to see together.

Instead of trying to allow for all the variables, let me dump you straight into a hypothetical that can test how subject you are to gluttonous thoughts.

The Quiz

You're in your middle thirties, and like most Americans, you're almost twenty pounds overweight. You never binge or purge, and you don't even really snack—but neither does your life often entail breaking a sweat. Your weight has been stable for several years—but concerned about your health and appearance, you've embarked on grim but steady restricted calorie intake, with exercise thrice (sometimes slipping to twice) a week. And you've already lost five pounds.

With co-workers, you're invited to a special dinner to be held in the poshest French restaurant in town—a place you never frequent, since your job doesn't pay enough. You all sit down to celebrate whatever it is the company thinks is wonderful. (Let's say the bigwigs finally settled that class-action lawsuit filed by all those midgets who'd claimed your company scientists experimented on them.) The bottles of Pinot grigio open up, and your supervisor announces, "Order anything you want. Lobster, foie gras, sky's the limit. This may never happen again, but I'm picking up the check. We totally came out on top. That midget lawyer *blinked*! We nailed them."

You take the menu and look through the elaborate appetizers—celestial stuff like *deep-fried Camembert with raspberry sauce* and *escargot mushroom caps in drawn garlic butter*. The entrees are even more brutal: *gratinéed scallops, flambéed veal chops in cream sauce,* and—oh crap, the single most exquisite dish in any national cuisine, *cassoulet*—a white bean stew cooked with duck and pork in goose fat. It takes Provençal housewives three days to make.[7] No wonder they charge $26.95 for it. And here's your chance to have it, on the suits.

As to desserts? You try not to look there, but your personal Screwtape gains momentary control of your eyes, long enough to show you *chocolate mousse* and *apricot crumble*.

All around you, coworkers are ordering multicourse fêtes with all the self-restraint of a pack of starving, feral dogs. And you face the moment of choice. You do one of the following:

a. You decide that your diet can start again tomorrow—that your meal tonight will in fact "count" as breakfast in the morning. And you'll have a salad instead of lunch. You won't think about how many calories you're chewing—or swilling, for that matter. Could somebody pass the wine? On the premise, "You only live once, if that," you purposely order the richest meal on the menu: *foie gras, sautéed in Calvados with toast points; cassoulet; and a pear soufflé with a glass of Poire William* (the best liqueur on earth). A meal like this isn't much to ask for from this Vale of Tears, and anyway, you've earned it (although not in a literal, physical kind of way). You raise a glass, a tiny liqueur

7. For the recipe, see *The Bad Catholic's Guide to Wine, Whiskey and Song* (New York: Crossroad, 2007), which offers a down-and-dirty, two-day version.

glass, to the win over the midgets. You're so intent on enjoying your evening that, in the morning, you won't remember it, and when you wake up barfing, you'll figure you've probably lost half the calories anyway. Remember this doesn't count as bulimia because *you didn't do it on purpose.*

b. As your eyes skim across each course, your brain automatically estimates the calorie count of each item. Ever since you started this diet thing, each item of food summons such a number—like a little price tag, neatly pinned to every chicken leg or muffin. What's worse, since you've made an algorithm of how many minutes of exercise it takes to burn such calories off, each meal disappears behind a vision of lengthy sweating. On the other hand, the bosses are paying for once, and you'd have to be a sap to skip one of the few perks this job offers. You're tempted to order the priciest possible meal (*madeleines with créme fraîche and caviar, lobster thermidor, chocolate-dipped strawberries in gold leaf*) just to sock it to them. But you figure that might be impolitic. So you order the *second* most expensive combination on the menu, which you experience in three courses: *$17.50 with thirty minutes on the Stairmaster, $35.50 with two hours of dreary running,* and *$10.95 with forty-five minutes of crunches.* Overwhelmed by all this math, you barely taste the food.

c. You're having a grand time and managing to pace yourself with the wine—remembering that these giggling trenchermen are *still* your co-workers, so whatever you say tonight may be examined under fluorescent lights tomorrow. But you still feel a tipsy camaraderie. Even that squirrelly guy who tried to get you fired looks kind of . . . human with a lobster bib around his neck. You're glad he's enjoying himself. And yes, your boss's glorious offer poses a real temptation. (You hope he doesn't get reamed out when the expense report comes in, and truth to tell, you feel a little guilty about the midgets.) You let yourself enjoy the richest dishes voyeuristically, leisurely reading the food-porn describing every one. Then you order the *baby green salad in a Gascon vinaigrette*, the *garden chicken supreme*, and the *mango-banana sorbet.* You eat slowly, savoring every bite.

d. You smile thinly when the boss makes his announcement, thinking how much you'd rather have the cash. Of course, there's some tax advantage entailed in dinners that can be written off as business expenses, and anyway, this guy is kind of a lush. It probably makes him feel like King Henry VIII, hauling everyone out here on their own time and ordering them to eat. You calculate the extra hours you'll have to spend with co-workers talking shop instead of sitting peacefully at home adding more entries to your social justice blog. But here you are, so you scan the menu, wondering how many families in Chad could eat for a week on what your firm is spending on this victory dance. When the waiter comes, you interrogate him on the provenance of the food: Are the chickens free-range? Were the veggies grown on sustainable farms? Is the boeuf really hormone-free? Your co-workers may be rolling their eyes, but at least they know somebody in this company has a conscience. (Anyway, food has never really caught your interest. You put on those extra twenty pounds in a fit of absent-mindedness, mostly from movie popcorn and soda you consumed while watching documentaries down at the art house. Not that any of these people care enough to educate themselves.) After ten minutes of wrangling, the waiter agrees to serve you a vegan meal: *walnut oil salad, ratatouille*, and *watermelon with toasted fennel salt*. You leave as soon as you're finished, waving farewell with an irony everyone misses. You decide, with a shrug, "Well, that was filling."

Here are the results:

- If you picked "a": If this is your reaction to a temptation as mild as a heavy business dinner, your will is woefully weak. Moralists have long said that addiction to one fleshly pleasure leads to others— something you know for a fact is true with drinks. One glass of wine leads to another, which leads to cognac, which leads to those little thimbles full of paint thinner you hazily recall was called something like *crappa*. Excessive drink, of course, lubes the skids for sins like Lust and Wrath, although in your case it's more likely Sloth—which explains why you were the only person to call in sick the day after the dinner. When you do toddle in, expect your supervisor to hand you a pamphlet about the Employee Assistance Program or (if he's Irish-American) a tract from the Pioneers.
- If you picked "b": You might be one of those people who'd be better off being fat. Really, if the only way to control your appetites is to turn them into idols you spend all day straining *not* to worship, yielding to them might be better than letting them twist you into an angry Pharisee. However, those aren't the only alternatives. Instead

of giving up on self-control, you should try to baptize the beast. Following Church fasts and feasts would be a start, but only if they help you develop a rhythm of gratitude to God for the good things of Creation and self-restraint in their enjoyment. When you're suffering from the necessary strictures of your diet, think of Christ fasting in the desert, and try to unite yourself with Him. When you're lifting the bar on your Soloflex, be thankful it isn't a cross. Your spiritual reading should start with Julia Child and continue with Joanna Bogle's *A Book of Feasts and Seasons (Herefordshire, U.K.:* Gracewing Publishing, 1993)—a delightful guide to marking the holy days of the Church year with recipes and festivities.

- If you picked "c": It sounds like you've got a wholesome balance going on here. Eating more mindfully will help you do it more healthily, if only because you're making yourself go slower and giving your stomach time to catch up with your palate. One way to do that is to stop buying premade, frozen, or "ready-to-eat" foods and start  making things from scratch. Yank out your microwave oven and give it to St. Vincent de Paul. (He always was a big fan of gadgets.) Taking time to actually cook things using fire and water—instead of, well, magic—will keep you from sliding into excess and waste. Also consider cutting your rations and "dieting" from some of the labor-saving devices you spent all that money on. Read Wendell Berry on how to do that—and start by using the stairs instead of the elevator, especially at the gym.

- If you picked "d": You sound like you suffer from Insensibility, the culpable lack of enjoyment in the things God made for our happiness. This typically goes with a harsh austerity toward other people and their pleasures and can culminate in Envy—in the wish that everyone lived stark and rigorous lives and pruned away every pleasure, to maximize utility or serve some ideology. Go back to Orwell's *1984,* and read about how the higher-ups in his totalitarian party were happy to sacrifice creature comforts in exchange for the power to inflict this discipline on others. If the political system outlined in that novel sounds the tiniest bit attractive ("We could tweak this a little, and infuse it with Catholic Social Teaching. . . ."), you've got yourself a serious problem.

Activities

❑ If you find yourself sliding down the gutter of Gluttony, it might just be time to take up Dom Guéranger's idea of keeping medieval-style Catholic fasts. The key to fasting and abstinence, remember, is not that they cause suffering; otherwise, on Fridays we'd be choking down Big Macs instead of peeling shrimp. The purpose of fasting is to subject your body to the rule of the mind and your will to a rule outside itself. Maybe it's time to call in that Higher Power. Think of Him as your personal trainer and designated driver. Whenever you find yourself chafing against the moderation you've embraced, try to think of St. Benedict and his men—those men in drafty, isolated abbeys who saved the great books of the ancient world, preserved the art of wine making, and invented the best beers in Europe. They couldn't have managed that if they were lushes—and if you don't believe me, think of the ancient Romans, lolling on their divans, eating lark's tongues before heading off to the vomitorium. How many of their recipes do we still use today? There's a liqueur named for Benedict; only pretentious restaurants mention Lucullus.

❑ If, on the other hand, you've wound yourself up into a knot of prudish Insensibility, it's time to climb down, efface yourself and embrace Creation. You could start by paying attention to all the human work and care that goes into growing wholesome food and preparing it elegantly. Try reading Wendell Berry on agriculture and cooking your way through Joanna Bogle or Julia Child. Remember that cooking is the single art that common folk have pioneered, leaving experts and gourmets to dash about collecting recipes from peasants. Anything that has consoled the laboring masses over the centuries—serving as a much better opiate than religion—must have something to recommend it. As you grind that basil with a mortar into a pesto, try to offer your work as a prayer.

Greed Is for the Good

I quipped on the eve of a recent election that the Vice of Greed was associated with Republicans and Envy with Democrats. But these questions are never so simple. A Wall Street "banksta" who offers reckless mortgages might be one of those men who love too much—too much foie gras; too much vacation time in Barbados; too many antique pistols, snifters of brandy, and hand-rolled cigars. These things are all quite innocent in themselves, and in proper doses, they add the spice to life. On the other hand, that banker might be driven by competition and by resentment at the sight of his classmates from Wharton living just a little bit better. That kind of man could watch his own house of cards collapse and still be happy when he sees the "For Sale" signs on his classmates' condos and watches his boss's Lamborghini get towed by the repo man: Republican Envy.

Conversely, the slacker who votes to "redistribute" the wealth might not in fact be envious. Let's say he's eager to get a monthly government check or have his sex-change operation paid for by the state, but he doesn't take an evil glee in taxing families out of their ancestral homes to pay for it. He simply shrugs and cashes the check: Democratic Greed.

So let's leave politics out of this. Our country is blessed with just two competitive parties, but we've got Seven Deadly Sins, and there are plenty to go around.

And that's what Greed is all about: the happy, carefree feeling of limitless life and lucre. The gumbo pot is full, the keg is overflowing, Victorian homes are sprouting fully decorated from the ground (at only 3 percent, with no down payment), and all is right with the world. It's the same fizzy *frisson* we felt in New York through the Internet boom, accepting instead of salaries "options" in stock that hadn't been issued, which we'd someday sell to investors who didn't know better, who'd buy up shares of a business that didn't make money—and we'd all retire at thirty.

This sense of plenitude is what Adam enjoyed in Eden, when he turned to Eve and said,

It's summertime and the living is easy
Fish are jumping and the cotton is high
Your daddy's rich and your mama's good-looking
Hush, little baby don't you cry. (Gershwin 2:11–15)

No wonder we want to bring back that loving feeling. And it's no surprise that we all hate economics, the science of scarcity—a fact of life the Bible tells us is as unnatural to us as death. (Some theologians have boldly asserted that without the Fall, even animals wouldn't have died—which raises the ugly image of antediluvian critters like the velociraptor munching carrots.)

Regardless of how literally we take little details like Adam's rib, there are solid facts conveyed in Genesis which the Church won't interpret away. And one of them is this: barring the whole "Apple scandal" (about which the less said the better), man was meant to live forever with an unlimited supply of whatever he needs.

I don't pretend to understand the mechanics of this, since we were also supposed to breed. If nothing else, space would have gotten scarce after fifty thousand years of people giving birth but never giving up the ghost. Would the planet have ended up as overcrowded as Hong Kong—till finally somebody got so sick of it that he started baking Forbidden Fruit into strudels and passing them out to thin the herd? Medieval theologians, who spent their time sweating such details, had another answer. They pointed to the fate of the Virgin Mary—who, ever since the early Church, had been famous for ending her time on earth by rising up to heaven, body and soul. Would that have happened to everyone, absent the Fall? That's a pretty big Assumption.

So we're all designed to crave endless life and limitless wealth—but we're born into a world full of sharp edges, raging bulls, and grisly bears. The very first human couple to walk the earth wrecked our credit rating, and while Christ came to pay the tab, He left us with the penalties and interest. He promised us life after death and eventual resurrection, but you'll notice He didn't repeal the second law of thermodynamics. It's still on the books: all created things speed toward their own decay—as you might have noticed in the mirror this morning if you're a day over twenty-three.

So is it really such a sin to try to regain a piece of Eden, if only as a time-share we use off-season and deduct as a business expense? That's all Greed amounts to. We yearn for a life without limits, for a second jar of Gerber minifranks, just one more ride on the Tilt-A-Whirl. We're reaching out for the Fruit of the Tree of Life and keep burning our hands on the Flaming Sword.

Now, it's not at all true that wealth is zero-sum; some systems work better than others. (If you're curious which is which, check the countries people are sneaking into and those they're sneaking out of.) There's not a strictly limited pie, which the nice man from the government ought to slice for us so we each get an equal share. We don't all deserve the same. The folks who develop a safer treatment for cancer deserve a richer reward than people caught shoplifting cigarettes. Fashion models who brighten our lives by simply existing in front of a camera deserve elaborate French meals— which, alas, they'll never eat.

But there are limits, so many limits, to the wealth each of us can earn. When we crave much more than that, sometimes we steal. If we lack the enterprise for that, we sulk or simply beg. On a small scale, guilt works pretty well; able-bodied panhandlers often make more money than the workers whom they harass. But begging on a huge scale relies much more on threats—for instance, give

us $700 billion or we'll bring back the Great Depression. You don't believe us? Just try it and see. . . .

Which brings me to the great economic collapse of recent years. People say that the best cure for a hangover is a hair of the dog that bit you. The people who say that are typically alcoholics. They're using the logic of an addict, whose reason has been fried by a short-circuit in the pleasure centers of the brain. Such people think it's *funny* when they fall down at a parish Christmas party (even if they're the monsignor) or when they puke on your champagne-colored carpet ("Good thing that's what I was drinking!"), and they'll probably think it's funny when, one morning, their liver slides out in the shower.

And that, boys and girls, is what happened to the American economy. As it lies there on the porcelain, we want to pick it up and put it back in, but we're scared it might just dissolve. Anyway, the process would probably hurt. Do we really need it?

But that's really what it means, when the Magi of Left or Right discuss the need for economic "stimuli" and bailouts or when financial journalists worry about the decline in consumer spending—by consumers who are losing their jobs. Just to break things down: In 2008, our country crashed into a wall because of our addiction to spending money we didn't have for stuff we didn't need. We overdosed, ran through our stash, and now we're thrashing around in a cold-turkey withdrawal—but here comes that nice man with the methadone. . . .

Economy. The word, which comes from a Greek term for household management, once had a connotation, now obsolete: "economy" meant the careful, prudent stewardship of limited resources—and was used sometimes when speaking of an author whose language was terse and concise. Hence Hemingway might be praised for his "economy of expression."

I know it sounds strange today, when economists earn their bread by serving as experts in stimulating demand for goods and services, fueled by expansive credit and the incessant printing of money. But words can change their meaning—just as "diverse" now means "nonwhite," "special" means "mentally handicapped," and Nietzsche's *Gay Science* refers, it seems, to a lab that churns out poppers.

"Economy" also turns up in traditional manuals of theology, as in the "economy of salvation." This has nothing to do with bingo, sending food stamps to Reverend Ike, or selling indulgences, but rather with God's plan for managing the household of the Church. The analogy breaks down here, as analogies do, since we also know economy as the "science of managing scarcity." That problem doesn't apply to God, whose graces are super-abundant. Although sometimes it seems that scarcely anyone is interested in them—which, if true, would give rise to the "negative outcome" known as the "fewness of the saved." But I digress.

No, in fact, I don't. In 2008, America faced a major meltdown of the economy after eight years of governance by the president whose base was—to put things baldly—orthodox Christians. Pro-lifers, patriots, hard-working types who aren't sitting by the pool clipping coupons or out at the Palm Beach Country Club recruiting their friends for a billion-dollar pyramid scheme. These people—and I'm one of them, folks—must take responsibility for the policies they enabled, the lifestyles they led. *We* urgently need to examine them all in the light of the Faith we profess and figure out a new way for our country to do its business—one that's a little more . . . Christian. Or at any rate, rational.

Does it surprise any of us what happened when "wolf-hunter mom" Sarah Palin got hold of the Republican National Committee's Gold Card and went hog-wild at Neiman Marcus? It's the same thing that happens to good-hearted, churchgoing folks who win the lottery—and within a decade end up nearly broke and estranged from friends and family. What is missing from the equation is a virtue that our churches have long stopped preaching, since it's even more countercultural and unpopular than Chastity—namely, Thrift. In Plato's *Republic*, this appears as the governing virtue of the class he calls (with some disdain) the "producers," whom he hopes the philosophers would rule through the soldiers.

And Thrift has gotten short shrift at various points through the centuries—since it's easy to confuse it with stinginess, with the niggling, ungenerous spirit Jesus saw in the worst of the Pharisees. The greatest saints we remember are those who embraced voluntary poverty, selling all they had and giving it to the poor. As I mentioned, St. Benedict lived for a year in Rome in a cell the size of a coffin. (I've crawled inside it and bought a key chain at the gift shop for five euros; it broke.) The "Mendicant Orders," beginning with St. Dominic, combated the Albigensian condemnation of the world with a renunciation all their own. The lavish wealth of postplague Italy drove St. Francis of Assisi to cast off his clothes in the public square, dramatizing his love affair with "Lady Poverty." The Theatine order that preceded the Jesuits in launching the Counter-Reformation took poverty so seriously that it refused to solicit donations—relying solely on whatever gifts God sent over the transom.

It's easy to recklessly equate such an embrace of the poverty of the apostles with an aristocratic disdain for financial prudence. In a famous essay, "Catholicism and the Bourgeois Mind,"[1] Catholic historian Christopher Dawson does just that—elevating the spirit of the saint and (curiously) of the soldier over that of the solid burgher. Sensible about so many other historical and cultural questions, here Dawson commits to print the following howler: "The ethos of the Gospels is sharply opposed to the economic view of life and the economic virtues. It teaches men to live from day to day without taking thought for their material needs." If this simplistic reading of Jesus's complex statements about material wealth were accurate, Christianity could never have built a civilization that lasted 15 years, much less 1,500. Indeed, no father of a family has any business adopting the attitude appropriate to a friar—as the Church recognized, encouraging people throughout the Middle Ages to delay marriage until they had the means to support and educate their children. It also

---

1. Find it in Christopher Dawson, *The Dynamics of World History,* ed. John J. Mulloy (Wilmington, DE: Intercollegiate Studies Institute, 2002).

condemned as heretics the "Spiritual Franciscans" who tried to impose the great saint's poverty on laymen, on penalty of mortal sin.

A better, more balanced picture than what Dawson offers of the proper interaction among the human faculties of work, prayer, and play can be found in the writings of the German philosopher Josef Pieper, whose classic *Leisure: The Basis of Culture* rejects the pragmatic materialism he saw rising in postwar Europe but maintains a Thomist respect for the virtue of Thrift—which is simply the governing natural virtue of Prudence as applied to the management of money.

The practical result of refusing to preach the importance of Prudence in managing wealth, or respect for the honest efforts of "vulgar tradesmen" who do the hard work of matching up customers with products, is not necessarily an abundance of saints like Francis of Assisi. Given man's fallen condition, it is far more likely to generate economic stagnation; the fatalistic acceptance of tyrannical, exploitative government and a vulgar flashiness on the part of the rich: Renaissance cardinals showering urban mobs with bags of gold made out of widows' mites, monarchs like Louis XIV constructing elaborate chateaus and embarking on useless wars for the sake of "glory," and endemic corruption such as that which still prevails in Southern Italy. And by the way, when was the last time you met a Theatine?

Of course, the bourgeois zest for Thrift can be taken to its own ugly extreme. If Max Weber's picture of Calvinist culture is in any way accurate, the "iron cage" of Thrift and rational planning can crush the human spirit. According to Weber, the Calvinist doctrine that it is impossible to influence one's own eternal salvation, or even know if you're one of the Elect, had the perverse effect of secularizing Protestant Europe—turning human energies outward, into spheres of life where one could make a difference and expect a predictable outcome for one's hard work, namely, the acquisition of wealth. The rigid dichotomy between spiritual passivity and economic planning put an intolerable strain on the souls of Europeans—and generated wild, antinomian reactions like Romanticism. And anything that can lead, even indirectly, to the poetry of Percy Bysshe Shelley demands our sleepless vigilance.

The conflict between the aristocratic and bourgeois spirits can be seen in exaggerated form in the famous lines Orson Welles spoke in *The Third Man*: "In Italy for 30 years under the Borgias they had warfare, terror, murder, and bloodshed, but they produced Michelangelo, Leonardo da Vinci, and the Renaissance. In Switzerland they had brotherly love— they had 500 years of democracy and peace, and what did that produce? The cuckoo clock."

Of course, we postmodern Americans don't like to have to choose between stark extremes. When faced with two opposing vices, we scorn talk of the Golden Mean—and instead try to combine the worst features of each. In the past thirty years, we have somehow managed to meld the financial fecklessness appropriate to medieval Italian mystics with the grim acquisitive spirit of Kierkegaard's Danish burghers. And we managed this through the alchemy of debt; instead of developing the Patience that comes with deferred gratification and relying on wealth accumulated by savings to finance our pleasures, we simply borrowed the money. We wanted plenty of weapons to win the cold war and borrowed the money. (Fair enough—it needed winning. But why are we still outspending the rest of the planet combined for arms to fight the Soviets?) We wanted social programs that made us feel generous toward the poor, so we borrowed the money. We want to fight wars in the Middle East and finance elaborate schemes to micromanage education across the country from Capitol Hill, so we. . . .

You get the idea.

Indeed, whenever Americans start to show some realization of their true financial condition and cut back on their spending, the government panics and expands the money supply. Sometimes it simply cuts every American a check, mailing it out in the form of a "stimulus." One worry that was expressed the last time this happened—and I'm not kidding, folks—was the danger that Americans *might not spend* their checks but instead might (God forbid) *save* them.

We seem to have forgotten the Economics 101 axiom that investments come from savings—that is, wealth compiled through deferred gratification in the hope of increased future returns. Instead, we imagine that borrowing money to keep the economy whirring—to keep us giving each other pedicures and serving each other peppermint lattes—will generate wealth sufficient to pay off our tab . . . someday. When would "someday" come? What imaginable events could bring the binge to an end?

This could occur in one of three ways:

1. Human nature could change radically, and the vices of Gluttony, Sloth, Envy, and Greed could all disappear—for instance, through the election of a president who comes in our favorite color.
2. We could wake up to the fact that we're not really borrowing the money for our trips to Aveda from the Chinese but from our children. Instead of storing up wealth for them (like those despicable Swiss burghers) or remaining celibate like those Franciscans, we are storing up IOUs our kids will have to pay off. A large-scale moral renewal could result from

this realization, and Americans could start once again to save rather than spend. This would hurt the consumption sector of the economy, but the folks down at the mall would find new jobs in the productive industries financed by the savings we accumulated.

3. Foreign lenders could finally realize that we are a nation of compulsive gamblers wearing diapers in front of slot machines (so we needn't leave to go potty), and they could cut off our credit. Then the whole Ponzi scheme would collapse.

We picked #3.

Put bluntly, we closed down our country's physical plant and turned the place into a casino. We skimmed a lot off the top, but we offered the best games in town. Our waitresses were hotter, the watered drinks were free, our security guards had nukes, and the floorshow featured Siegfried and Roy. We tried to pursue prosperity by catering to the instant gratification of every conceivable human desire— and when we ran out of those, we got very good at coming up with new ones.

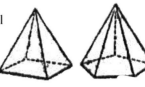

Figures shaped like pyramids

In 1980, who knew that we needed Twitter at the beach? Bariatric surgery? Transgender dorms at ex-Methodist colleges that charge $40,000 a year to teach women's studies? We didn't just feed the vices, we came up with new ones—and found ways to make them "pay." Of course, the people who'll really pay for our spending spree will be our grandchildren, who'll inherit the brain-bleeding debt we've run up, which both political parties are eagerly expanding as you read this. When the tight-fisted, hard-working Confucians who take receivership of Ameri-casino™ come in to assess the property and sweep up the pizza boxes, discarded condoms, and CrackBerrys, they will shake their brainy heads and wonder, "Why did we ever give these people gunpowder in the first place?"

Understanding America's Economy: A Pyramid of Ostriches

Perhaps all this sounds too black. The reader deserves a more detailed, nuanced account of the structure of the American economy, and I can provide it—based not so much on my study of economics as on my up-close experience of ostrich farms and pyramid schemes.

Having worked for a magazine that covered (i.e., promoted) network marketing businesses like Herbalife and Amway, I knew quite a bit about the structure of such organisms. They rely less on selling products than on recruiting. Whatever it is you're selling—and I've written about everything from ceramic patriotic *tsotchkes* to chicken-based weight loss supplements—you make only a modest sum on each sale. But if you can recruit an army of people under you to sell the stuff, you get a percentage of each of their sales. The goal is to build a pyramid—oops . . . never, never use that word—an "organization" that will pass their profits up the line to you. Their motive for signing up? Not the chance to sell chicken goop but to build a similar, er, three-sided geometrical figure. Of course, this can't go on forever, since the number of new recruits required for anyone but the top echelons to make much money soon exceeds the number of human beings who've ever lived. And there you have our Social Security system.

Perhaps the most bizarre such scheme I ever covered was the 1990s Louisiana ostrich bubble. Okay, there weren't just ostriches involved. There were also Australian emus and South American rheas—then camels, wallabies, alligators, "heritage" sheep and goats, and finally escargot. Desperate family dairy farmers, devastated by competition from federally subsidized agribusinesses, were trying to raise each kind of beast in the hope of keeping their farms. While the underlying story was deeply sad, at the time these hardhanded men were full of hope. They'd been shown the commodity prices of these exotics and were eager to try something new and entrepreneurial—instead of giving up and getting jobs at Jiffy Lube. I was rooting for them.

As one of those New York agrarians without a driver's license, I'd eagerly taken the assignment as a reporter for the *Baton Rouge Business Report*, bumming rides from friends to rural alligator farms and camel ranches. The alligators were easy profit: you fed them chicken giblets and made them into handbags. The camels were not for eating; it seemed that, in Louisiana, farmed camels could pay for a year's feed (plus a healthy profit) with the fees Baptist churches paid to rent them for Christmas pageants. Talk about the "invisible hand."

But the main focus of my article was ostriches and emus. These birds, you see, are an

Crocodile (14 ft. long)

excellent source of healthy red meat that's low in cholesterol and fat; indeed, it's so lean that the steaks are too easy to burn. You pretty much have to sear them—preferably in a nice little red wine demi-glace, with a strong spice like oregano, rosemary, or allspice to counter the "wild taste." With the promise of nursing homes and senior centers as lucrative markets, cattle farmers across the state were culling their herds and fencing off sections of their land to hold these large, exotic ratites. The Australian emu is like a wimpy kid brother to the African ostrich—smaller and tame enough that you can reach in and take its eggs. The oil that's rendered when they're slaughtered is prized, one promoter told me, "by NBA athletes," and sold for $32 an ounce.

The ostrich, on the other hand, as a Cajun explained to me—pulling me by the scruff of the neck away from the ostrich run—can "disembowel a lion with just one kick. Those critters are *mean*!" When it's time to remove their enormous eggs to an incubator, the mama birds must be distracted with feed—and the eggs quickly purloined before they come back, kicking and screeching.

There was just one problem with the way the birds were introduced into the states: they were part of a pyramid scheme. I'm not sure who first got the notion of packing up ratites from subtropical climes and shipping them to Acadiana, but whoever he is, he's probably reclining in a toga, eating grapes peeled for him by a team of naked supermodels. You see, the birds were brought over not as ordinary livestock but in carefully selected pairs of "special breeder stock," which sold for $30,000 each. The farmers were skeptical, of course—until the promoters explained how many eggs each female would lay, yielding birds that could be sold for (you guessed it), $15,000 a piece. So these poor ex-dairymen would mortgage their land, or spend their savings, to buy several pairs of these gold-plated birds in the hope of finding buyers (also known as "greater fools").

Emu (6 ft. tall)

This scheme, which eerily foreshadowed the tech and real estate bubbles, took no account of the fact that someone, at some point, would have to kill these golden geese and make them into steaks—which would cost, it was estimated, $4,000 a serving. Who would ever bother to slaughter one of these birds? The answer, of course, was no one—at least not until the pyramid had collapsed and the last round of buyers (the "greatest fools") gave up trying to break even—and in desperation, decided to "eat the damn things." Which is, I guess, what happened. I expect you'll find the farmers who made this costly mistake working at Wendy's. "Do you want ostrich with that?"

Not all of them failed. Some farmers bought cheaper birds expecting to breed them for meat. So I'm happy to say that at least one of the ranches I visited, Acadian Ostrich, is still in business. (The emus, on the other hand, turned out to cost more money to feed than their meat and oil was worth—which explains why you'll see the creatures running wild all across the Gulf Coast, ranchers having simply opened the gates, crying, "Fly and be free!")

And this is what happened all across the economy. The homes that Americans were told would go right on appreciating in price forever and ever were never actually worth the putative prices they (briefly) commanded—any more than ostriches were ever worth $15,000. The scungy two-family houses in blue-collar Queens where I grew up were never worth the $750,000 sticker price they'd attained by 2007. By which I mean, their proximity to Manhattan, their quality and attractiveness, and the features that made people willing to pay for them never added up to such a price. Instead, their estimated value was hugely inflated by the sheer expectation that someday, somebody would be willing to buy them for $950,000. Why would that happen? Because home values were going up. It happened because it was happening, and the only thing that would stop it from happening was the drying up of cheaply borrowed money to finance further purchases by speculating homeowners of ever-pricier ostriches. Er, homes.

Likewise, the paper "billionaires" of 1999, whose IPOs had yielded them options worth more than several American states, *were never really rich.* Their shares, which were "worth" $30 billion or something, were impossible to sell. The moment these thirty-year-old hucksters started trying to unload the stocks, their value would plummet—based as it was on nothing: no profits, meager earnings, nothing more than the fantasy that a greater fool would come along to pay hundreds of millions for shares in a company that sold Hindu devotional mouse pads made from recycled condoms. In the end, we ran out of fools.

So as I use my quarterly 401(k) statement to clean up after the beagles, I console myself with the thought that the annual gains of 25 percent that they earned throughout the 1990s never really existed. They were promises of consumption, based not on previous savings but on the hope of future loans. They were faerie, insubstantial creatures of light and air that vanished with the first ray of the dawn. The beagles, at least, are real.

A Visit to Richistan

One of my favorite lurid reads of the past few years is journalist Robert Frank's account of America's crassly, newly rich, titled *Richistan*[2]. Reading it reminded this rent-controlled kid from Queens of his first trip to the Whole Foods in Highland Park, Dallas. After a lifetime spent straining to take down one out of maybe seven brands of cereal from dusty, crowded shelves and squeezing through narrow aisles to pick between two kinds of milk (regular or skim), my maiden voyage to this supermarket was an awakening. Who knew there could be so many different *varieties* of baby greens? Or that lettuce, of any kind, could fetch $7.50 a pound? The vast, spacious shelves attended by tanned and toned Dallasites groaned with organic, local, sustainable, and "eco-friendly" foods. The carts were big, the aisles were wide, and your pricey provisions could be packed (your choice) in paper, plastic—or hemp! I learned at Whole Foods that goats also give milk, and that it is tasty—albeit $3.50 per quart. As I left the store, I felt stunned by the sheer abundance of it all, like a recent arrival from the old Soviet Union. In my best Russian accent, I told the bohemian chick who checked me out, "I LOVE Amerika!"

And I meant it. But there also lingered in me a sense of, well, excess. Was it really healthy to cultivate such delicate sensibilities? Did one really need this many choices of chard? It's one thing to shop at farmers' markets because you want to support the folks who grow apples in your area—and another to learn how to care, really *care*, about buying "pre-War" balsamic vinegar. C. S. Lewis dubbed such

---

2. Robert Frank, *Richistan: A Journey Through the American Wealth Boom and the Lives of the New Rich* (New York: Crown, 2007).

exquisite awareness the "higher gluttony," which consists not in excessive consumption but undue *attention* to food. He smelled it in vegetarians, food faddists, and others who made of their body not so much a temple as a fetish.

Reading *Richistan* brought Lewis's warning to mind. Frank follows the lifestyles and probes the souls of extraordinarily successful hedge-fund managers, Internet "instapreneurs" who cashed out before the NASDAQ crash, and a least one ceramic figurine magnate. (The book was written before the Crash of 2008, but I suspect

these people landed on their Pradas.) These men and women live in gated communities or isolated estates, are attended by "concierge doctors," and use private airports for their teak-lined private jets. They are citizens of another country altogether, the republic of Richistan.

Along the way, issues arise of interest to policy wonks, such as the alarming growth of inequality in America and the wage stagnation of the lower middle and working classes alongside the burgeoning ranks of billionaires. The book parallels the recent explosion of astronomical wealth with historical moments when the "wealth gap" between the richest Americans and the rest of us yawned equally wide—the Gilded Age and the Roaring Twenties. Each period gave way to "progressive" reforms designed to redistribute that wealth, frequently through confiscatory taxation that funded the large-scale expansion of government—a nice excuse for regulating markets to enshrine the power of existing economic giants and insulate them from future competition. In the end, measures such as the ones Theodore Roosevelt took against the "trusts" and Franklin Roosevelt undertook to manage the entire American economy (i.e., the National Recovery Act) ended up empowering not the common man but managerial elites—the sorts of people who are adept at rising in bureaucracies, be they corporate or governmental.

None of this is to defend such Richistani excesses as wealth camps for sons and daughters of the privileged, where participants scoff at sums like a mere $10 million and playact how to someday inform their fiancées of the necessity of signing prenups. And I don't even want think about the Freudian competition among male software execs to build the biggest yacht—ending in four-hundred-foot-plus monsters with their own Olympic swimming pools.

In an otherwise damning portrayal of a rising class that has little class, Frank finds men to admire. He is positively gushy on the subject of "socially conscious" magnates like the Colorado Gang of Four, left-leaning entrepreneurs who worked together in the late 1990s to target socially conservative public officials and "take down the religious Right." (Unsurprisingly, we learn that two of the four are gay.) Indeed, while most of the merely "affluent" (folks with net wealth of just a few millions) tend to skew conservative or libertarian, as one climbs higher in the ranks of Richistan, the politics slant swiftly leftward. Frank lauds "one education philanthropist" who says, "When you look at what I spend compared to what government spends on schools, it's like pissing in the wind." Frank goes on, "So to have impact, today's philanthropists also want a say in directing government funds."

Translated, that means these magnates prefer to spend other people's money, so they use their own cash to grab political power so they can do good works on the taxpayer's dime. In case you ever wonder why movie stars traipse around demanding U.S. government aid to places like Darfur instead of—well, sending their own money—here's your answer. There's more "impact" to be gained by buying or bullying senators.

More admirable by far is a man like Philip Berber, whom Frank colorfully describes as a "Jewish Irishman who now lives in Texas." Shocked by poverty he saw once in Ethiopia, Berber is spending his considerable fortune digging wells and providing economic opportunities in a country ravaged by drought and decades of Communism. Businessmen like Berber—the *real* philanthropists depicted here— are revolutionizing the field of foreign aid, demanding fiscal accountability of nonprofits, and squeezing out the waste endemic to such assistance.

But the heart of the book lies outside the political realm and goes to questions of culture. Frank points out vividly the difference between families possessing "Old Money" and new arrivals in Richistan. Of course, there's the difference in taste; old families tend to hide their wealth, invest conservatively, consume inconspicuously, and fund the arts. Richistanis compete to own the largest estate in Palm Beach, continue to sweat fourteen-hour days to accumulate that next $100 million, and view artworks as commodities.

But then, new money has ever been vulgar, and it has always taken a decade or two to turn filthy lucre into social and cultural prestige. European nobility began as warlords wearing bearskins and the Medicis as *arriviste* usurers who endowed Renaissance painters to outdo the aristocrats. The Kennedys before establishing Camelot founded their

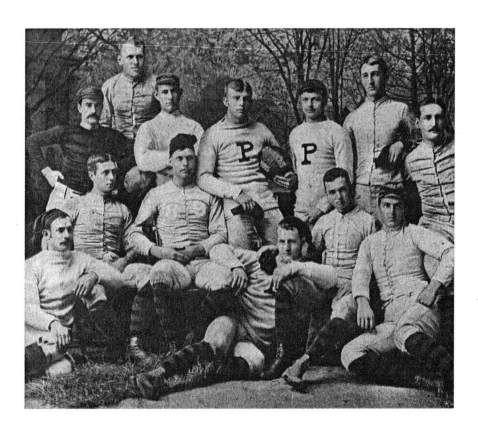

fortune on bathtub gin, and their political ambition was fueled in part by Joseph Sr.'s rage at his exclusion from the ranks of Boston Brahmans. It would seem natural to expect that Richistanis would proceed through the same process of assimilation to the cultural norms of the established wealthy classes and gradually shed their extravagance in favor of Old Monied reticence and civility.

Except that those norms no longer exist—or at any rate, the Richistanis don't care about them. As Frank recounts, when today's newly rich encounter exclusion at the hands of established elites, they don't bother toning down their behavior and attempting to "pass" by aping the ways of those who came before them. Instead, they found their own country clubs, throw their own (higher-priced and hence more prestigious) charity events, and thumb their noses to the old farts in J. Press jackets who furrow their eyebrows at the glare from a $40,000 wristwatch. Nor does the second monied generation feel pressure to conform. The old guard, according to Rockefeller cousin Nelson Aldrich, honed the mores and morals of their youth at boarding schools. Frank quotes Aldrich on the prevailing ethos of these schools: "When I grew up, the ethical tradition was this weird combination of Christianity and manliness. There was a heavy emphasis on sports, especially the most painful sports, like ice hockey and football. It was all about stoicism and patience under great stress." At his parents' insistence, Aldrich spent his summers at jobs that entailed digging trenches or tending bodies at the morgue. Whatever the shortcomings—which have been endlessly detailed in resentful novels and snarky films—of this old "way of the WASP," such stoicism had its virtues. But it no longer shapes the scions of Richistan. In fact, as Frank relates, "nearly 40 percent of today's millionaires give their kids unregulated access" to their inheritances.

And the outcome is easy to sum up in four bitter syllables: Paris Hilton.

Mao Tse-tung's Greed for Mayhem

Not every villain in history can be confined to a single vice. In pointing out, for instance, the Gluttony of François Mitterand, I didn't mean to clear this polygamous socialist of any suspicion of Lust or Envy. Quite the contrary, as St. Francis de Sales implied when he suggested that giving way to Lust made men effeminate, allowing any Deadly Sin to conquer part of one's will merely softens up the rest for easier conquest. Think of your moral life as a small, developing country, surrounded by enemies, kept going by a lifeline to a single, benevolent patron (say, your one-time colonial ruler). The more you allow corruption to take hold in business and government, the slower and more inefficient everyone's work will be, as the vicious cycle of distrust leads even honest folk to get in on the game—till at last you're actually nostalgic for the sight of the Union Jack. Think of God's grace as the squadron of British gunboats that steams upriver and restores order in the capital.[3]

Likewise, a will that has compromised left and right with passionate perversities has little defense against the next temptation to come along. As a man deepens in malice, he can learn to take a Luciferian thrill in flouting his conscience, tossing the rules of decency into the outhouse like the Sears catalogue. One truly dark example, whom my research has led me to dub as the *most successfully evil man in history*, is the late Chinese dictator Mao Tse-tung. One of the governing passions of Mao's life seems to have been Greed—for luxury, privilege, and most of all the power of life and death.

I cannot hope to do justice to this man here. Indeed, to make a dent would require not so much a book as

---

3. Is it possible to find a more politically incorrect simile? If so, I can't think of one. Enjoy!

a series of horror films. Not so obviously demonic as Adolf Hitler[4] or thuggish as Uncle Joe Stalin, Mao was portrayed by his propaganda machine as a wise, reflective leader of China's long-oppressed peasants—a man given to philosophical musings and short, inscrutable poems. This Oriental stereotype got eaten up like a pint of late-night takeout by a long string of gullible Westerners—from journalists like Edgar Snow to generals like George Marshall, who forced Chiang Kai-shek to stop attacking Mao's guerillas when victory was still possible. At least these people had the excuse of operating before Mao came to power. In the late 1960s, after Mao had already racked up most of his estimated 70 million deaths, Western intellectuals with a taste for utopian tyranny turned from Moscow's brand of Communism to Mao's; radicals like Michel Foucault[5] and Julia Kristeva camped it up for years, calling themselves Maoists—even as Mao's regime crushed every flicker of independent thought among almost a billion people, starving or working millions of them to death in the process. Mao's system organized committees to micromanage the public, private, and sexual lives of millions at the point of a bayonet. This won it praise from pampered professors as the "purest form" of socialism. And on this point, they were right. The essence of every form of collectivism boils down to one person's craving to organize other people's lives on the model of a termite colony. Few have so spectacularly had the chance to indulge this fantasy as the spoiled scholar from Hunan.

Courtesy of Photofunia.com.

---

4. Pope Pius XII told any diplomats who would listen that Hitler was "possessed by Satan."
5. A gay sadomasochist nihilist literary critic who died of AIDS, he is famous for asserting that holding schizophrenics in institutions is arbitrary and oppressive.

Mao has never gotten the credit he deserves. Vendors sell little statuettes of him in New York's Chinatown. American college students sometimes sport green hats with Mao's infernal red star.[6] Andy Warhol (see Chapter 9) made a nice pile of American dollars decorating portraits of this dictator with garish silkscreened colors—raising none of the questions that might have emerged had he been issuing pictures of Hitler. But then, Mao killed very few Europeans, and those Asians just have a terrible habit of dying like flies, don't they?

Such a tacit, crass assumption is the only way to explain the genial disregard in the West for Mao's atrocities—which were most fully documented in *Mao: The Unknown Story* by Jung Chang and Jon Halliday.[7] I pretty much ruined Thanksgiving last year working my way through 801 pages, and six decades, of villainy. From the copious documents and quotations Chang and Halliday cite, what sets Mao apart from ideologues like Lenin, Hitler, and Pol Pot is his comparative lack of interest in ideas. His youthful conversion to Marxism seems perfunctory, and his political writings never attained the theoretical sophistication even of Stalin's. Mao would have been equally at ease adopting Nazi ideas, had they been less parochially German, since his focus from a young age seems to have been less on improving the lot of industrial workers (whom he scorned) or peasants (whom he hated) and more on the following three-point program:

1. Avoiding work
2. Attaining power and privilege
3. Causing mayhem and destruction largely to see what would happen

Mao's solipsism emerged early on, as Chang and Halliday document, pointing to his philosophical jottings at age twenty-four:

> Mao's attitude to morality consisted of one core: the self, "I" above everything else. "I do not agree with the view that to be moral, the motive of one's actions has to be benefiting others. Morality does not have to be defined in relation to others. . . . People like me want to . . . satisfy our hearts to the full and in doing so we automatically have the most

---

6. Having learned about Mao's crimes from seminars by refugees in Manhattan, I confronted one clueless fellow student about his Mao cap, asking him where he kept his "Hitler hat." A great way to make friends, I can tell you.
7. Jung Chang and Jon Halliday, *Mao: The Unknown Story* (New York: Knopf, 2005).

valuable moral codes. Of course there are people and objects in the world, but they are all there only for me."

Mao shunned all constraints of responsibility and duty. "People like me only have a duty to ourselves; we have no duty to other people."

[Mao further wrote]: "All our actions . . . are driven by impulse, and the conscience that is wise goes along with this in every instance. Sometimes . . . conscience restrains impulses such as overeating or over-indulgence in sex. But conscience is only there to restrain, not oppose. And the restraint is there for better completion of the impulse." (13)

No wonder Mao became so popular in the 1960s. His ethical core—which could have been cribbed from the writings of the Marquis de Sade—was precisely what the New Left was peddling, in the form of "free love" and the Dionysian frenzies of drug-fueled musical orgies such as Woodstock. But there's one crucial difference: the New Left, following the gradualist revolutionary tactics of Antonio Gramsci, promoted egoistic hedonism as an acid to eat away bourgeois Christian society—the better to replace it with a Puritanical, egalitarian anthill. It seems that Mao was doing the converse—creating a dictatorship in the service of his own narcissism. Unwilling to serve Heaven, he carved out a vast Hell on Earth where he could reign.

Mao saw himself as part of a small elite he called "Great Heroes":

For this elite, he said: "Everything outside their nature, such as restrictions and constraints, must be swept away by the great strength in their nature. . . . When Great Heroes give full play to their impulses, they are magnificently powerful, stormy and invincible. Their power is like a hurricane arising from a deep gorge, and like a sex maniac on heat [*sic*] and prowling for a lover . . . there is no way to stop them." (14)

That's a picture-perfect description of the capital sin of Greed—the fetishization of animal instincts and simple whims, incensing them on an altar as ends in themselves.

Now, a lesser, better man might take from such a credo mere hedonism and follow the path of a wretch such as Hugh Hefner (see Chapter 1)—ending up not as the absolute ruler of 900 million souls but rather as one of those guys you hear about on Viagra ads who end up in emergency wards thanks to "erections that last longer than eight hours."

But Mao combined Hefner's juvenile narcissism with a tectonic will to power. Mao regarded lesser humans (those of us who aren't Great Heroes) the way a sadistic schoolboy might see the ants in a hill he was savaging with fireworks. Mao yawned that long-lasting peace

is unendurable to human beings, and tidal waves of disturbance have to be created in this state of peace. When we look at history, we adore the times of [war] when dramas happened one after another . . . which make reading about them great fun. When we get to the periods of peace and prosperity we are bored. . . . Human nature loves sudden swift changes. (14)

What model of change did Mao have in mind? According to Chiang and Halliday,

When he came to the question, "How do we change [China]?" Mao laid the utmost emphasis on destruction: "the country must be . . . destroyed and then re-formed. . . . This applies to the country; to the nation; and to mankind. . . . The destruction of the universe is the same. . . . People like me long for its destruction, because when the old universe is destroyed, a new universe will be formed. Isn't that better?" (15)

Mao's attitude didn't change after his conversion to Communism, although he learned to cloak it in social justice rhetoric, to frame his pronouncements in the jargon of Marxism-Leninism and lard them with concern for peasants and workers. However, it was precisely those "little people" of China—who, despite the vast inequalities of the old imperial system, had in many places built up small savings and larger plots of land—that suffered most directly at Mao's hands. The first victims were his supporters and the unlucky residents who came under control of the guerrilla bands Mao came to command in the lawless China of the 1930s, where bandit kings ("warlords") and Japanese invaders fought the legal government of China, headed by the well-meaning but naïve and nepotistic Chiang Kai-shek. Regions Mao commanded on behalf of the fledgling Communist Party of China were raped for resources, the peasants stripped of all their savings and often reduced to near starvation, while the Red cadres themselves endured horrific privations. Those worst off were the Communist soldiers serving under leaders whom Mao envied or feared. Repeatedly, Mao would maneuver entire Red armies commanded by his rivals into hopeless battles or hostile terrain, killing off tens of thousands—but weakening his competitors for leadership. Other competitors Mao had poisoned or tortured to death, sometimes in his presence. Mao would continue in these habits once he ruled the country. His need to wipe clean every trace of independent thought would culminate with the Cultural Revolution (1966–76), Mao's attempt to purge the country of its 2,400-year-old Confucian culture, to destroy all family loyalty, to liquidate most of the educated class (except for industrial and military specialists), and to eliminate the last traces of Christianity. Instead, all the philosophical wisdom his citizens would need could be found in Mao's *Quotations from Chairman*

Mao—a collection of platitudes that was printed by the tens of millions, which Chinese carried everywhere, if they valued their lives.

All through his rise to power, Mao insisted on living like an emperor. The desperate 1934 to 1935 retreat across thousands of miles of arid Chinese terrain that Mao's publicists dressed up as "the Long March" did indeed involve a great deal of marching—but none of it by Mao. As Chiang and Halliday record, his feet rarely touched the ground: Mao and other leaders were carried on litters like Manchu aristocrats. Indeed, while the elite consumed wholesome food, dozens of litter bearers dropped dead from exhaustion or hunger.

This hypocrisy set the pattern for the rest of Mao's career, as he rose in the party ranks, and especially after Russian intervention and American interference helped bring Mao's party to power: even as ordinary people paid the price for Mao's ultra-Marxist policies of collectivizing the land, seizing all surpluses, and working peasants to death by the tens of thousands every year, Mao ate multicourse meals—flying in his favorite fish, still alive, across thousands of miles—built elaborate villas, and commandeered gifts from international aid groups for his own use. (During World War II, Mao seized an ambulance funded by donations from Chinese-Americans as his personal limousine.) When Mao craved superpower status to rival the Soviet Union, he sold massive quantities of food, cutting the diets of average Chinese to just a few hundred calories day. To fund his industrial "Great Leap Forward," Mao squeezed the farmers even harder, opining, "Half of China may very well have to

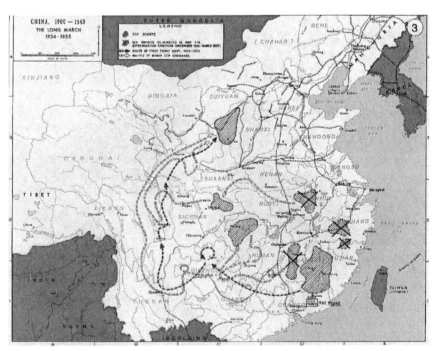

The route of the "Long March," which, for Mao, was more like a magic carpet ride.

die." When he faced possible attack by the United States because of his involvement in the invasion of South Korea, Mao

> wrote to Krushchev confirming that he would be only too happy for China to fight a nuclear war with America alone. "For our ultimate victory," he offered, "for the total eradication of the imperialists, we [i.e., the Chinese people, who had not been consulted] are willing to endure the first strike. All it is is a big pile of people dying." (407)

Mao's attitudes hadn't changed since his early twenties, when he played at being Raskolnikov. When reports would come to Mao of mass starvation and thousands of suicides, Mao replied that people were

> "not without food all the year round—only six . . . or four months" [*sic*]. Senior officials who invoked the traditional concept of conscience (liang-xin) to beg him to go easy found themselves being slapped down with remarks like "You'd better have less conscience. Some of our comrades have too much mercy, not enough brutality, which means they are not so Marxist." "On this matter," Mao said, "we indeed have no conscience. Marxism is that brutal." (387)

For once he was telling the truth.

Generosity: How to Give without Being Taken

It's easy to make fun of Twelve-Step groups, given their curious jargon and the fact that there are so many different varieties of them filling church basements across the country with shaky participants and their pamphlets. In case you didn't know, the movement has gone far beyond offering hope to alcoholics and drug users, expanding to fill the empty space in a wide assortment of modern hearts and heads. There are deep resemblances between the moral path traced in the steps and Ignatian spirituality—a fact that impressed the Jesuit Reverend Edward Dowling, whom Alcoholics Anonymous (AA) founder Bill W. befriended in 1940. Given Bill W.'s ignorance of the existence of St. Ignatius, Fr. Dowling chalked up the similarities to Providence and threw his support behind the fledgling group. Countless lives and souls have been saved by AA and related organizations.

The Twelve Steps come to mind here because I'm examining Generosity, the Virtue opposed to Greed. If Greed is a disordered hunger for the good things God created, then its opposite is equally bad. Scorning the wise use of wealth and wasting your substance in riotous spending is every bit as evil as covetously hoarding stuff. Dante damned the Prodigal right alongside the Greedy and set them rolling stones like Sisyphus in opposite directions, with both sides slamming into each other and vociferously heckling. If this sounds like modern politics, that's not exactly an accident. Since the fully Christian, sacramental view of the world runs aslant secular ideologies, secular political parties tend to miss the point—although the folks at the "tea parties" that sprang up in 2008 seem to be closer than most.

The Twelve Steps make the distinction between extending kindness to an addict—let's say, your cousin who volunteered in Caroline Kennedy's truncated campaign for U.S. Senate—and "enabling" him in ways that lubricate his slide into self-destruction. True Generosity means not only treating an addicted person charitably—avoiding sarcasm and gossip—but also as an adult who has a behavioral disease. You respect his independence and (this is the kicker) do not try to step in and control his disordered behavior. That's between him and God, and when you insert yourself, you're playing God. Or, in Twelve-Step parlance, "trying to become his Higher Power." Instead, be humble enough to pray for the person—and not to tell him that you're doing it. Sure, take away his car keys when he isn't fit to drive, but don't become his volunteer, unpaid chauffeur.

Tough love is a very hard balance to tread, as family members of addicts can testify. Indeed, the temptation to "enable" is such a powerful one that it's actually addictive. It may sound funny to those unfamiliar with it, but there are Twelve-Step groups devoted not just to addicts but also to their family members. And for very good reason: living constantly in the presence of someone enslaved by behavior that's self- (and other-) destructive is morally grueling. It provokes an overpowering anxiety and saps your trust in God. You may start out as Mary, sitting at Jesus's feet and listening to him, but a few years of living alongside a drinker, druggie, or gambler and you're likely to turn into a high-octane, power-hungry caricature of Martha—rushing about cleaning up people's messes, wiping the noses of adults, and all but changing their diapers, while feeling like a genuine victim soul. You'll "offer up" your suffering—all caused, of course, by the addict—and make sure that he knows how well you're doing your Job. You'll learn along the way a wide array of domineering and manipulative behaviors that help you survive the addict's presence. And in good fallen, natural fashion, you'll start using them on everyone you meet.

Or seeking out other damaged folks you can "fix." I know someone who grew up the son of a full-on compulsive gambler. She started by nibbling away at her husband's blue-collar salary with simple games of bingo. But the Diocese of Brooklyn in the good old 1970s—when it never turned down an annulment—had its sights

MARY AND MARTHA

set on higher things, like high-stakes poker games. Instead of nickel and dime, the games would be "dollar and two," watched over by local cops named Pat and Brendan, frequented by guys in pointy, roach-killer shoes with names that rhymed with RICO. They'd play against little old ladies with teased-up, Marge Simpson hair and serious gambling problems. Some priests would make change for players, playfully "blessing the money for luck." One pastor even scheduled games on Friday nights during Lent—and when a pious addict pointed out he was serving bologna sandwiches, the priest solemnly conferred on the assembly a special dispensation so they could eat them.

This housewife would drop some $300 per week, often borrowing extra money from slick-haired men who took repayment with . . . deadly seriousness. Her husband took to dealing cards to make back in tips what his wife was losing. When they weren't at parish poker, they were fighting like feral cats over the family's death-spiral finances—all of this while their children were applying to top-tier colleges. The fruits of these family dynamics were the following:

- To this day, the daughter can't open bills or even deposit paychecks without a panic attack.
- Having listened to so much screaming about so many parish games, when she hears terms like "Precious Blood," "St. Joseph," or "St. Margaret Mary," she doesn't think of saints or sacred mysteries but of . . . poker.
- Over the years, the son assembled a collection of parasitical "friends" who relied on him for make-work and short-term "loans."
- When she meets someone with a deep-seated problem or raging addiction, the daughter actually gets excited, rolls up her sleeves, and gets to work. Pretty soon, she's dragging the person to the sacraments, giving him reading lists, calling him up for status reports, and generally acting like a third-rate substitute for God. She views such micromanagement of other full-grown adults as falling under various "works of mercy."

This case may seem extreme, but it points out the distortions to which the Virtue of Generosity is subject.

This virtue business is a puzzler. If picking up the tab for a raging alcoholic or keeping one's gambling-addict grandma in bingo cards doesn't add up to Generosity, what does? Isn't the New Testament full of admonitions like "Give till it hurts" and "It's 10 PM. Do you know where your children are?"

It's true that the Gospels include injunctions to give away your cloak, walk the extra mile, and sell all you have so you can give it to the poor. I used to deal with such baffling dicta in the Scriptures by gritting my teeth and reading past them quickly, till the next really interesting miracle. I mean, are we actually meant to turn ourselves into "eunuchs" for the Kingdom of God (Mt 19:12)? Even if we're talking about the clergy, that passage fairly screams out for a reassuring footnote from the editor (i.e., the Church). It's one I'd skip altogether if I were a biblical literalist . . . like the eggless theologian Origen, bless his heart!

Then I came to think that Jesus purposely spoke in parables with potentially fatal side effects just to force His followers to organize a hierarchical Church, with a sturdy Magisterium to explain away the crazier implications of His words—like T. S. Eliot, who I think wrote obscure stuff just to keep us English professors employed. (Thanks, Tom!)

I mean, someone who misread Christ's advice about turning the other cheek, plucking out an eye, lopping off a hand, becoming a eunuch, and getting himself born again, then combined it with Paul's statements on serpents, could end up a blind, pacifist, single-handed snake handler in diapers singing soprano. Which is one more reason I'm glad that I'm a Catholic.

Getting back to Generosity, think of the passage where Jesus told the young man who sought perfection that he should sell everything he had, give it away, and follow Him. As the wise theologian Rev. Gilbert Graham, O.P., once explained, Jesus could read human hearts. He knew the spiritual problems of each person He encountered—and answered them accordingly. So when Jesus met the woman at the well, who was something of a tramp, He called her on the carpet. He explained to her the real reason she was so insatiable and offered her "living water" instead. Likewise, the well-meaning, pious Jew who accosted Christ and explained in detail all his virtues was actually eaten up with guilt, he knew that he was holding something back, which is why he kept pestering Christ about what he needed to be "perfect." So Jesus willingly handed him one of the "counsels of perfection," which the Church later cataloged as Poverty, Chastity, and Obedience.

These three sacrifices of pretty much everything that makes earthly life worth living quickly formed the vows of monks and nuns—who, by living them out, serve as prophetic signs of faith in the afterlife. (I mean, why else would anybody bother?) But does that mean these goals are for everyone or even that it would be better if they were? Does the Church really wish that everyone were called to Poverty, for instance? Was Chairman Mao's China, where everyone dressed identically, ate six hundred calories a day, and bicycled through the rice paddies, a model of Catholic society? (Sometimes, from reading bishops' pastoral natterings on the economy, you might be forgiven for thinking so.)

Likewise, the Church doesn't secretly wish that everyone were called to monastic Chastity so that the human race could vanish in the course of seventy years; it leaves such fantasies to radical ecologists.

Nor does the Church yearn to impose on the laity the Obedience proper to monasteries— which, if imposed universally, would yield a totalitarian state. (Those of you who have worked for lay-run Catholic institutions know exactly what I mean.) Instead, within the broad parameters of the natural law and the gospel's call to Charity, we each are meant to discern our vocation as individuals, within our state of life and our particular station in life, to cultivate Generosity. As Pope Leo XIII wrote in *Rerum Novarum*,

> True, no one is commanded to distribute to others that which is required for his own needs and those of his household; nor even to give away what is reasonably required to keep up becomingly his condition in life, "for no one ought to live other than becomingly." But, when what necessity demands has been supplied, and one's standing fairly taken thought for, it becomes a duty to give to the indigent out of what remains over. (#22)

This means that some who are born fabulously wealthy, like St. Katharine Drexel, may well be called to sacrifice everything to the service of the weakest and most neglected—in her day, blacks and Indians; in our day, the unborn.

But not every calling is so dramatic or (in its own way) glamorous. For most of us, Generosity means consistently, day in and out, doing just a little bit more than the minimum—working a little harder on an article, grating fresh cheese into the soufflé instead of shaking it from a can, putting flowers on the table, wearing makeup for one's husband, spending extra time on the yard work or the exercise bike to please one's wife. . . . It's humdrum stuff that's typically the hardest to do consistently, but these small sacrifices of self—usually done not for strangers but family members, colleagues, or customers—make the difference between a society of civic virtue, trust, and excellence . . . and the shabby, dreary, litigious nest of snakes we call "the real world."

It isn't real. In fact, it's less real, because it partakes less in the ultimate Good than a faithful monastery, a healthy Christian family, or a conscientious business. Religious orders that abandon their charisms are hardly more than phantasms—which is why few young folk are bothering to join them. In the same way, marriages entered into frivolously are annulled fairly routinely, and businesses built on hype and empty promises get bailed out for billions by the taxpayer—then go right on dispensing bonuses. That's the "real world," my friends—an enormous, faintly obscene Thanksgiving Day balloon filled with methane. And here comes Jesus with a blowtorch.

Generosity at Gunpoint

I've often heard people talk about their most beloved aspect of our Faith. When asked "What's your favorite thing about being a Catholic?" some well-instructed souls

will cite the Eucharist, while others will speak of their devotion to Our Lady. Still others will cop to "bingo." The pointier heads in the room might cite the Church's rich storehouse of worldly and heavenly wisdom. In the old days, people pointed to the liturgy—but that was before its "renovation" in the 1970s with orange shag carpet and cheap wood paneling. Reading what many Catholics have to say on economics and politics lately, it seems to me that if these folks answered honestly, they'd have to say, "Being Catholic gives me a high-minded rhetoric of noble-sounding values, a sense of moral superiority, and unrestricted license to speak and write as a crank."

I'm reminded of people I used to meet at Latin Mass, whose Faith was past reproach but who hadn't spent quite enough time on the care and feeding of Reason. Some would wave at me yellowed copies of a schismatic Catholic newsletter, citing the latest column proving that heliocentrism is a heresy. But I'll never forget the sweet old lady who took me aside one Sunday.

"Do you know what I read?" she whispered. "The environmentalist scientists are planning to reduce the world population to 700,000 people and turn the rest of the planet into a nature park."

"Er, really?"

"And you know how they're going to do it?"

"Well. . . ."

"They're going to clone dinosaurs and unleash them on us," she said, almost giddy with glee. Apparently some columnist had read Al Gore's *Earth in the Balance,* rented *Jurassic Park,* and connected the dots.

Unsure of the charitable response, I restricted my remarks to these: "Well, you know what I heard? For the past thirty years, the Freemasons have been faking the weather."

"Really?"

"Yeah. I don't have time to tell you how they do it, but I promise I'll give you all the details next time I see you." And I never came back.[1]

I'd made the woman's day. From then on, whenever it seemed to be spitting smog on Lexington Avenue or blazing heat on the asphalt, she knew that behind the Masonic façade there really was glorious, temperate, Catholic weather—if only we could see it.

---

1. The scandal titled "Climate-Gate" raised suspicions that much of the scientific consensus over climate change had been created through force and fraud. Maybe an international conspiracy of secular humanitarians really has been faking the weather. . . .

That pretty well describes how too many Catholics look at economics and public policy. Whatever the facts of the matter, regardless of learned arguments, they know without thinking too hard or reading too much that the "Catholic" answer (as they dimly understand it) must be correct . . . so they need not bother going through the trouble of doing any research. Having read about an issue (perhaps for the first time) in some Church document or other, they seize upon a relative good it recommends:

- The Church supports a "living wage"
- . . . and decent conditions for workers
- . . . and opportunity for the poor
- . . . and "economic justice"
- . . . and "rights for immigrants"
- . . . and health care.

Then they treat this desideratum as an unconditioned absolute, as binding as the right to life, more important than liberty or property. They don't feel the need to master even the basics of the discipline they're considering but rather grab left and right at whatever facts will help them build a case. If they're talking about economics, they'll cite a Gospel verse here, quote St. Francis there, throw in some abuse of "usury," maybe even summon some half-remembered Chesterton—then wrap it in a pretty pink bow with a long quotation from a bishop's pastoral letter and act as if they've made a genuine argument. If you ask about the costs of the policies they propose or the dangers of bureaucratic management, they won't respond

to specifics but rather start pounding the table and accusing you of "dissent" from Catholic teaching . . . as if you'd marched right out and joined Planned Parenthood or the Klan. Instead, you're simply suggesting that maybe, just maybe, the hailstorm outside the window isn't being faked by the Masons.

The learned Thomas E. Woods, Jr., in his indispensable book *The Church and the Market*,[2] complains of his violent frustration at Catholics who grandstand about "distributive justice" and offer Rube Goldberg schemes for reengineering our country's economy, without knowing or caring how wealth is produced in the first place. He's right on target. Too many well-meaning Catholics treat our country's relatively recent, hard-won, and fragile prosperity as if it had descended in pennies from heaven, and the only question now is how to

2. (Lanham, MD: Lexington Books, 2005.)

divide up the windfall fairly. All property and all labor are owned in common. It may suit the state to allow you to hold a "title" to your house or keep some portion of your wages, but fundamentally you belong to the U.S. Congress, just as a Russian serf and every stick of furniture in his house was the property of the tsar. Left-leaning bishops who wish to make this point note that Creation was given to man in common; they leave out the fact that our labor is our own and that taxes enforced by the threat of imprisonment can mount up to a kind of slavery. You and I pay up to 50 percent when federal, state, local, Social Security, and sales taxes are added up—which means that half our time is spent working with a bayonet at our backs.

What's missing from the happy, totalitarian picture painted by certain advocates of what they claim is "Catholic Social Teaching" is something fundamental to the West, a fruit of Christian culture that it took Vatican II for the Church to fully recognize: the fact of human dignity. In the early Church, up through the first writings of St. Augustine, the Church asked only for liberty of worship, confident that the Gospel would sway people on its own. In his later years, frustrated by the intransigence of the Donatist heretics, Augustine changed his mind and asked the now-Christian emperors to "compel them to come in." Building on Augustine's later work, many popes and countless Christian kings used the coercive power of the state to persecute heretics—arguing that the  free will of these individuals was outweighed by the danger to the souls they might lead to hell. Besides, they said in a phrase that became a little bit infamous, "Error has no rights." Since no one has a right to do what's wrong, how can those with false beliefs have a right to hold and practice an inaccurate religion? Do they have the right to lie about the gospel?

At Vatican II, the Council Fathers (under pressure from American prelates, as an unsympathetic Michael Davies argues in *The Second Vatican Council and Religious Liberty*) were more concerned about the very real persecution of Christians throughout the Communist bloc than the duty of (now-deposed) Catholic monarchs to uphold orthodoxy. They reframed the question as follows: error may have no rights, but the person holding the error does. In *Dignitatis Humanae*, the Council teaches that the dignity of the human person forbids religious coercion by the state. Pope John Paul II was not, I think, misguided when he apologized for the actions of his predecessors that violated this precept.

Nor does human dignity stop at the church door. Throughout the Catechism, the Church insists on the rights of the human person to liberty of thought, association, and action—within the limits of Justice and the countervailing rights of one's fellow men. Only when our actions violate Justice—not Charity, but Justice—is it right to use the violent, coercive power of the state to curb and restrict them. Indeed, it is only Justice that can be enforced by the state. Mandatory Charity is as moot as mandatory Faith or Hope.

Courtesy of Wikipedia Commons.

So in all our discussions of economic issues, let's keep in mind that part of loving our neighbor entails not enslaving him at gunpoint to suit our vision of the good—be it religious orthodoxy, economic equality, or anything else. On a prudential level, we must take with grim seriousness the threat that every government program to replace the Corporal Works of Mercy will expand—irrevocably—the power over our lives of a grimly secular state. That's power we won't get back, and it won't (given our Constitution) be used in the service or with the guidance of the Church. "He who is not with me is against me" (Mt 12:30).

Penitence and Penury

My old parish in downtown Nashua, New Hampshire, is a reverent, slightly battered Irish parish, with painted wood that bravely substitutes for marble, a bathroom that always smells funky, and a mostly empty rectory. Built for ten or twelve, the red brick fortress houses two of the best priests in our diocese, who offer the Latin Mass twice a month, assisted by a surprisingly able choir. The pastor is brisk and informative in his sermons. He's also a bit of a

"card"; a late vocation who used to belong to a rock band, he's said to vent excess energies by hammering his old drum set.

One Sunday, the last of the Octave of Easter, the pastor taught me something—that each day of the Octave serves in a sense like one long liturgical "day." *I didn't know that*, I said to myself, resolving to put something extra into the basket: the laborer is worthy of his hire. But I got something more from the Mass that day, an insight into a spiritual issue

I struggle with that writhes at the heart of the things I write, the arguments I get into, the doubts I fight against. This insight came to me during the Mass, although it has taken some days to fully articulate to myself. That in itself is unusual; most times if I can't figure out a theological problem in twenty seconds, I dismiss it as an irresolvable mystery or, at any rate, something a council or ex cathedra statement will have to sort out some day.

But the conflict I encountered that Sunday is one that pervades our life and faith as Catholics, and I don't think it's one I'll see resolved this side of the grave: the tension between the orders of Nature and Redemption, between God's Creation and crucifixion, and the claims they make upon us.

My difficulties started with the reading from the Acts of the Apostles, which was brief and went like this:

> The community of believers was of one heart and mind, and no one claimed that any of his possessions was his own, but they had everything in common. With great power the apostles bore witness to the resurrection of the Lord Jesus, and great favor was accorded them all.
>
> There was no needy person among them, for those who owned property or houses would sell them, bring the proceeds of the sale, and put them at the feet of the apostles, and they were distributed to each according to need. (Acts 4:32–35)

This apostolic model of Christian life has clearly had its echoes through the centuries in the form of monastic life and mendicant orders and the ongoing aspiration of Christian thinkers that societies formed by men of faith make provision for those in need. Such provision was largely unknown in pagan Rome, where the only largesse provided to the poor came in the form of bread and circuses, dished out to keep the mob from storming the Capitoline.

What is more, for many Christians, the fact that the Church in its earliest (and, presumably, purest) days practiced voluntary communism would serve as a rebuke, a perfect model from which the hierarchical, manifestly unequal societies of Christendom had fallen through human sin. Medieval heretics and orthodox mendicants alike aspired to apostolic poverty, and movements such as the Beghards and the Beguines spread the idea that true Christians even among the laity would share in this aspiration. The most radical of the Franciscans, who split from the recognized order and called themselves the "Spirituals," went so far as to say that owning private property itself was a mortal sin.

The political implications of this were clear, and clearly dangerous, to the Christian authorities of Church and state; as Norman Cohn documents in *The Pursuit of the Millennium*, most of the movements that embraced ideas like these, from the Spirituals to the Flagellants, got mired in heretical anticlericalism and sometimes resorted to violent revolutionary politics. (They also displayed a disconcerting proclivity for attacking and sacking the local Jews.)

These movements were quashed, but their spirit reappeared with the Peasants Revolt in Reformation Germany and again among radical Protestants in the English Civil War. The notion that inequality and property were sinful structures went on to infuse the socialist movements until at last Karl Marx coined the maxim "From each according to his ability, to each according to his needs."

That's almost enough to sour a soul on the ideal of equality. But still, a small voice speaks to you when you hear this Scripture reading: the apostles lived this way. Are we sure they were wrong? That their mode of life is suited only for men in religious vows? Are you sure that isn't a cop out?

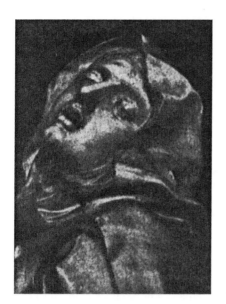

In fact, there is a deeply Christian impulse toward detachment from things of the flesh, toward focus on the next life rather than this one. One sees it, for instance, in the (frankly creepy) longing felt by some saints like Teresa of Avila for martyrdom during childhood. In its deeper, more serious forms (like her adult spiritual writings and those of St. John of the Cross), the urge toward renunciation, the willing embrace of suffering and mortification, makes up a major strain in Catholic spirituality. Think of St. Ignatius's infamous third degree of humility, the deal killer for me at my one and only Ignatian retreat:

In order to imitate and be more actually like Christ our Lord, I want and choose poverty with Christ rather than riches, opprobrium with Christ rather than honors; and desire to be rated as worthless and a fool for Christ, Who first was held as such, rather than wise or prudent in this world. (Spiritual Exercises, #167)

I was so scandalized by this that I could only retain my good opinion of the Jesuits by meditating on the exquisite Baroque churches they had built, their role in the court of Louis XIV, and their presence as chaplains on the ships of the Spanish Armada.

As I chewed this biblical cud at Communion time, something else happened that brought home to me the reasons for my resistance. A mother was hauling her squirming, adorable two-year-old blonde daughter up the aisle. The child, with the face of a Renaissance angel, was terrified and squalled with perfect clarity that echoed off the walls. *"But what about my toys? I want my toys!"* She was scared to leave them behind, afraid her trip up to the altar of the Lord would take some joys out of her youth.

St. Augustine might have muttered to himself (as he did when he spoke of crying infants) that original sin was clearly operative even before the age of reason. But I had a different reaction: I wanted to run up and kiss the little girl. Her reaction to leaving the pew echoed my feelings about the reading. Her fear was palpable, and her mother kindly reassured her that her toys would still be there when they got back. (How unlike certain parishes I remember from New York City. . . .)

And I couldn't help thinking, doesn't God feel the same way toward us? While surely there is evidence of the Fall in the inordinate, obsessive attitudes we can take toward earthly pleasures—aren't they also thumbprints left behind when He created us? If pleasures are only put here as hurdles for us to jump over, snares we are meant to renounce, then how can we justify offering them to our children, our friends, our lovers? Most of the simple acts of kindness and charity we perform in daily life consist of giving each other such pleasures—cooking a tasty meal, providing a spouse the pleasure of . . . well, let's just say a back rub. If the truly Christian thing is to disdain and despise such things, and suffering is (as the Reverend Frederick Faber once was bold enough to suggest in *At the Foot of the Cross*) the only currency acceptable in Heaven, then what business have we making the lives of others more pleasant?

As I wrote in *The Bad Catholic's Guide to Wine, Whiskey and Song*,[3]

> If suffering is such a good thing, why keep it to ourselves? If it's the key to salvation, we should be spreading it, far and wide. Instead of serving as the single largest social welfare agency in the world—running hospitals, clinics, hospices, and shelters on six continents—all with the goal of diminishing suffering, the Church ought to be promoting it. (271)

---

3. *The Bad Catholic's Guide to Wine, Whiskey and Song.*

This tension between the wholesome, animal drives God implanted in us through His creation and the call of Christian perfection isn't one I can resolve in the next twenty seconds, so I'll leave it to the reader to sort out the conflict between the apostolic aspirations of serious Christians and the innocence of a child, "for of such is the kingdom of God" (Lk 18:16).

The Generosity of J. R. R. Tolkien

In the 1930s, a young Catholic professor at Oxford University began writing stories to read his children at Christmastime. They were tales full of well-known magical creatures—elves, dwarfs, knights, wizards, witches—but what made them unique was a race of Tolkien's own, the noble, plump little halflings he called "hobbits." The best description for them is this: imagine Chesterton's idealized Englishmen—generous, earthy, self-mocking but deeply courageous—shrunk to the size of six-year-old boys, equipped with pipes and mugs of beer.

Professor John Ronald Reul Tolkien[4] started with no thought of publishing this story, *The Hobbit*, although he'd idly dreamed of issuing his longer, unfinished epic *The Silmarillion.* When he did submit *The Hobbit*, the publisher's eight-year-old son, who loved the book, vetted it. It sold respectably, and the publisher begged him for more. Largely to feed his growing family, Tolkien spent the war years writing *The Lord of the Rings.* The books started strong and became wildly popular in the 1960s, serving as Tolkien's subtle apostolate, inspiring tens of millions of readers around the world, helping to steer back from the abyss of modern nihilism many a shaky soul—one of them mine. But more about me later.

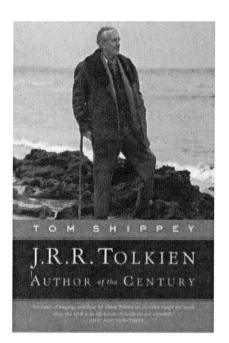

Besides teaching Anglo-Saxon at Oxford, Tolkien graded hundreds of university entrance exams each year for extra income to support his family. (No one who hasn't taught high school or college can imagine what kind of hell Tolkien put himself through.) While at

---

4. For the best account of Tolkien's life and work, see the book by his heir as Anglo-Saxon scholar at Oxford, Tom Shippey, *J. R. R. Tolkien: Author of the Century* (Boston: Houghton Mifflin Harcourt, 2001). Since Shippey knows the literature that fed Tolkien's imagination, his account of Tolkien's works is deeper and richer than any other.

Oxford, he joined luminaries such as C. S. Lewis, Charles Williams, Dorothy Sayers, and Owen Barfield in the Inklings, an informal club of Christian writers. Tolkien was instrumental in winning C. S. Lewis back to Christianity, as that great apologist recounts in *Surprised by Joy.*

Tolkien spent his scant free hours constructing the parallel world "Middle-Earth" found in his books. He acted as its loving father, peopling it with a vast array of species. Instead of doing what most writers[5] settle for, the minimum needed to move the story forward, Tolkien showed all the Generosity of those medieval craftsmen who would carve even the backs of pillars that no man would ever see—since they worked for the glory of God, Who would. Tolkien crafted for his creatures' use entire languages with alphabets and whole continents with maps. He limned out their history for thousands of years, from the mists of our own faded legends (such as *Beowulf* and the *Brothers Grimm*) all the way back to Creation. The opening of *The Silmarillion* describes the fall of a mighty angel and his expulsion from heaven. It begins, "There was Eru, the One, who in Arda is called Ilúvatar; and he made first the Ainur, the Holy Ones, that were the offspring of his thought, and they were with him before aught else was made. And he spoke to them, propounding to them themes of music; and they sang before him, and he was glad."

Tolkien didn't see his work as a piece of Catholic apologetics but as something more ambitious. Tolkien hoped to create for the English-speaking peoples a literary myth—as the Germans had in the Grail legends and the French in chivalric romances. The stories of King Arthur, Tolkien sniffed over his pipe, were actually Celtic and too mixed up with French infusions for his Anglo-Saxon tastes. So he spent his life creating a replacement—which, to his cackling delight, took root. Let's test that assertion. If you're reading this in English,[6] write down the names of as many Knights of the Round Table as you can think of. Now name all the hobbits you can. Case closed.

But the Catholic element in Tolkien's work keeps peeping up from the shadows—which isn't really surprising, since he grew up enduring a kind of persecution for the Faith. The young widow Mabel Tolkien lived with her two sons J. R. R. and Hilary in slumlike conditions in Birmingham. Her family had cast her out and cut her off for the crime of converting to Catholicism. After four years of bitter work, Mabel died, leaving the boys to the care of Fr. Francis X. Morgan, one of John Henry Cardinal Newman's protégés at the Birmingham Oratory.

Tolkien became a daily communicant and a weekly penitent. He especially held the Eucharist in awe, as he made clear in a letter to his son:

> Out of the darkness of my life, so much frustrated, I put before you the one great thing to love on earth: the Blessed Sacrament. . . . There you will find romance, glory, honour, fidelity, and the true way of all your loves upon earth, and more than that: Death: by the divine paradox, that

---

5. Trust me!
6. A good bet, since there aren't any translations.

which ends life, and demands the surrender of all, and yet by the taste (or foretaste) of which alone can what you seek in your earthly relationships (love, faithfulness, joy) be maintained, or take on that complexion of reality, of eternal endurance, which every man's heart desires.[7]

Tolkien's Faith carried him through a lonely childhood, then through the squalid futility of the Battle of the Somme—where he saw three of his four closest friends die pointlessly in the trenches. Tolkien's dogged prayer life sustained him through a sometimes difficult, always tender marriage to Edith Tolkien. Their romance was the basis for the poetic love story of Beren and Lúthien in *The Silmarillion*—a fact now carved on his and Edith's tombstones.

As a teenager, J. R. R. Tolkien had neglected his Latin and Greek to study Norse. And Finnish. And Anglo-Saxon. Tolkien thrilled at studying medieval *eddas* and

sagas, and mastering dusty grammars to decode half-forgotten tales. At Oxford, he made himself the university's expert in Nordic literature and won a prestigious chair that he'd hold for the next four decades. Indeed, his love for Nordic languages is what first led Tolkien to set pen to paper; delighted by the Finnish epic the *Kalevala*, Tolkien decided to create his own language that mirrored its structure. The result was the language that geeks like me know as Elvish.[8] Once he'd developed the language, Tolkien felt the need to invent a race that spoke it, then a history for that race . . . and thus were planted the seeds of *The Silmarillion*. It all started with Finnish.

While Tolkien always insisted he wasn't writing allegory—twisting his story to fit a hidden agenda or comment on current events—he was happy to see the truths he'd laid out applied to understanding the (all too) real world. So here is Tolkien on moral relativism and "situation ethics":

---

7. J. R. R. Tolkien, *The Letters of J. R. R. Tolkien*, ed. Humphrey Carpenter (Boston: Mariner Books, 2000), 53–54.
8. If you go to the right Renaissance fairs, you can hear it spoken. If you do hear it spoken, *run!*

Good and ill have not changed since yesteryear; nor are they one thing among Elves and Dwarves and another among Men. It is a man's part to discern them. (*The Return of the King*)

On suicide and euthanasia:

Authority is not given to you . . . to order the hour of your own death. . . . And only the heathen kings, under the domination of the Dark Power, did thus, slaughtering themselves in pride and despair, murdering their kin to ease their own death. (*The Return of the King*)

On our current culture of death:

But the fear of death grew ever darker upon them, and they delayed it by all means that they could; and they began to build great houses for their dead, while their wise men laboured unceasingly to discover if they might the secret of recalling life, or at the least of prolonging Men's days. But those that lived turned the more eagerly to pleasure and revelry, desiring ever more goods and more riches. (*The Silmarillion*)

And finally, on Satan:

From splendour he fell through arrogance to contempt for all things save himself, a spirit wasteful and pitiless. Understanding he turned to subtlety in perverting to his own will all that he would use, until he became a liar without shame. He began with a desire of Light, but when he could not possess it for himself alone, he descended through fire and wrath into a great burning, down into Darkness. And darkness he used most in his evil works upon Arda [Creation], and filled it with fear for all living things. (*The Silmarillion*)

Tolkien's books have deepened and enriched the lives of countless millions of readers—and helped save not a few souls, including (I hope!) mine.

At age eleven, having no idea who Tolkien was, I read *The Hobbit*. To me it was a simple story of an unexpectedly heroic little person who finds a magic ring. That book led me to its sequels. I thrilled to read about Gandalf, a wise old wizard in long gray robes, whose hands wielded magic to strengthen good creatures and fend off the wicked; of bravely bearded dwarfs named Oin and Gloin, Thorin and Ori, who delved the earth's bowels for treasure; of the greedy dragon, Smaug, who must be slain; of long-lost languages, realms, and lore. It was the kind of world that really should exist, that must exist—and in a sense, does exist. It profoundly complemented the mysteries I glimpsed each week at Mass.

I learned of the fallen Kingdom of Numenor, the noblest human realm ever founded, which failed in its piety, embraced a culture of death, and rebelled against

the Creator—only to be swallowed by the waves. I dreamt of Elbereth Giltholniel, the pure-hearted Queen of the Stars invoked by pious elves at the hour of danger. I dreaded the Ring of Power, an evil talisman that granted its wearer the might to master other men's wills and make them slaves—a ring so evil that even the wisest and best might not use it, even to fight against demons, lest they too be corrupted.

Best of all, I walked in the footsteps of the hobbits—a race of pudgy, homely men about three feet high. (I was tall by comparison.) Their quiet courage and humility suited them alone to bear the ring through mine and mountain, goblin-pit and poisoned swamp, without succumbing to its sinful urgings. These hapless, home-loving hobbits, in some ways like the boy I was, must carry the Ring like a cross into the kingdom of death and beyond.

Then I met another mentor. At age fifteen, in Catholic school, I sat hearkening to a bearded sage—Mr. Faustus, let's call him. Trained at top seminaries to the brink of priesthood, he'd been chosen by the nuns and the chaplain to hand on the ancient mysteries of the Faith.

Mr. Faustus's eyes glinted cleverly as he tossed off the names of wise men we would learn about in his class: "Tyrell, Loissy, Teilhard, Rahner, Kung. . . ." He traced words in Latin and Greek in spidery lines across the dusty blackboard, glints of erudition that shimmered like gold.

Thunderstruck, we drank it all in. Here at last was secret knowledge—to which not even the pope was privy! Pope John Paul II had been blinkered, Mr. Faustus explained, by his narrow upbringing in a faraway land among backward peasants (like hobbits?). We should view him as a lovable but slightly befuddled grandfather who told us fables containing grains of truth—fables, Mr. Faustus added, like the New Testament.

By learning the secrets of *sophisticated* faith, he promised, we would emerge smarter, savvier, and more upscale than our immigrant forebears. We'd be *modern, American* Catholics, fair and free. The mists of ignorance that had cloaked our pope and parents would pass away in the cool modern winds of research. So would our sexual guilt—one promise that perked up our pubescent ears. Things we'd been taught were sins were actually complex and morally ambiguous—and sometimes allowed. Ethics depended on the situation.

My youthful skepticism took fire as Mr. Faustus nuked one myth after another. The virginity of Mary? A mistranslation from the Greek. An infallible pope? Undemocratic. The devil? A symbolic bogeyman. Women priests? Inevitable. Christ's resurrection? A psychological event. Christ's ban on divorce? Rendered irrelevant by longer modern life spans. The Eucharist? Mr. Faustus warned us against "magic theology" and pointed out that *Hoc est enim corpus meum* was the origin of the term "hocus-pocus." What's more, as Mr. Faustus quipped to us, "Jesus didn't have a Master's in Theology. I do."

I felt enlightened. When I went to see Pope John Paul at Madison Square Garden, I looked down on him benignly, savoring this irony: at fifteen, I understood (as the poor pope couldn't) the truth about Catholicism.

I had lost something in return. Mr. Faustus's world lacked romance. My boyish love of kings and popes, of miracles and sacraments could not attach itself to dissident biblical scholars and feminist nuns. Attempting to remystify my world, I even borrowed manuals on the occult from a creepy, drug-dabbling schoolmate. (In retrospect, he reminds me of one of the Columbine killers.) Compared to what I remembered of the works of Tolkien from childhood, these books seemed spooky and shallow, and I soon lost interest.

I went back and dug grimly through my pile of old hobbit books, wondering, do these stories hold a key to Creation's real mystery and wonder? If Mr. Faustus was right, that was impossible. The universe was just a lab experiment, and God a disengaged bureaucrat Whose memos kept getting garbled by His staff. I poked at the books, depressed, and wandered off to Sunday Mass, not sure why I still bothered.

I looked past the liturgy, the sermon, and the grimly "contemporary" music and waited for the Consecration. I watched the "presider" elevate the small white wafer and wondered what on earth it meant. Then I heard the bells and felt my knees buckle. My wise guy's wisdom trembled for a moment, as boyhood fancies, loves, and dreams awoke, sputtering like the fuse on a Roman candle. The wide, mysterious world for which Tolkien had prepared me *might really exist.* There might be a Virgin Queen of Heaven, a Dark Lord whom she fought, and a reason for any hobbit to shoulder his cross. I might be a dupe, a fool. Thank God!

I went back to Tolkien for inspiration, to an old catechism for answers, and employed some real skepticism at last. I saw that my newly cultivated doubts were cheap excuses, blasé retorts to the ultimate questions, graffiti sprayed across the Sistine ceiling. As once I'd read *The Silmarillion* to explicate *The Hobbit*, now I delved into the *Catholic Encyclopedia*, delighting in the real complexity, the exquisite depths and heights and breadth of God's love and truth, His works and world. I found my very own Gandalf in Fr. John Hardon, S.J., who graciously let me sit in on his college classes.

I decided that Mr. Faustus was more like Saruman, the brilliant wizard who turned his lore to evil; I spent the next three years or so debating with him and the colleagues who seconded his opinions; I reported them to my parents and the principal, and then to bishop and papal nuncio, in a carefully detailed document that nearly got me expelled. When consequences came—when angry fellow students confronted me, when a radical sister stood me before the class alone to defend *Humanae Vitae* "in the face of a starving world," when I went in alone to face the teachers, and chaplain, and principal, who demanded to know what I was doing and why, I simply thought of Frodo, carrying the ring to the brink of doom. And I wasn't afraid.

For me, as for every believer, Faith came as a gift. While God was its origin, it passed through many human hands—and Tolkien's were the gentlest. He wrapped the starkness of mystery in the exquisite fabrics of myth, in gold-wrought watered silks that proclaimed its preciousness. The Pearl of Great Price can only come from Christ, but Tolkien packed it up for me in a bright blue Tiffany's box. In an age when "experts" and "specialists" teach us the price of everything and the value of nothing, the Generosity of artists may yet work our redemption. As Fr. Zossimov promised Alyosha Karamazov, "Beauty will save the world."

Trademark-Busting Cosmo-Style Quiz™ #4: Where Do You Fall on the Gordon Gekko[9] Scale (It Can Affect Your Credit Rating)?

In dealing with Greed and Generosity, you might say I've ranged pretty widely— drawing so far as I know the only direct connections yet between Chinese Communism, Elves, ostrich farms, and the banking crisis. But that's what being Catholic (from *katholikos*, or "according to the whole") is all about—learning to look at the whole world in all its dimensions, exploring its murkiest shadows in the light of remembered truths. And most questions that vex current politics can be best understood by understanding the relationship of Justice and Charity. It's a simple one: Justice is the foundation of the house and its stress-bearing walls, while Charity provides the windows and the doors. Neglect the first, and you live in a tottering ruin; the second, and you're in a prison.

But the point of these reflections isn't to change the way you vote but to help you achieve the Golden Mean of virtue in daily life. That means avoiding the sin of Greed without lurching over sideways into Prodigality, learning to give liberally without enabling the wasteful. We must not, to paraphrase Scripture, eat up our substance with prodigal giving— particularly when we're speaking of wealth or rights that belong to our fellow citizens. Taking part in a partly free economy, many of us are offered frequent temptations to act greedily, and it's hard to know where or when to stop. In a culture that has tacitly decided (in 1688, to be specific) to shelve religious questions and concentrate on getting rich, it's all too easy to see accumulating property as a virtuous end in itself. Dostoevsky, of all people, called money "coined freedom," and who wouldn't want more of

9. For those of you who aren't as bloody old as I am, that's the name of the Michael Douglas character in *Wall Street*. It's a movie, and yes, I watched it on something called a "VCR." Gekko made an infamous speech proclaiming, "Greed is good," then spent the rest of the movie proving it isn't.

that? Well, Dostoevsky for one, who threw his wealth away most prodigally at the gambling tables and only embraced Christianity while serving in a labor camp.

So we're ringed round with paradoxes, and the issues aren't simple. In search of those clinking little icons of liberty, we can easily enslave ourselves to workaholic habits or corrupt our friendships and even our families by commercializing them—for instance, when you try to recruit your college pals into a pyramid scheme or nix your chance at marriage by wrangling over a prenup. Perhaps the best answer is that of Catholic philanthropist Frank Hanna, whose book *What Your Money Means* proposes a deeply biblical approach. Going back to the parable of the talents (Mt 25:14–30 and Lk 19:12–27), he suggests we think of every natural good that God has given us as something precious we've been entrusted, to use in unique ways. Had God other plans for each gift, He would have given it to someone else. With that fact in mind, we should husband our resources prudently, aware that, on Judgment Day, we'll be called to account for each of them. That's not the time you want to be on your hands and knees with a trowel.

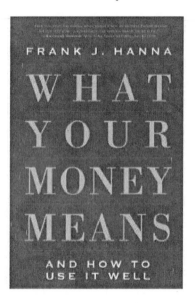

The Quiz

If someone you know who runs a successful business—say, a friendly acquaintance—approaches you to do a job for him and offers you a fee that's three times your going rate, what do you do? (Assume for the sake of argument that you're not in desperate financial straits—which nowadays means either you've been hoarding gold or you live and pay taxes in Switzerland.)

a. You take the money and run. It's a free country, and this fellow is free to make his own mistakes. It's not your job to run his business for him. Let him learn from experience—or better still, keep throwing money your way. You do a decent job, but don't exert yourself, since this guy is clearly not on the ball. When you're paid, you go to your investment research and find the highest-yielding stocks you can, which it turns out are in companies producing antipersonnel landmines—a business that's positively booming over in Africa.

b. You take the money and agonize about it, worrying that you might be doing something dishonest but finally reassuring yourself on that point. Then you start to fear that your client will figure out his mistake and never hire you again. In fact, he's liable to figure things out and bad-mouth you to other potential customers. You're tempted to give the money back, but then you'd have to explain yourself, and he'd think you were an idiot. You spend far too much time on this job, to the detriment of other projects. In the end, you feel so rotten, you stick the money in a mattress. And you never approach this client again.

c. You genially tell the fellow he's offering you too much moolah and you want to keep his business. You're careful not to make him feel foolish, and you feel a bit magnanimous. So you undertake the task at something closer to your regular price and do a bang-up job, confident that you'll likely be working with this guy again in a healthy, cooperative partnership. Still, you're kind of wistful about what you could have done with the extra money.

d. Sure, take the money and get the job done quickly because you're busy. This fellow obviously doesn't need the cash, but you do—for instance, to help your brother-in-law pay off that loan shark who's on him for his gambling debts. Or to "lend" as first and last months' rent to your old college pal who flunked out of rehab and has been living on your couch for seven months. Come to think of it, maybe you're just going to spend it all on bourbon. God, could you use a drink right now. Might as well get the good stuff. You deserve it.

Here are the results:

- If you picked "a": You are clearly a Gekko and have just grown a bright new layer of green, spotted skin. While you might come out ahead for the moment, you are indeed likely to lose this fellow's business. A thousand little decisions like yours are what make people skinflints and break down the trust that makes a free market possible in the first place. A few decades of this business culture and what you end up with is Russia—not Commie Russia, but Yeltsin's Russia, where oligarchs tool around in armor-plated Bentleys with hulking skinhead bodyguards named Boris and only take payment in cash, opium, or vans full of blonde teenagers. I suggest you try to internalize the catchy biblical dictum, "Do unto others as you would have them do unto you." Imagine that Christ meant it literally, and try—just for today—to put it into practice.

- If you picked "b": Stop torturing yourself. The money isn't worth it. Yes, you've been taught that it's your prime directive to acquire as much wealth as you can without breaking the law, to work as many hours as required to stockpile extensive financial reserves that can serve as a cushion in case of disaster, and even to buy yourself a burial plot well in advance so you can get it on clearance. But this might just be the time to remember the Gospel verse about the lilies of the field and the little birdies. To take some time off and make a retreat—with Franciscans, the hard-core kind who sleep on the floor and don't have telephones or Web sites.

Meet Boris.

- If you picked "c": You're approaching the proper balance of ethics and acquisitiveness. It's not surprising you found the offer tempting, and if the circumstances had been different (say, your family really needed the money), you'd have acted differently. But given your situation, your sense of integrity was worth more to you than the money. Now don't start getting smug or blasé about this. Who knows if next year you might be in such dire straits that you'd act differently. Remember that it's easy to feel magnanimous when things are going well. Pray for guidance in wise stewardship of all your resources and talents.

- If you picked "d": It sounds like you're good at your job—the problem is that you're no longer a carpenter or psychiatrist. You've become a full-time enabler, and there isn't even a union. By trying to siphon "extra" resources from those who "don't need it" to give to "poor souls" who will waste it, you've set yourself up as a tiny microcosm of the European Union's Common Agricultural Policy. You've been using Danish taxpayers' money to grow a mountain of cheese in France, and the smell is finally getting to you. I'd say it's high time you meditated on the parables of the talents and did some research on Misguided Compassion (see Chapter 14) by finally renting the movie *Longford*. Get hold of Hanna's book and keep it by your bedside next to *Codependency for Dummies*.

Activities

The key to this Virtue is balancing a grateful appreciation of the good things in life with a healthy detachment from them. Imagine you're sitting in a restaurant and you see the waiter carrying a really scrumptious tray of appetizers. (And I don't mean some greasy, nasty belly-bomber like deep-fried jalapenos stuffed with Velveeta—the culinary equivalent of crack; we're talking buffalo mozzarella with balsamic vinegar and cherry tomatoes.) If you've truly mastered Generosity, your appreciation for them won't be spoiled when you see that they're headed for the guy at the next table. Not even if he's shaped like a guy who has eaten more than his share of multicourse dinners over the years. You'll just see the food, appreciate it, and be thankful that you're in the same restaurant, fed by the very same chef.

Here are a few tips for cultivating a sane perspective on Mammon:

- ❏ If you find you're suffering from Greed, reflect on how much actual suffering it causes you. You look at your own possessions and attainments, but instead of being grateful for them, all you can seem to do is pick out their flaws and wish for something better. It's as if you were wearing jaundice-colored goggles all through life—which is really only appropriate if you're a beekeeper.
- ❏ Toss this monkey off your back, and learn to appreciate what you have—by doing without it. Make an inventory of your appetites, and find the single nonessential item you're least satisfied with— let's say that TV set you're sick of watching because it isn't HD, like your older brother's. Box it up, and give it to a trusted friend to hold for you for a month. Of course, you shouldn't replace it with the higher-end model you've been coveting. Leave its niche in the house starkly empty, a silent (and increasingly irritating) reproach to you for your worldliness. Pretty soon, you'll be pestering your friend to help you renege and take the thing back ahead of schedule. But your friend is a holy hardass, and he holds you to your word. When the month finally expires, you'll claim that box and unwrap your old possession like a hungry teenaged boy ripping open a shiny new Atari, circa 1982.
- ❏ If your problem isn't Greed but Prodigality, and you find yourself funding the undeserving poor in the form of various parasitical friends or relatives, it's time to remember the story of Our Lord and the barren fig tree. Misguided Compassion isn't something you can wean yourself off gradually; it needs a clean break. So take a strictly biblical approach. The next time this person hits you up for undeserved favors or cash to waste, instead of detailing patiently (and pointlessly) the importance of his "finding his independence," remember what Jesus would do. Say to him, in a calm, cool voice, "May no one ever eat figs from you again"

(Mk 11:14). When he asks for an explanation, just repeat yourself once, shrug, and smile. If the person persists, walk away—and when that whiny voice calls after you, stop only to literally kick the dust from off your feet (Mk 6:11).

❏ If you find yourself preoccupied with money, instead of thinking about how much you haven't got, you should meditate on what money means. Too many of us have learned to think of cash and credit not as value markers but as magic—tools for transforming ourselves into better, cooler, higher-status beings. I remember skulking around the entryways to apartment buildings on Sutton Place[10] and feeling like they were doorways into Narnia. If I could somehow finagle the price of one of those places, just living there would turn me into Prince Caspian, grant me a friendly centaur, and teach all my beavers to speak. Now, I've never had the cash to make the experiment, but I strongly suspect that even New York real estate doesn't work quite that way. In fact, all money amounts to is information. Each dollar you spend is a message you send to other people to keep on producing some good or service. Each dollar you get is a kind of thank you note from some stranger whom you have served. There is no other way to organize a cooperative society—short of setting up a totalitarian state where everybody wears green jumpers and gets their orders on little slips through pneumatic tubes. If you've honestly accumulated a large number of these thank you notes, you can trade them in for something you really want. If you haven't got very many, it's because you haven't been doing things that make other people happy. Maybe it was more important to you to work on private projects of significance only to you and God. Rest happy in what you have, and know that He'll repay you in other ways.

---

10. That's where the folks on Park Avenue move once they have "made it."

The Joy of Sloth

First of all, the word "slothful" is offensive. The polite term is "inertful." There are millions of Inerto-Americans, and the only reason they haven't raised up their voices till now is . . . well, why attract attention? If you put up your hand, you might get called on. Then the teacher will know just how much of the reading you really did. No reason to ruin his day. In fact, it's uncharitable.

SLOTH

Studying—okay, skimming—the Gospels, the inertful man can appreciate that Jesus means well but wonders just how well He appreciates human nature. When Christ says that the Creator of the universe "numbers all the hairs on our heads," the natural response is, "Enough with the baldness jokes! I have a hard time just reading my Dish Network bill to figure out if they're ripping me off."

In matters religious, there are certain fundamental questions that vex each human soul. Each of us has a governing passion, a distinctive thorn in our spirit or flesh. Those of us who dwell in that mild, middle state we call inertia have our own question, which is asked not so much of God but of ourselves: "Is it really *worth* it?" This simple criterion can be applied to every area of life, and it nearly always serves to lighten the pressure. Try this at home: *Is it really worth it*

SANDWICHES

• to brown that sandwich in a skillet? The microwave would get it nice, hot, and spongy in under a minute—with nothing left over to scrub.

• to train the church choir to sing something difficult, something written before 1970? And those old songs are all so heavy.

• to put on a tie (or shave your legs) for Mass? What is this, a funeral or something?

• to iron out the last few details in that assignment they gave you at the last minute, as usual? What do people expect from you, perfection? Then they should be paying you more.

• to repeat all those mind-numbing prayers? Once you've hailed Mary once, do you really have to keep on pestering? Doesn't that cross the line into stalking?

• to go to Mass, fast, or pray a single time more than the absolute requirements you read about, twenty years ago, in that . . . Catholic book you had to read? Inspired by Jennifer Aniston in your favorite movie, *Office Space*, you think, "If you want me to wear thirty-seven pieces of flair, why don't you say so?"

• to get all enthused about the godforsaken sporting event, dance recital, or drug intervention your wife insisted you attend? Your parents never went to your games. You had to go cold turkey from nasal spray all by yourself. Won't coddling your kids like this turn them *soft*?

And that list only covers our ordinary, day-to-day duties. Start concerning yourself with what those religious fanatics call "Christian perfection," and your sense of weariness can bring you to the very brink of a coma.

For the inertful, it's a tough enough slog from the morning coffee to the nightly melatonin capsule without asking for one more thing to worry about. Introduce the (frankly creepy) idea of eternity, and you bring to mind a Monday that drags on for millions of years. Here's how the organizer on your celestial phone will read:[1]

7:00 AM: Praise to the Celestial Father and Creator of the universe.

8:15 AM: Praise to His Consubstantial and Coeternal Son.

9:45 AM: Praise to His Holy and Life-creating Spirit.

10:50 AM: Praise, adoration, and thanksgiving to the Coeternal Majesty of the Three Divine Persons.

11:30 AM: Ambrosia break.

12:05 PM: Gratitude workshop with patriarchs and confessors. Optional: Break-out sessions with victim souls, incorruptibles.

1:35 PM: Exercise period; sacro-cardio sessions and glorified body-building.

And so on, *ad aeternam.*

I know it's intrinsically impossible to get across the kind of ecstatic something-or-other that holy people will enjoy in the next life, so I'll cut the saints some slack. But most of the descriptions I've read of beatitude in Scriptures and devotional books lean pretty heavily on promises of golden streets connecting palaces made out of diamonds and freakish animals performing amazing tricks, like opening scrolls and speaking. Frankly, the whole thing sounds to me a lot like Vegas—without the showgirls. (Mohammed knew a thing or two about addressing the Everyman.) No wonder most of us go through life thinking of Heaven as "the place that isn't Hell."

If you want a picture of paradise that will interest the inertful, it had better include fuzzy slippers, bubble baths, and radio comedy hours with sempiternal Lutherans like Garrison Keillor, who gently lob nice, simple jokes right over home

---

1. This schedule is based loosely on the strict daily regimens observed by cloistered Benedictines. Think of Heaven as a really big, really high energy monastery from which there is no escape. Of course, they *say* you'd never want to. Those same people say they love their jobs and never want to retire. . . .

plate. Or, if we have to do some work, we'd appreciate a clearly labeled series of straightforward tasks that will keep our minds occupied, drowning out that drone of praise and adoration. And maybe a pair of shades to dim the glare you see in all those icons. Don't those painters know that candlelight is a heck of a lot more flattering?

How about a little soup? What would it hurt? Nothing too hot or cold. Serve it up Goldilocks-style . . . just right.

Sloth in Drag

Now, it would be easy, too easy, to toss off Sloth as a sin that only afflicted the lazy. But there's another and subtler form it takes, which occurs among the busiest workaholics. You know, the kind of person targeted in Harry Chapin's insidiously catchy song:

> And the cat's in the cradle and the silver spoon
> Little boy blue and the man on the moon.
> When you comin' home, dad?
> I don't know when, but we'll get together then, son.
> You know we'll have a good time then.

It's one of those 1970s saws you've heard wafting in the waiting rooms of bail bondsmen and psychiatrists more times than you care to admit, and it's *stuck in your head* now, isn't it? You might try driving it out with another tune,[2] but you'll find that this is the kind of song that requires prayer and fasting.

Sorry I had to do that. But the song really does point to the fact that millions of modern people are content to fill the void that is their spiritual lives with incessant, often invented activities. Speaking of the 1970s, remember all the pointless crazes that filled that abysmal decade? In a mere ten years, our culture was subjected to the following:

---

2. Try "Gather Us In" or "This Is the Song That Does Not End." Just makes matters worse, doesn't it?

- jogging
- streaking
- mood rings
- biorhythm calculators
- CB radios
- roller disco
- pet rocks
- swingers' retreats
- antidisco rallies
- hair metal
- neoconservatism
- cocaine
- the Novus Ordo Missae[3]

BIORHYTHMS

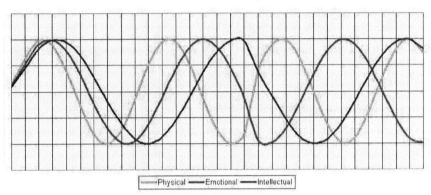

Physical ━━━Emotional ━━━Intellectual

Clearly, we had way too much time on our hands. The energy we'd stopped putting into wholesome (if on the surface, oddball) activities such as fasting, all-night vigils, Eucharistic processions, and child-rearing needed some outlet, however pointless. A few Catholics really did become committed to serving the poor under the rubric of "social justice," but for most of us, the gradual demolition of the "oppressive" structure of pre-1970 Catholicism became a pretext for self-indulgence of the lowest, dullest order. Remember that in the 1920s (and 1820s, 1720s, go back all the way to the 420s on this one), the mass of people lived in sparsely functional homes but lavished their extra wealth on decorating their places of worship. In the 1970s, we threw this engine into reverse. We focused on making our homes into comfy,

---

3. As Josef Cardinal Ratzinger wrote, "After the Council . . . in place of the liturgy as the fruit of organic development came fabricated liturgy. We abandoned the organic, living process of growth and development over centuries, and replaced it, as in a manufacturing process, with a fabrication, a banal on-the-spot product." See Ratzinger's preface to Klaus Gamber, *The Reform of the Roman Liturgy* (Ft. Collins, CO: Roman Catholic Books, 1993).

high-tech palaces, while churches were stripped of ornament, thrown together out of cheap concrete, and decorated with chintzy abstract windows, crappy banners, and Ficus trees. But at least the pews and kneelers had plenty of padding. Indeed, there's an almost perfect ratio, I've found, between how *ugly* a modern church is and how *comfortable* is the seating. Go to churches in rural Italy or Mexico, where people either stand or kneel on floors to gaze up at jewel-encrusted masterworks devoted to glorifying God, then toddle off to some monstrous new cathedral that looks like a Sam's Club, and you'll see the point: Sloth can also take the form of misplaced priorities. We're ignoring that mysterious lump we keep feeling under the skin, sending Twitter updates to all our friends about the progress of our acupuncture.

Those of us who have filled up our days with works and tasks that, piled up, really do seem like legitimate reasons for keeping our religious life to a minimum need to make a sharp turn in the opposite direction. One might start by violently truncating a single range of activities—by getting rid of your iPad and BlackBerry, for instance, and insisting on some time during the day when you are both silent and unreachable. Use that time for some idiot-simple repetitive prayer, like the Rosary or Divine Mercy chaplet. It might seem useless at first, but it surely can't do any harm. (Indeed, we have assurance in the forms of dozens of creepy, wonder-working apparitions that such prayer makes a huge difference in the world, but never mind that for now.) Spend more time with nature, even if it comes in the form of a long walk through Central Park.[4] A good meditation to counter workaholic Sloth can be found in the work of Catholic poet Charles Péguy. In fact, the busier you are, the more you should make time to read his beguiling *The Portal of the Mystery of Hope*. It pictures Hope as a little girl who leads the other, adult virtues of Faith and Love along by the hand. As Péguy writes,

Human wisdom says
Don't put off until tomorrow
What can be done the very same day.
But I tell you that he who knows how to put off until tomorrow
Is the most agreeable to God
He who sleeps like a child
Is also he who sleeps like my darling Hope.
And I tell you

---

4. People who aren't from New York City, please fill in . . . one of the names of the parks you have in those . . . other places.

Put off until tomorrow
Those worries and those troubles which are gnawing at you today
Put off until tomorrow those sobs that choke you
When you see today's unhappiness.
Those sobs which rise up and strangle you.
Put off until tomorrow those tears which fill your eyes and your head,
Flooding you, rolling down your cheeks, those tears which stream down your
  cheeks.
Because between now and tomorrow, maybe I, God, will have passed by your
  way.
Human wisdom says: Woe to the man who puts off what he has to do until
  tomorrow.
And I say
Blessed, blessed is the man who puts off what he has to do until tomorrow.
Blessed is he who puts off.
That is to say, blessed is he who hopes. And who sleeps.

Still another form that Sloth takes—indeed, the very reason it was included in the Seven Deadly Sins—is the rather elusive syndrome called Acedia. The monks who struggled with it called it the "noonday devil," and spiritual writer Kathleen Norris has penned an instructive book on the subject called *Acedia and Me*. This condition entails spiritual weariness, even dreariness, and it often afflicts the most pious or industrious souls partway along their journey toward holiness. Those whose vocation is marriage might know it as the "seven-year itch." For parents, this is the age at which most children cease to be quite so cute. Slowly but insidiously, the good things we have striven and sacrificed for no longer seem entirely . . . worth it. Instead of keeping our eye on the prize, we start to total up the *costs* a goal has imposed upon our lives and look forward to the unending decades of effort that still lie ahead of us. We realize the stark ugly truth that

- at age fifty, and again at age sixty, I will still be married to this person.
- till the day I turn sixty-five, I will be teaching these same damn books I used to love. Why did those bloody monks have to save them from oblivion?

- they're going to bury me at this desk. Or take me to the taxidermist and have me stuffed and mounted.
- at age thirty-five, this kid will still be living in my apartment. Is being a mammal really worth it? At least reptiles can lay eggs, then scurry away.

Day in, day out, the same thing over and over again—we seem to feel that burden all at once, and the theological truth that God will never burden us beyond our strength starts to sound like a pious fable. Our favorite Bible verse becomes the line from Job, "Curse God and die" (which makes, by the way, an imposing bumper sticker).

Acedia afflicts priests and religious parents, activists in worthy causes like the pro-life movement (those on the other side never seem to burn out quite as quickly—

Charles Péguy.

they have "little helpers" with names like Moloch), dedicated teachers, brave firemen, and honest cops. Aquinas warns that Acedia, unacknowledged and unanswered, is a sure road to despair and can lead even to suicide. It rarely urges us to sin, even by omission, but rather allows us to slog through our daily duties, jaundiced by a sickly tint of dismay and even disgust. Pleasures can start to weary us, and the prospect of Heaven seems not so much unattainable as irrelevant.

Having never really suffered from Acedia, I can't offer expert advice at how to counter it, but I can draw on my ethnic heritage to help those uninterested in Heaven: think of Hell instead.

The Source of Sloth: Sneaking Back into Eden

One night, as I was chattering on the phone instead of writing more on Sloth, something very strange happened. I made a comment that struck someone as "profound." As readers will by this point have realized, this is not the reaction I'm used to provoking. Raucous laughter, yes, sometimes milk-spraying guffaws, occasionally a driver steering off the road at one of my anecdotes. There's even an old Cajun friend of mine whom I can at will force to laugh until he vomits, using only my Bob Dole imitation. Imprudently, he invited me to his wedding. (I really should use my powers for good instead of evil.) And I've learned to live without profundity. In fact, I steer clear of folks who throw that word around. Ditto the kind of people who do the following:

- claim to have read and been "really changed" by von Balthasar's *Theo-Drama*
- collect holy cards of victim souls and pray for "extra suffering"
- try to browbeat all of their friends into doing the Montfort consecration. "Oh, so you don't trust Our Lady?"
- insist that their favorite movie is Tarkovsky's *Andrei Rublev*—a four-hour, mostly silent, black-and-white drama depicting Russian icons drying.

Call me a Chesterton-style Catholic. And yes, I have no Bernanos. My brush with profundity took place on the phone with my whip-smart girlfriend who was deploring with me a new scientific monstrosity, along the lines of cloning embryos to grow new livers for rock stars in rehab.

Then I said, "I think that most of our modern sins are the result of our trying to sneak back into the Garden of Eden"—in other words, to gain back the "preternatural gifts" Adam lost, which, according to traditional Catholic theology, were pretty impressive.

While our records are scant of human society before the Fall (St. Thomas Aquinas speculated that it happened in a matter of hours, even before Adam and Eve had the chance to consummate their marriage), authoritative tradition teaches that the following were included in God's gift bag:

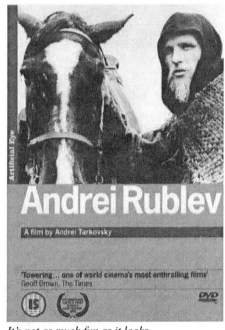

It's not as much fun as it looks.

- *Immortality.* We wouldn't have tramped from golden youth through crapulous middle age to decrepitude, then dust. No wrinkles, sagging, sore joints, or colostomy bags. Had Eve showed more Humility, and Adam more moral courage, man's world would have been a vast but pious nudist colony that didn't make you cringe, look away, and wish for "quality control." No

one knows how long we would have dwelt on earth, but medieval theologians speculated that after a time, each embodied soul might have been Assumed as Mary was—our only "test case" of a sinless human being who wasn't also the incarnate Son of God. That's why she was the only candidate considered for the Vatican Space Program.[5]

• *Impassibility*. We wouldn't have been subjected to mental or moral suffering, and our bodies would have been preserved from any serious pain—although one assumes that kids who stuck their hands into the fire would still have felt some urgency to pull them out eventually. Unless, of course, our bodies would have been immune from any destructive force—a viable reading of the doctrine. If so, then an unfallen Olympics might have included Volcano Diving, Alp Jumping, and Chainsaw Swallowing.

• *Freedom from concupiscence.* Our desires would never have exceeded what was appropriate for our needs or goaded us into sin. No one would take "all you can eat" as a personal challenge, hog both lanes of a two-way country road, look longingly at someone else's spouse, or gasp at the results of a pregnancy test. Each child would be a wanted child.

• *Freedom from ignorance.* Everything would be on a strictly need-to-know basis, and we'd know everything we needed. Our private theological opinions and the "common sense" that was prevalent in the culture would match up with the actual state of affairs in heaven. Following, our conscience would never entail rebellion or dissent, and there'd be no call for papers like the *National Catholic Reporter* or, for different reasons, the *Wanderer*.

• *Freedom from sin.* We wouldn't carry around inside our heads a tiny Miltonic Lucifer, ready to scream *non serviam* at the drop of a hat or one's pants. While sin would be possible, it would seem to people

_____

5. Pope Pius XII beat Stalin into space by seven years. For video footage see http://www.badcatholics .com.

strange—a deviation from the norm, like a dog walking on its hind legs, instead of going back to its vomit. Our wills would match our consciences, and when we did what we thought was right . . . it would be.

- *Lordship over the earth.* One hopes man would not have remained a naked, rural vegetarian but would have built wondrous cities. Imagine New York without the attitude, New Orleans without the crime, Vienna without the socialists. Our use of natural resources would never outstrip what was prudent or fair, so innocent third parties wouldn't have to suffer from the waste we dumped in rivers, the filth we pumped into the air, or the nonsense we wrote on Twitter. We would just know better than to do such things, and our mastery of the earth would be seamless and eco-friendly.

Most of the project of secular modernity could be summed up as the technological and ideological crusade to achieve all these ideals—and shove the pesky business of the Fall and the Redemption down the memory hole.

It's perfectly legitimate to try, within the limits of justice and the natural law, to mitigate the suffering that came to us from the Fall. (There are some Catholics who fetishize suffering, but they aren't reading this book—they're off watching *Andrei Rublev.*) Too bad the human race—thanks to its fallen will and darkened reason—typically blows past those stop signs like a Humvee plowing through a tollbooth. So we seek immortality by turning ourselves into stem-cell cannibals and impassibility by downing drugs or asking the "cause" of our suffering for a divorce. We conquer concupiscence by changing the rules to match our cravings and ignorance by clubbing the intellect into submission to the will. We keep ourselves sinless by defining deviancy down and spreading our conscience like Silly Putty to pick up the op-eds in the newspaper. And we lord it over the earth by shifting the costs for our self-indulgence to innocent third parties who live downwind, or to future generations.

Nice work, if you can get it.

Technology and Sloth

I wasn't homeschooled—thank God. As you'll read some day in my memoir of an Irish-American childhood, *Angela's Ashtray*, my churchgoing, chain-smoking, agoraphobic mom wasn't up to the task: to buy chalk, she would have had to leave the house. And the store that sold chalk was owned by Koreans—all of whom Mom warned us must be "Moonies." (As a gag, I once subscribed her to the *Washington Times*. She tossed it aside with disdain: "Crossword puzzle's too hard.")

I went to an ordinary Catholic grammar school, which had made the transition from rote learning to modern educational methods—which meant we sat around doing SRA cards in every subject while the teachers read magazines. (Okay, I didn't actually do any of the cards. Instead, I roamed the room, hopped up on Captain Crunch, tormenting the cute Italian girls.) I pretty much educated myself at home, reading encyclopedias for fun and watching college credit courses on PBS. Then I went off to a low-end Catholic high school, which wasn't much better than the average New York City teacher's union special. We were spared stabbings and shootings—a fact for which I'll always remember the auld school fondly. But the main difference was religion class, which featured disaffected, leftist nuns showing us Sandinista propaganda films and denying the resurrection of Christ. In public schools, this is the task of the social studies teacher.

I'll never forget the last lesson I had in my last math class. The teacher, overwhelmed by our youthful zest for lethargy, announced with a sigh, "Well, we didn't get through all of trigonometry. If some of you had done the homework . . . aw, screw it. Anyway, one day, some of you are going to come across something called a logarithm," she said, closing the textbook. "But you won't know what they are. . . ." There we sat, smiling, a support group for math sloths.

Our teacher was right. When I got to college, I tried to kill off the science requirement by taking Physics for Fools. But Professor Horvath, an earnest, brilliant Hungarian, began to sling around that "math jargon," including the dreaded "logarithm." I looked around and confirmed that I was not alone ignorant, seeing hundreds of scrunched-up, empty eyes. Since I was born without the chromosome for shame, I raised my hand and asked this refugee from Communism who now taught at William F. Buckley's alma mater, "Excuse me, professor. What's a logarithm?"

He paused and went into an explanation of how to derive the *confabulatory scrutative precipitates* of an *ordinal imaginary fraction* from the. . . . No, and none of the other kids understood, either. So my hand shot up again.

"Excuse me, professor. My math's not so strong. . . ." He breathed the harrumph of the just and explained more simply, speaking more slowly. The words sounded pretty.

This time I put up my paw more timidly. "I'm sorry, professor, I still don't understand. . . . What's a logarithm?"

With flashing eyes, he admitted at last, "It is a *button* on ze *calculator!*"

We wrote that down, every word. "A logarithm is a button on ze calculator."

For millions of Americans, technology indeed becomes a means of enabling their Sloth. People e-mail instead of writing or even calling their loved ones. "Touching" urban legends involving kittens who miraculously cure their owners of lupus choke up our inboxes until we end up spam-filtering our siblings,[6] and friends show they *almost* care by sending imaginary bottles of champagne over Facebook. I knew a woman whose ex-boyfriend asked her to reignite their relationship via *text message*. The scary part is that it worked. The sad part is that she and I were out on a date at the time.

There's no need to go to the movies when you can download them on your couch. At least that way the "urban youths" talking back to the screen will be your own, poorly disciplined children. I haven't been to a record store in years—and it's rare that I buy CDs from Amazon since I heard about Pandora. com, which lets me design my own station that will play nothing but Palestrina and "Weird Al" Yankovic. Thanks to Playstation, even city-bound schlubs like me can downhill ski without getting our trousers damp. Games like Guitar Hero mean that no one needs to spend all those tedious hours with Mel Bay's beginner books practicing those chords entailed in playing an actual *song*. Just

---

6. Yes, I really did have to do this. Sorry, sis!

pop in the DVD, and pretty soon you will be rocking and rolling before a crowd of obsessed, fanatical fans.

I think that even the explosion of Internet pornography has less to do with Lust than it does with Sloth. While it's true there is no comparison between actually committing a serious sin with another person and indulging yourself on the Internet, at least it doesn't entail losing weight, buying better clothes, and arranging an actual date with a whole *other human being*—refractory, needy, demanding. . . . Is it really worth it? the inertful ask themselves. Just wait until Wii gets on the stick for this industry. Millions of lonely men will simply disappear into their homes and never be seen again. We will call it the Frapture.

Anyone concerned about the connection between technology and Sloth really must read Wendell Berry, the poet and novelist who quit a plumb teaching job at New York University—smack dab in the middle of the best part of Manhattan—so he could move back to Kentucky and . . . farm. I know, I know. Seems incomprehensible to me, too. I've always said that it's all fine and dandy to live outside New York City when you're single—but once it's time to have kids you owe it to them to move into The City. Your offspring need asphalt to play on, whizzing traffic to hone their reflexes, and subways so they can go to their soccer games without you. Berry disagreed, and in 1965 began to grow corn and grain at his farm, Lane's Landing. There he wrote novels, and sharpened his critique of modern living, secular capitalism, and the effect of technology on the soul. A fervent Christian, Berry devoted himself to living in harmony with Creation.

Reading Berry didn't drive me back to the land, but it did inspire me to resist acquiring more technological devices than I needed. Indeed, apart from essentials like rent, whiskey, and ethnic restaurants, I tried to spend no money at all.

I was sure that I had dodged the temptation to Sloth inherent in modern technology. I praised myself for refusing to adopt the same doodads as my peers. When I still lived in New York City, I would feel a tiny bit smug that I possessed

- no cell phone
- no laptop
- no iPod
- no television
- no car
- no driver's license
- no exercise equipment
- no wristwatch
- no comb.

I didn't own a suit that had cost me more than $60 at the thrift shop, and I slept on the same $300 mattress I'd bought "reconditioned," which means, I guess, that they deloused the thing and pulled out all the bullets, but it suited me just fine.

For many years, I got along comfortably—watching Netflix sometimes on the PC that I used to work from home, using payphones when I needed to make a call while on the road, cadging rides on those rare occasions when I needed to leave The

City (e.g., to go pick up yet another rescue dog). At events that called for formal dress, I'd wear a turtleneck—and experience a tiny frisson of "artistic," rebellious bravado.

I'll admit I even felt a little condescending toward my friends who carried BlackBerrys to beaches and bars. When their pockets hummed and they had to interrupt our conversation to answer an e-mail, squinting and pecking at that tiny little keyboard, I thought, "How free I am. How bohemian. . . ." I'd played on my boss's technological phobia (which I'd reinforced by sending him Berry's book) to make myself unreachable at will. Whatever he needed from me, it would have to wait.

Of course, my ascetical attitude sometimes caused inconveniences to others. Once I was called down to visit a director in Virginia to work on a screenplay project. When I spoke with his assistant who was to pick me up at Dulles, he asked for my cell phone number. "I don't have one," I said with a smile in my voice. "We'll just find each other." Annoyed, he pointed out that neither of us had ever seen each other's face and this process could last for hours. At last, I agreed to wear a green Tyrolean hat. Since this was springtime in Virginia, I explained, chances were that I would stand out. And indeed, I did.

Long-distance dates have wasted, cumulatively, hours, driving around airports waiting for me to emerge from the baggage claim. Sometimes I would simply pester some stranger to use his or her cell phone. The person would always agree but stare at me—suspicious that I was, in fact, an extraterrestrial or a pervert. Then he'd carefully swab the phone with an antibacterial wipe.

And so on. Over the years, I have surely put friends and family to enormous, complex trouble in my pursuit of simplicity. I've certainly overlooked a hundred subtle or blatant hints and shaved a few months off their life spans with the stress I blithely inflicted—all the while patting my very own, turtlenecked back for my Franciscan austerity, which amounted, of course, to passive-aggressive Sloth.

But my regimen broke down—caved in like some post-Communist cabinet in Hungary. Moving from New York City to New Hampshire and taking a job that entailed getting dressed and going out, I was forced to surrender on every front:

- Trapped in a large house five miles from the nearest micro-brewery, spending sometimes $40 daily on cabs, I finally purchased a car—albeit a decaying Chevy that would earn derisive snickers in Havana.
- I finally took driver's ed—paying $45 per hour for some guy to hold my hand as I merged on the freeway, for which I never did get up the nerve—so now my GPS, which I've set with a British accent and nicknamed after the royal concubine "Camilla," guides my every turn through the back roads of New Hampshire. Who knew there were so many dour Yankees straight out of Robert Frost poems standing sullenly outside so many gas stations?
- For my teaching trip in Italy, I had to buy a cell phone. The pay phones in Rome look just like their condom machines and are just as awkward to speak into.
- For the same trip, I had to buy a laptop—and use it every day to pour out the two thousand words I was writing for a website. Since Internet access was hard to find, I even had to spring for a satellite modem—which let me upload Internet columns from Orvieto.
- Surrounded for three months in a foreign country by American college students, I had to buy an iPod to drown them out.
- Ordered by my doctor to lose forty pounds, I bought an elliptical trainer and set it up in front of

my new . . . television, for which I ordered (for the first time in my life) cable. So I can bribe myself to work out with reruns of *Law & Order: Special Victims Unit.*

But I refuse to buy an iPad or a Kindle. And I still haven't sprung for a decent suit. Writing teachers can get away with turtlenecks, and I have yet to master that godless innovation they call an "iron."

The Art of Sloth: Andy Warhol

> "Charles," said Cordelia, "Modern Art is all bosh, isn't it?"
> "Great bosh."
>
> *—Brideshead Revisited*

You needn't be quite so blithe as Evelyn Waugh's Charles Ryder to know that visual art has gone far astray in the past one hundred years. While the works of individual geniuses still arrest us with their idiosyncratic beauty—painters like di Chirico, Chagall, and Schiele come to mind—in the vast bulk of what has been accepted as worthy, "interesting" art by critics, teachers, galleries, and collectors, beauty is *beside the point.* Indeed, the very word is sneered at, conflated with mere *prettiness,* and disdained as the sort of thing that philistine, *bourgeois* dunderheads look at and nod, saying, "I don't know much about art, you know, but I do know what I *like!*" "Beauty" is relegated to beauty magazines and the nineteenth-century prints that seventh-grade girls put up on their walls. The great tradition of representational painting, which we trace in the West back to Greece and Rome via the Renaissance and the Baroque, is conflated lazily with paintings of weepy clowns, droopy sunsets, and poker-playing dogs.

Instead, contemporary art features piles of trash laid out on the floor of art galleries (one such "installation" by Damien Hirst was accidentally cleared away by the janitor, God bless him), bisected sheep carcasses preserved in embalming fluid, and works like the following, described by Roger Kimball in his witty, immensely informative *Art's Prospect*:

Consider Matthew Barney, a hot young artist whose oeuvre consists of things like *Field Dressing (Orifill)*, a video that depicts the artist "naked climbing up a pole and cables and applying dollops of Vaseline to his orifices." That description comes from Michael Kimmelman, chief art critic for *The New York Times*, who recently declared Barney "the most important American artist of his generation."[7]

Now, I went to college with Matthew Barney, and I never saw him climbing any of our flagpoles. Maybe you need an MFA to learn about that.

This isn't the place for a learned essay on how Christian theology came to renounce the iconoclasm of Moses and baptize the classical tradition of representational art, first via simple graffiti pictures of Jesus as the Shepherd or statues of Apollo rechristened as Christ. Suffice it to say that the Church's insistence on the goodness and orderliness of Creation, reaffirmed by the Incarnation, created a culture that valued visual beauty and didn't feel guilty about it. The dignity of the human form reflected man's creation in God's image, and even the grotesqueries of extreme suffering might be elevated by comparison with Christ's. So Western art had room alike for the tranquil Annunciations of Fra Angelico and the war-induced nightmares of Goya. To assert that a tradition this rich and flexible is too constricting for a modern artist's vision is itself an act of philistine ignorance that only the graduate of an expensive art school could commit.

The great rebels against the Tradition, beginning with the Impressionists, had first been forced to master figurative drawing—so that their departures from it might, and often did, *mean* something. But their influence on art education meant that the next generation never learned the techniques of Renaissance and Baroque painting, so the chain of craftsmanship was almost broken. Indeed, most contemporary artists come of age never learning how to *draw*. Art critic James Panero quotes Randall Jarrell's novelized memoir of teaching art at Sarah Lawrence College way back in the 1940s (Jarrell calls it "Benton"): "If you had given a Benton student a pencil and a piece of paper, and asked her to draw something, she would

7. Roger Kimball, *Art's Prospect* (Chicago: Ivan R. Dee, 2003), 50.

have looked at you in helpless astonishment; it would have been plain to her that you knew nothing about art."[8]

In his hilarious dismissal of the whole of modern art, *The Painted Word*, Tom Wolfe makes the case that ideologies of various sorts have replaced Creation as the subject matter of art in our time. One no longer paints portraits of the poor, like Millet's, or even of suffering workers, as Diego Rivera did. Instead, the truly modern (or postmodern) artist depicts ideas or ideological constructs such as "suffering," "struggle," or even "the Dialectic." The next step in the artist's secession from external reality comes when *his own struggle* becomes the subject of the art. A lingering Romantic myth of the artist not as a patient craftsmen but a genius possessed, a tortured Promethean rebel, helped fuel in the 1950s the fascination with "action" painters like Jackson Pollock. Of course, there really is nothing intrinsically interesting about a single tortured soul—except perhaps as the subject of our compassion. If the artist, not the art, is now the point, then why not choose, instead of anguish, *irony*? Painters such as Roy Liechtenstein chose to craft on enormous canvases recreations of strips from comic books, and the critics and collectors lined up to jack up the prices of his paintings—as reflected in the ever-reliable Art Market Index, which I'll note always outperforms the Standard & Poor's. So instead of the infinitely complex, visually demanding world of man in nature, the subject matter of art became the jaded sensibility of the artist.

Enter Andy Warhol. Born in working-class Pittsburgh, the son of a Byzantine Catholic coal miner, Warhol was a sickly, effeminate child. He took refuge from bullying and ostracism in an obsession with Hollywood movie stars and other trinkets of popular culture. Trained as a commercial illustrator, Warhol had a little more practice drawing actual objects than the graduates of Jarrell's Benton, although his skills ran to pictures of products rather than people. So it's not surprising that when he made his strategic move into the addled world of art, products are what he chose to draw. They are also very easy to draw, and Warhol never pretended to spend much time on the work he exhibited. Indeed, what quickly made a media sensation was not so much his banal reproductions of soup cans, Coke bottles, and silkscreen Chairman Mao portraits as his unique persona as a languid, affectless dispenser of ironic, iconic quips, such as the following:

- "In the future, everyone will be famous for fifteen minutes."
- "Fantasy love is much better than reality love. Never doing it is very exciting. The most exciting attractions are between two opposites that never meet."
- "I love Los Angeles. I love Hollywood. They're so beautiful. Everything's plastic, but I love plastic. I want to be plastic."
- "Just look at the surface of my paintings and films and me, and there I am. There's nothing behind it."

---

8. "Pictures from an Institution," *The New Criterion,* December 2004.

- "I suppose I have a really loose interpretation of 'work,' because I think that just being alive is so much work at something you don't always want to do. The machinery is always going. Even when you sleep."
- "Art is what you can get away with."

Warhol's Instamatic success reminds one of Oscar Wilde's premature fame, which came before he'd produced much work of note, as the fruit of his campy public appearances and acerbic commentaries on current events. (The difference, of course, was that Wilde was a tireless craftsman; it takes a lot of work to look that effortless—at least it did in Wilde's time.)

It's dreary to recount the parade of celebrities and hangers-on who trooped through Warhol's Factory in search of fame, sexual hookups, or a better grade of dope. What matters is Warhol's attitude toward art, which he made clear with his series of "piss paintings," created by oxidizing a canvas so it would react with body fluids, then taking turns with his epicene male companions in relieving themselves on it.

And the critics drank. In an essay that really, *really* should be the last word on the subject, "Drunk on Andy Warhol," Kimball pays a long visit to the vast and

expensive Andy Warhol Museum in Pittsburgh, sorting through the garish ephemera that constituted Warhol's lifelong production. This alone is worth the purchase price of *Art's Prospect*, but then Kimball opens the museum's catalog:

One essay is by the American philosopher Arthur Danto, who for many years has been a champion of Andy War-hol, both as an artist and—a more provocative claim— as a thinker. In the essay he contributed to the catalog, Professor Danto reaffirms his high opinion. It all started in 1964 when he saw the exhibition of Warhol's Brillo Boxes at the Stable Gallery in New York. Since then, he writes, he has felt that Warhol possessed "a philosophical intelligence of an intoxicatingly high order." (216)

Andy Warhol got away with it. A manipulative sexual voyeur of minimal talent who never worked very hard, he grabbed the imagination of a rudderless postwar culture and for three decades lived at the pinnacle of society. His paintings—often consigned, dismissively, to be actually crafted by assistants—still sell for millions. Two separate museums are dedicated to him, a bridge in Pittsburgh is named for him, and there is actually something called the Andy Warhol Art Authentication Board, to help prospective speculators on the Art Market Index ascertain that their soup cans really are by Andy instead of Campbells.

There are even some well-meaning, addled Catholics desperate for secular validation trying to claim Warhol as a postmodern Catholic artist—citing the fact that the deeply superstitious Warhol sometimes attended Mass and, in his later years, scrawled some cringeworthy, cartoonish imitations of da Vinci's *The Last Supper*. And the Warhol industry encourages them. Kimball notes how the museum catalog sprinkles its philosophical elaborations on Warhol's deadpan pranks with Catholic terminology. Citing along the way the titles of two of Warhol's cinema verité efforts, which we coyly render here as *Bl** Job* and *F****, Kimball quotes the effusions of chief curator Mark Francis, who said that Warhol's urine paintings

> continued to refer to his preoccupations with the human body, the exchange of value between money and objects, and what can only be described as a religious desire for communion and human interaction. . . . The *Oxidations* are metaphors for transubstantiation, the transformation of base metals into precious objects. (220)

And despite his blasphemous rhetoric, Francis is right. No man in history, not even P. T. Barnum, could equal Andy Warhol for turning crap into cash.

10

Diligence: Blessed Are the Sweaty

While working on this book, I found myself starting with Sloth and putting off Diligence to the end. Procrastination isn't so much an art as a science, in the old sense of the word that predates Descartes, which means a quest for knowledge of the cosmos and one's self. Since that high-strung Frenchman redefined "science" as the project of making man the "master and possessor of nature," we learned to sniff condescendingly at "knowledge work" that doesn't involve white coats, beakers, and electrified fetal pigs. That's how theology traded its crown as "Queen of the Sciences" for the little paper hat called "Religious Studies" and learned to ask, "You want Christ with that?"

But in the old sense, procrastination is a scientific experiment that reveals what most troubles us—since it's literally the last thing that we get to. If you're like me, you put off organizing your house till the last possible moment—for instance, half an hour before your guests arrive. Once I've shoved the last neglected dish into the washer and the final sock into the sack, I step back and learn something about myself: cleaning the house induces panic attacks because the thing I most fear is disorder.

Scratch my surface *Gemütlichkeit*, and underneath you'll see a panic of anarchy, an unholy terror of rats, mobs, and bandits. Unsurprisingly, the thing that drew me first to the Faith was the *Summa*, the edifice of apparently crystalline perfection that is the Church's deposit of Faith, its treasury of theology and apologetics—okay, all that and the Crusader armor I used to gawk at in the treasury room at New York's Met. No wonder that between writing chapters on the vices, I while away the hours conquering and reconquering the Holy Land through the computer game Medieval Total War.

As a nervous teenager in the roiling, crime-soaked New York City of the 1970s (see Spike Lee's *Summer of Sam* and you'll understand), I took peaceful refuge in the carefully thought-out defenses of the Faith found in the old *Catholic Encyclopedia*, whose sandy, cracked black volumes survived in our public library. I owe my faith not to the Bob Dylan songs we sang at folk Mass, or even the scorching sermons of our old Irish pastor, but to the dogged Diligence of the men who, over the centuries, patiently answered every heresy, laid down firm limits to reckless speculation, and spent their lives setting in order each iota.

I like, really like, that the Church doggedly resists accepting miracles, views up-and-coming Marian apparitions with a skepticism that shames Christopher Hitchens, skewers superstition, and sneers at phony mysticism (i.e., most of it, according to John of the Cross). It helps keep the supernatural firmly in its place—at the top of the pyramid, of course, but set up high in plain sight of the sun, instead of sneaking around in caves, in the whispers of fortune-hunting "visionaries," or secret traditions slipped through tangled codes for the enjoyment of elites. The Faith is at once a mystery and a massive radio transmitter, and I like to think of it sitting on top of the Chrysler Building.

Photo by David Shankbone, courtesy of Wikipedia Commons.

Of all the Virtues, Diligence wears the least perfume. Its odor of sanctity is honest sweat, wafting through the subway car at day's end as you schlep back from the city. The book of Genesis says boldly that scarcity, like death, comes to us as punishment for sin. Absent the Fall, we still would have worked, St. Thomas teaches, but every task would have felt more like a hobby. Our hunter-gatherer ancestors wouldn't have teetered on the brink of malnutrition, and when we built our cities, they needn't have had enormous walls to keep out ravening hordes—or slaves to build the walls.

We might well have lived in the earthly paradise imagined by Karl Marx, whose real enemy wasn't the bourgeoisie but something much more fundamental: what economists (the scientists of scarcity) call the "division of labor." On the Big Rock Candy

Mountain[1] to which Marx offered to lead us, he promised each could be a philosopher in the morning, a poet in the afternoon, and in the evenings . . . perhaps an eye surgeon. This fantasy was what attracted so many beaten-down workers and hungry intellectuals to embrace his messianic system—an Eden, rebuilt on the ruins of a pulverized civilization, populated by a bold new creation, "socialist man," who'd shed like an old, dead skin the faith, the art, and the traditions of the past that belonged to another species. The New Man would look back alike at factories and cathedrals as we do at artifacts of the Neanderthals—all this in service of Sloth.

The essence of sin is to shuck off the duties of the day, taking refuge in wishful thinking or the assertions of the ego. To deny one jot or tittle of the implications of the Fall, to pretend we can reverse it by political or scientific techniques, is to take once more the fruit the serpent offered Eve, which Adam lazily ate. It would be very nice, now, wouldn't it, if we didn't have to trundle off daily to jobs serving other people's needs, merely to make some dirty *money*? We could keep on for decades noodling around on our pet projects, not worrying whether anyone appreciated them—while organic snacks grew on Ficus trees, health care fell from the skies on the just and unjust alike, and our houses cleaned themselves so we could focus

---

1. See the anonymous hobo song referenced by Orwell in *Animal Farm*:

> One evening as the sun went down and the jungle fire was burning
> Down the track came a hobo hiking and he said boys I'm not turning
> I'm headin for a land that's far away beside the crystal fountains
> So come with me we'll go and see the Big Rock Candy Mountains
>
> In the Big Rock Candy Mountains there's a land that's fair and bright
> Where the handouts grow on bushes and you sleep out every night
> Where the boxcars are all empty and the sun shines every day
> On the birds and the bees and the cigarette trees
> Where the lemonade springs where the bluebird sings
> In the Big Rock Candy Mountains
>
> In the Big Rock Candy Mountains all the cops have wooden legs
> And the bulldogs all have rubber teeth and the hens lay soft boiled eggs
> The farmer's trees are full of fruit and the barns are full of hay
> Oh, I'm bound to go where there ain't no snow
> Where the rain don't fall and the wind don't blow
> In the Big Rock Candy Mountains
>
> In the Big Rock Candy Mountains you never change your socks
> And the little streams of alcohol come a-trickling down the rocks
> The brakemen have to tip their hats and the railroad bulls are blind
> There's a lake of stew and of whiskey too
> You can paddle all around'em in a big canoe
>
> In the Big Rock Candy Mountains
> In the Big Rock Candy Mountains the jails are made of tin
> And you can walk right out again as soon as you are in
> There ain't no short handled shovels, no axes saws or picks
> I'm a goin to stay where you sleep all day
> Where they hung the jerk that invented work
> In the Big Rock Candy Mountains

on the window treatments. If only sexual love was all about clean young fingers entwining around a martini, instead of serving as a snare set to drag those paired romantics into the grubby world of diaper buckets, crusty dishes, and teenaged hysterics. We crave such a magical world and wield our technical or biochemical gadgets, endlessly seeking the spell that will uneat the Apple.

To nail a Virtue means rediscovering one solid square foot of reality. The idea that work can sanctify wasn't original to St. Benedict, but the way he said it helped make Western Christendom a healthier, holier place. If we think of our work *as* a prayer, we can find ourselves fulfilled by digging a ditch and digging it as well as ever we can. Likewise, in answering emails, baking casseroles, bathing squirming toddlers who accidentally whizz in one's face—and even though the blood drains from my face as I say it, in *grading student essays.* Any work that isn't intrinsically a sin[2] can serve to sanctify.

And the best way to do that, indeed to do anything, is to turn our gaze away from ourselves, to think of the customer whose needs we hope to meet, the family we're supporting by our work—and most of all, I think, the *excellence of the thing itself.* A wall well made, a meal lovingly crafted, a coruscating essay that really obliterates its target—all these can be, if only we make them, Platonic ideals that glow in our souls, which we pursue through all the muck and mire of their making.

As we sweep up the sawdust from the shop floor, we might even think of St. Joseph, the patron of workers. He wasn't some pale, emasculated figure forever holding a huge stalk of lilies. He was an independent contractor, a skilled Jewish businessman who probably haggled with the best of them. From him, Our Lord no doubt learned His skill at winning arguments, His joy in a job well done. In each of His miracles and parables, we can see a human delight as well as divine intention.

2. Liturgists, this means you.

If we could harness a little spark of that in our daily drudgery, we'd each be a little less likely to shrug and slump and turn in stuff we think of as "good enough for government work."

Looking for Diligence in All the Wrong Places

So there I was at the 21 Club, eating raw meat with the Gun Lady. . . .

That was the best journalistic lede I ever wrote—and it never saw print (till now). My editor snipped it right out of the profile I'd done of a high-powered female gun rights activist on Capitol Hill.

This large-caliber dowager—"Gun Lady" was a nickname she made up for herself—had the close-cropped steel hair and roller derby shoulders of every scary nun I'd ever known. Her favorite political philosopher, she told me in her brawny voice, was Ayn Rand (see Chapter 11). The lobbyist had invited me to interview her over lunch at 21, the swanky Manhattan spot where Michael Douglas brings Charlie Sheen in *Wall Street*. (Douglas orders Sheen steak tartar and leaves him staring puzzled at a plateful of hamburger meat topped by a shiny raw egg. So I ordered the stuff myself.[3]) That film is not the socialist diatribe you might expect from Oliver Stone but instead a cinematic parable about the evils of seeking easy money instead of diligently using the sweat of your brow to earn your bread. Or for that matter, your raw meat.

It was a lesson I needed to learn. Having spent the better part of nine years taking courses and using up fellowships studying to be a literature teacher, instead I was slothing around, avoiding the Great Books of the West. I used my literary skills to make a decent living writing on subjects I didn't know or care about—like the secrets of business success. I'd never taken a course (or even read a book on the subway) about either business or journalism . . . so I became a business journalist.

The stakes were lower and the pay was higher than I could expect from scholarly

---

3. It was the first time I'd tried the dish, and I've since come to like it—to like best of all the Ethiopian variant called *kitfo*, which mixes ground-up, uncooked beef (in some places, you just have to hope that it's beef) with berbere pepper, butter, and farmer's cheese. You wash it down with *tej* (the African honey wine that puts out the fire), rinse hands, and repeat. You scarf down Ethiopian food with all five fingers, scooping up balls of flavorful meat and sauce in this nutty, spongy bread they call *injera*. Then, if you're me, you curl up in the fetal position by the toilet for the rest of the night—groaning that you'll never eat Ethiopian food again. But it's so damn good, you always come crawling back, sure that this time, this time, it will turn out differently. It's a lot like dating. . . .

work, and I could put off the prospect of writing a 250-page dissertation that exactly two people might read. So I conned myself into thinking that I was Diligent: I was going to work five days a week, drawing a decent paycheck, even for the first time wearing a tie. But I was really just procrastinating. I'd come to the very brink of finishing my Ph.D. and embarking on a life as a scholar and author—the vocation I'd dreamed about since childhood. Instead of completing the last and hardest step to finish my degree, I was noodling around on the neutral ground between journalism and public relations.

So would I spend my weeks, having luncheons at some of Manhattan's finer bistros with eager representatives of companies trying to boost their stocks, then going back to the office to paraphrase what they'd told me. (Just in case you were wondering what happened to your 401[k]: it was invested by brokers who relied on articles like mine.) I never could quite grasp accounting terms, so when some executive used jargon like "gross earnings" and "amortization," my eyes would glaze over and I'd think about Gothic architecture or sex, until he came around to some topic I understood, then I'd go back to taking notes. By the end of each day, I was drowsy enough to feel virtuous if instead of watching TV, I listened to NPR. I'd pick up the Walker Percy novels I was supposed to be writing about. I wouldn't reread the things but just flip through them counting pages, wondering how on God's earth I'd ever be able to explain them.

I'd honed my journalistic skills at an upbeat business magazine (which has since gone bankrupt), whose focus was less on the specifics of fiscal whatchamahoozits and fiduciary thingamabobs and more on emotional uplift and positive thinking. It focused more on inspirational cant, of the kind you see on those Successories posters with eagles and mountaintops and incantatory quotes:

- "What you can conceive, you can achieve."
- "Live your best today, for it is your only preparation for tomorrow."
- "The Little Choo-Choo . . . Could."
- "There is no 'U' in 'winner.'"

Other business magazines might take as their bible Adam Smith's *The Wealth of Nations*, but ours was a book called *Think and Grow Rich* by Napoleon Hill—an early twentieth-century pauper who did indeed become a millionaire . . . by peddling thousands of books door-to-door on how to become a millionaire. The book's philosophy was a weird mix of elements from Ralph Waldo Emerson, Faust, and Machiavelli. Instead of practicing virtues like Prudence and Diligence, the book taught that the key to success in any field was essentially . . . sorcery.

Do you think I'm kidding? *Think and Grow Rich* argues that either God or "the Universe"[4] responds to our thoughts like warm Play-Doh in the hands of a five-year-

---

4. The book's author used them interchangeably, but I would argue that there are important differences. Whatever God's will might be for an individual, what the Universe wants for each of us is clear: to break us down into subatomic particles and scatter them randomly through empty space.

old. Think dark thoughts, and the sun will set. Think green thoughts, and you'll attract big, tottering piles of money, and so on. The creepiest section of *Think and Grow Rich* was the part where Hill encourages readers to write down the precise day and month by which they will have earned a million dollars, then repeat that date to themselves hundreds of times a day, every day, for years, until it happens. Kind of like the Jesus Prayer—except, you know, for Mammon. Instead of accomplishing something by working hard, you do it through magical thinking. This is Sloth served up on a silver platter to people seated in business class.

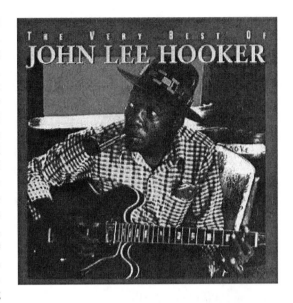

As a dour, blue-collar monarchist, this drivel went down pretty badly with me. I used to walk around the office muttering, "Think and grow mushrooms. . . ." But my girlfriend Sallie Mae had expensive tastes, and I really didn't want to go back to reading long books and having long thoughts about them. On the up side, writing for a business audience taught me to drop the phony Chestertonian style I'd picked up. When you have exactly five hundred characters (not words) in which to make a point, you learn the virtues of economy—if not of economics. Also it turned out that my workshops in screenwriting would prove

the perfect prologue for my new line of work. The ideal story for the magazine followed the format of VH-1's "Behind the Music."

Act I: A poor kid, with a brilliant idea, through hard work, pluck, and luck, makes a business out of nothing. He starts a whole new industry, or builds a better mouse pad. The money rolls in. He gets a John Edwards haircut and buys his aging mother a Cadillac.

Act II: He gets cocky. Or lazy. Or his best friend steals his company, his wife, and his Siamese cats. He verges on despair, starts watching pole dancers through the bottom of a shot glass at 3:00 PM on Mondays, and gets investigated by the SEC. Pretty soon he's selling used spark plugs from a garbage bag just to fund his heroin habit.

Act III: The newly poor entrepreneur has one hand on a bottle of tranquilizers, the other on the trigger of a shotgun—when Something Special happens. He finds his Higher Power. On his way up the clock tower with a sniper's rifle, he stumbles into a self-hypnosis seminar. His mom brings home a kitten that looks like Buddha. Whatever. The point is, his life turns around and he figures out how to go back to making money. He buys back his old company, bankrupts his enemies—but forgives them— and earns three times the fortune he'd frittered away. *Resurrexit, sicut dixit, Alleluia!* The key to such turnarounds was never hard work applied in a principled manner to attain just and rational goals but sudden insight that fell like pennies from heaven and landed the tycoon back on his yacht off Margaritaville.

By God's grace, my next job in the field brought me face-to-face with real exemplars of hard work and determination—indeed, you might say I was assigned to the Diligence beat. My task was to sort through names of leading innovators and managers in a wide array of fields, then tell the story of their success. And here I really did find folks whose tales were inspiring:

- Guitarist and composer John Lee Hooker, who'd followed his muse from grinding poverty among the ground-down sharecroppers of Mississippi. He wrote hundreds of songs, played thousands of juke joints and segregated music venues, and became a worldwide legend. (The best Rolling Stones songs are still their covers of Hooker hits.) I tracked Hooker down—back in Mississippi, but this time living large— and quizzed him by phone about what inspired his early hit, "Boom,

  Boom, Boom, Boom." His Delta accent was so impenetrable that his answers sounded to me like "Ahz lifn round Greenville batden n'I'd dis gurlphren werkt in a genamens club. . . ." I stammered, completely baffled, until his manager jumped on the other line and translated John Lee's answers into Yankee.

I learned, among other things, that the author of the immortal "One Bourbon, One Scotch, and One Beer" was now a Jehovah's Witness, so I wouldn't see him at Last Call. Nor did his sect believe in eternal damnation; it turned out that his classic "Burning Hell" blues was in fact intended as a religious tract. It was a real honor to speak with this musical genius and heretic.

- Filmmaker Elia Kazan, who, like the (now-late) Hooker, was still then clinging to life. But he wasn't giving interviews. As the detail-driven, quality-obsessed director of some of America's greatest films (*A Streetcar Named Desire* and *On the Waterfront* are the most famous), Kazan is now chiefly famous for blowing the whistle on Communist agents who'd wielded power over the film business in the 1940s. Born the son of impoverished immigrants, Kazan was a real self-made man, who transformed American theater and cinema—okay, and plowed his way through a fair share of starlets, since he had the libido of a rutting goat. Still, Kazan was an artistic maverick who flouted forces of evil that had infiltrated his industry. No wonder Hollywood hates him.

- Music legend Wynton Marsalis. A jolly and canny character, this scion of a New Orleans musical family has made a career out of rescuing jazz from the critics—irritating white guys who have been wearing berets since 1955, snapping their fingers, and going, "Oh, baby!" to

Napoleon Hill plans his invasion of Russia.

ever-more chaotic and crackpot atonal noodling . . . as the popular audience excused themselves and sneaked out the back. Marsalis is a champion of "classic" styles of jazz—the kind with melodic lines, discernible structures, and other features once considered important to music. I call it "nonsuck" jazz, for short. By reviving nonsuck jazz and patiently teaching it to young musicians at Lincoln Center, ignoring the scorn of critics, Marsalis has done more for the genre than anyone alive. His Diligence helped save an entire style of music from cacophony and obscurity. It was not only great fun speaking with him but also a little frustrating: when he answered the phone, he announced that as he talked to me, he planned to eat a plate of fried chicken. And so he did, through our whole conversation. Just the kind of colorful detail a writer can't resist—which, of course, I couldn't use.

- St. Ignatius Loyola, founder of the Jesuits. This one was easy. Again, I couldn't get an interview, but using a few biographies, I explained to my business audience how a handsome, successful soldier and

lothario had—through grueling psychological effort and harsh physical penances—transformed himself into an impoverished, celibate missionary who took all his orders from the pope. I offered "take-away" lessons on how they could do the same—for instance, by following St. Ignatius's Principle and Foundation, which starts the first week of his Spiritual Exercises:

Man is created to praise, reverence, and serve God our Lord, and by this means to save his soul. And the other things on the face of the earth are created for man and that they may help him in prosecuting the end for which he is created. From this it follows that man is to use them as much as they help him on to his end, and ought to rid himself of them so far as they hinder him as to it. For this it is necessary to make ourselves indifferent to all created things in all that is allowed to the choice of our free will and is not prohibited to it; so that, on our part, we want not health rather than sickness, riches rather than poverty, honor rather than dishonor, long rather than short life, and so in all the rest; desiring and choosing only what is most conducive for us to the end for which we are created.

Inspired by these men, I found myself scratching around the service entry to the Virtue of Diligence. I started waking up an hour early to work on writing projects. From 7 to 8 AM, five days a week, I banged away at a story I'd been brooding over for years—which I sold as a script to a real-live Hollywood director.[5] I discovered techniques to keep myself keyed to the task, such as putting on the same music every

---

5. Like all scripts, it was never filmed.

morning as I worked on the story. (This made me really popular with my room-mate.) I actually dove back into the Walker Percy novels that had long ago seemed so important. And I found to my surprise that they still were.

But it's hard to switch from writing articles for pay that someone will actually read to carving scholarly scrimshaw that even your dissertation committee is likely to skim. And opportunities are never scarce to fritter away your talents. Lured by the promise of higher pay, I switched to a magazine that profiled and promoted business schemes for getting rich quick on the labors of other people (see Chapter 7). Back I went to spinning tales of "entrepreneurs" who'd climbed up pyramids of unearned wealth through the power of positive lying. I even had to catalog in "lifestyle" pieces the flashy crap they'd bought with all that money. I used my newfound Diligence in the service of such Sloth, but the cognitive dissonance began to eat away at my brain.

I started trying to slip stuff past my editors. So an article about some mogul's pricey, ergonomic office would appear . . . that mentioned Evelyn Waugh. Or I'd amp up to the point of self-parody the New Age rhetoric of a Tony Robbins–type we were profiling. I once even pitched a cover story on how to "Harness the Power of . . . Luck." It made as much sense as some other stories we ran—like profiles of how CEOs learned leadership skills by walking barefoot over hot coals during deductible, weeklong junkets to Hawaii. We'd run these alongside ads for airlines and travel agencies. (Now there's integrity for you.) Well-paid but completely dispirited, addicted to my new income, I found Southern novels once again unreadable, and the prospect of writing about them at last unthinkable. It was time to stop wasting money on long-distance tuition, to withdraw from graduate school at last. The pig had returned to his trough.

God[6] protects drunks and idiots, and I was a little bit of both. Given how I've planned out my career, my guru is Mr. Magoo, who would walk straight out a window—onto an I-beam that carried him safely to the ground. In this case, the I-beam came in form of an April Fool's prank. One disgruntled day, from thin air I made up a detailed story proposal that applied the principles of positive thinking and entrepreneurship to post-Soviet Russia. It seemed that two out-of-work KGB guards had found the capital to turn their former Gulag camp into an executive "toughness training" facility. For only $5,000, CEOs could come for six whole weeks of the Total Gulag Experience™: chopping logs barefoot in the snow, being

---

6. Or the Universe.

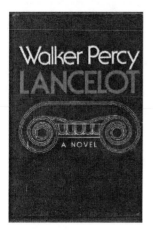

prodded from barracks to the mess hall with bayonets, all-night interrogations, and a diet of fish head soup. I included spurious quotes about what they'd gained through the experience from the serious business philosopher Peter Drucker (then in his late nineties), and corporate guru Tom Peters, whom I had saying, "It's pretty hard to be set in your old corporate patterns, when six guards in top coats with Kalashnikovs are chasing you across the taiga." Most of my smart-ass fellow editors saw through the parody right away. Not my boss, who loved the piece, and wanted to run it in the magazine. Then he looked around the room. How everyone laughed. . . .

Six weeks later, I found myself 1,300 miles away in Baton Rouge, watching snakes from my back window, eating red beans, and finally writing my goshdurned dissertation. My Act III had begun.

Role Model: Mother Angelica

Leaving aside the popes, the person who has served as the public face of the Church in the United States for the past two decades is a crippled, chronically ill old Italian-American lady who chats with Jesus daily, used to speak in tongues,[7] and leaps before she looks. As I write this, she is quite ill, and we can't predict how long she will be with us. But the global media empire planted by this contemplative Poor Clare has put down mighty roots, with millions of viewers who love its dogged loyalty to the teachings of the Church. Indeed, in large swathes of the country where parishes have either closed or turned de facto Methodist, Eternal Word Television Network's broadcasts serve the isolated faithful like Allied broadcasts into occupied Europe.

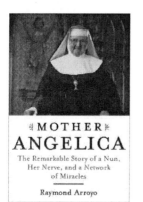

Given the crisis of faith of the 1970s and 1980s, building EWTN sometimes meant flouting the power of worldly bishops who'd learned more than golf-tricks from their liberal Protestant colleagues. Indeed, too many clerics had soaked in the pastel, fuzzy uplift that for "mainline" denominations has largely replaced the Faith. By building, without these gray men's by-your-leave, a media operation that reached millions of the most devout and generous Catholics in the country, Mother Angelica

---

7. Hey, it was the 1970s. Cut her some slack.

did an end run around the bureaucratic institutions that modernists had co-opted—and built an enduring bridge between ordinary believers and the teaching office of Peter.

Born Rita Antoinette Rizzo to a fragile, fashionable mother and a worthless tomcatting father, she grew up desperately poor in a Mafia-infested Canton, Ohio. John Rizzo left her mother to fend for herself while Rita was still a toddler—an abandonment from which Mrs. Mae Rizzo would never recover. (She would end up becoming the single most crotchety nun in Angelica's own community.) Marital meltdown wasn't taken for granted back then the way it is now; indeed, at my own Catholic school in the 1970s in New York, we all knew the one kid whose parents had gotten . . . *divorced.*

And we felt bad for him—a pity he flouted by learning to fistfight and becoming the neighborhood's best garage-band drummer. He kicked my butt more than once. (He was also Italian.) But I digress.

Or perhaps I don't. On a natural level, it just might have been the vicious scorn pharisaical nuns poured on Rita in school for her father's sins and the sight of her mother slaving at odd jobs during the Depression that made Rita so beatifically implacable. Out of place at school, treated sternly by her mother's disappointed family, and afflicted with chronic abdominal pain that forced her as a teenager to wear a corset, Rita developed a rich inner life that more than made up for missing the Lindy Hop. Having heard of a homebound lay mystic, Rhoda Wise, who bore the stigmata, Rita befriended her—behavior that wasn't, in the 1940s, typical for a Midwestern teenager. Wise's intercessory prayer helped win for Rita a cure to her debilitating illness and launched her on the road to a vocation. Scornful of the fidelity that men seemed to offer, Rita didn't get out much. As she told her biographer

and longtime collaborator Raymond Arroyo, "I was never a sexpot, and I never wanted a date. Sexually, I'm a eunuch. I could care less. It's just not my bag."[8]

Lest that sound not chaste but actually frigid, Arroyo records the torrid, Mediterranean love affair the adolescent Rita embarked upon with the One she would come to call her Spouse. After slogging through high school with middling grades, she went to work at Timken Roller Bearing Company. There, Arroyo writes,

> A picture of Jesus impaled by a crown of thorns sat on the edge of Rita's desk. When accused by a co-worker of "pushing her religion," Rita responded, "If you have a picture of a movie star or someone you love, you put it out there. Well, this is my love, and it's going to stay there." (34)

Soon Rita realized she wished to wed the Man she loved. She applied to a strict Franciscan contemplative community—and persevered despite a long list of obstacles that ranged from her rebellious personality to chronic knee pain that made it excruciating for her to join in communal prayer. (Angelica would later write that in the convent her knees were like "two puffy water-filled grapefruit.") On November 8, 1945, Mae Francis Rizzo took her first vows as a religious, marking the occasion with a letter to her mother that reads like a wedding invitation.

Angelica would carry that conjugal conviction through the decades, living with an almost constant sense that Christ was her faithful, high-maintenance spouse. Intense reading in spiritual authors like St. Teresa of Avila, St. John of the Cross, and Brother Lawrence of the Resurrection helped Sister Angelica school herself in *radical trust*. What's puzzling to us worldly folks is that this trust would only grow stronger in the face of suffering and disappointment. In an incident that Angelica has retold hundreds of times to live and televised audiences, the young nun was cleaning the monastery floor with an unwieldy electronic polisher when the contraption got out of control—injuring her so seriously that she would eventually need a full-body cast and weeks of traction. No treatments helped very much, and Angelica was left with chronic numbness and back pain, forced to wear a back brace just to get around. Her response to this crippling event?

She decided to found another monastery. For some time, sisters in her community had talked of creating an abbey that would pray for and minister to black Americans—whose civil rights activists were then being murdered and churches were being bombed. But no concrete plans had been made. So in her hospital bed, with no prospect of ever walking normally, Angelica offered her Spouse what she calls her "outrageous bargain." Arroyo cites a letter she later wrote that laid it out:

---

8. See Arroyo's moving, candid account of her life and struggles in *Mother Angelica* (New York: Doubleday, 2005).

A year ago when the doctors were doubtful that I would walk again, I turned to our Lord and promised that if he would grant me the grace to walk, I would do all in my power to promote a cloistered community among the Negroes. It would be dedicated to the Negro Apostolate by prayer, adoration, sacrifice, and union with God. It would ceaselessly make reparation for all the insults and persecutions the Negro race suffers and implore God's blessings and graces upon a people dear to the Heart of God. (75)

While her healing was slow and incomplete, Angelica didn't wait around to see if Christ was keeping up His end. With permission from her superior, she found other nuns who'd be willing to take up this unlikely mission in some hostile zone of the Bible Belt—finally settling on an area outside Birmingham, Alabama, in 1961. Ironically, fear of actual violence would lead the new community to keep its mission of racial reparation a closely guarded secret. In the long run, the nuns would end up serving another persecuted minority—faithful American Catholics.

Selected to head the new community, Angelica would raise the money to build it and keep it running through a wide array of holy schemes, from marketing fishing lures to Protestant anglers with promises of blessings from St. Peter, to roasting peanuts whose "nun appeal" made them novelties at ballparks. In the end, the only reason the self-educated Angelica started writing books and recording religious tapes was to raise much-needed funds for her abbey. The popularity and profitability of the tapes soon led her to television, which she grasped instantly as the tool needed to "reach the masses." That was when her movie came out. As Arroyo tells it,

When the local station she contracted to film her video series decided to air a movie denying the resurrection of Christ, Mother . . . blew her top. She insisted that the station drop the movie, or she would walk. The station manager got nasty, threatening that she'd "be off television permanently" if she left. "I don't need you, I only need God," Mother fired back, "I will build my own studio, buy my own cameras, and tape my own shows." (145)

Coming from anyone else, this might have been a peevish boast or an empty threat. But Angelica had come to see a pattern in her life: faced with grinding pain and apparent futility, she would always respond with several steps, in this order:

1. Ask God His will in prayer.
2. Once she knew it, throw caution to the wind and trust that He would make her efforts fruitful.
3. Work like a madwoman, wheedling support from the uncertain and shunting aside doubters and dissenters who got in her way.
4. Rinse, repeat.

In other words, Angelica would follow the Ignatian dictum to "pray as if all depended on God, and work as if all depended on you." While some tenured Jesuits may resent what Mother Angelica has said over the decades on her talk show—and she's not one for undue tact—they must appreciate how well she lives out this charism.

The source of Angelica's Olympic-level diligence was the fiercely protective love a woman bears her husband—especially when he suffers innocently for others. She couldn't bear to see her loved One mocked, and she wouldn't stand idly by. So when that network flippantly questioned the Resurrection, she did found her own network. When U.S. bishops greeted a visit of Pope John Paul II with a show that featured Christ as a female mime, she stopped accepting their programming, despite their string pulling and threats. When Cardinal Roger Mahony of Los Angeles issued a pastoral letter that watered down the Real Presence, she critiqued him, point-by-point, on television—and refused to offer a false apology, even when Mahony's machinations got her threatened with interdict (the loss of the sacraments) and the closure of her community. When still other bishops tried to gain control of EWTN and stifle her loudly orthodox voice, she famously said, "I'll blow the damn thing up before you get your hands on it." Her eyes always focused on the eyes of her Beloved, she was almost blind to the worldly obstacles thrown in her way. She stepped right over them.

Angelica has flouted powerful men, the conventional wisdom, and the voice of prudence so many times that for her it's almost routine. Her intimate contact with Christ has helped her to keep, in the midst of outrageous success and mounting power, the simplicity of her founders—Francis and Clare. What drew her to those saints, Mother Angelica has said, was "their absolute dependence on the providence of God. They saw Him in all. And what they undertook was not planned by them, but through their love and detachment they fit into whatever was happening in the present."

It takes a broadly Catholic imagination to see the strand connecting the threadbare life of St. Francis to the basilicas, hospitals, and colleges built in his name. Likewise we won't know till Judgment Day how many conversions, "reversions," vocations, and deepened lives of faith can be traced to Mother Angelica's influence. And that's just as well, since she'd never take the credit, attributing all her successes

to Providence rather than personality. That said, it helped that Angelica knew how to hornswoggle Baptists into laying free pipe for nuns, charm the socks off jaded cable-TV execs, bend the ears of visiting cardinals, and impress the pope. She worked without ceasing, except to pray. It's hard to imagine that she will ever rest, even in Heaven.

Perhaps those with really high-end satellite dishes will someday be able to tune into "Eternal Life with Mother Angelica."

Trademark-Busting Cosmo-Style Quiz™ #5: Score Yourself on the Scale from "Thomas Edison Workaholic" to "Unionized Belgian Soldier on Strike"

Practicing Diligence may seem simple, but it requires its own discernment. We're not wrestling with a simple polarity of Sloth versus Diligence. If that were true, then questions of how much energy to put into pursuing natural and spiritual goods would end with the simple answer, "More is more." But this Virtue (like all the others) can be caricatured. Move far to the right of the Golden Mean, and you're liable to the neurosis of Fanaticism. It isn't always easy for outsiders to distinguish heroic efforts of Diligence (see St. Ignatius and Mother Angelica, discussed previously) from unbalanced zealotry. At some point, we have to judge things by their fruits.

We can also gauge intentions; if a person or group's public statements seem more grounded in *hatred of an evil* than love for a threatened good, it's time to be suspicious. Even obvious, almost metaphysical evils such as Communism or Nazism can goad us to oppose them in the wrong way, overzealously, in a way that can corrupt us. For instance, at the end of World War II, outrage at the evils of the Vichy regime gave the French Left the cover it needed to simply massacre thousands of its enemies, most of them innocent Catholics, under the cover of de-Nazification (*épuration*). There were countless Americans who joined the Communist Party because it was the strongest group fighting Jim Crow (see W. E. B. DuBois, Chapter 3), overlooking mass famines and purge trials, the better to integrate lunch counters. Conversely, the U.S. government was all too ready to lend support to "anti-Communist" dictators over the years—and to Islamist guerrillas in places like Afghanistan, one of them named Osama bin Laden.

It's easy to spot zealotry in others, of course, but much harder to know when we're slipping into it ourselves. I'll speak for myself here. I'll never forget the day back in 1994 when I realized I was a fanatic. Overwhelmed with grad school research, a part-time job, engaged with a wide array of pro-life and pro-family projects and groups, I heard the following run through my head: *I can't seem to conquer my own sins, but at least I can change the world.*

If that kind of crazy talk is running in your head, if you're rushing about trying to save other people's souls so you can offer them as a dried-flower bouquet on Judgment Day, it's time to tune out, turn off, and drop in. If you want to keep on being Martha, you'll need to spend some time with Mary. Replace one of your most exciting activist projects with serious, silent time spent before the Blessed Sacrament, and look into making a real Ignatian retreat. (These are rarely offered by Jesuits, by the way—I'd try the Fraternity of St. Peter instead.) Remember how the 9/11 hijackers spent their last days before murdering thousands for Allah . . . in strip joints, drinking beer.

The Quiz

You have a worthy charitable work that's both intrinsically good and compatible with your vocation. You have made the time to do it through some sacrifice—less Twitter time, not so many episodes of *House* on Tivo, or rounds of drunken miniature golf. You've embarked on the project and already burned through the fun part. Now you're slogging through the tedious detail work, encountering frustrations, maybe starting to miss the Miller Lite and mini golf. Let's say you volunteered to help maintain a homeless center, and you've already planted all the flowers that will fit, then gotten the lawn nice and spiffy. But now it's time to help with cleaning the bathrooms—something you only reluctantly do at home. When the nice lady in charge hands you the toilet brush, you react as follows:

a. Feel an overpowering *heaviness* that can only be answered by taking a long, much-needed nap. You start to total up how few hours you might have left on earth and wonder whether God really wants you to waste them cleaning up after strangers—some of them druggies who *got themselves* into this mess or drunks so out-of-touch with reality that they won't even notice how clean are the toilets *they think are telling them to kill the president*, and anyway it doesn't matter because this is the limit—you're going home. This decision fills you with energy and hope.

b. Nod grimly, and focus on all the spiritual benefit you can obtain by offering up your valuable time in such a grimly squalid cause. Imagine the Purgatory you're burning off here—and remember all the dire warnings of Holy Souls who appeared to solitary, malnourished nuns, to report that Purgatory is only a little better than Hell. Compared to that, hobo toilets are child's play. *Too bad*, you observe, as you clean under the rim, *the Church stopped just selling indulgences.*

c. Shudder, and remind yourself of Dostoevsky's dictum: "Love in action is a harsh and dreadful thing compared to love in dreams." If you feel a little resentful, even humiliated, you try to remember occasions when you were praised beyond your merits and chuckle as you think of this as balancing out the scales. If you're deeply pious, you might imagine that Jesus has a stomach virus and you're cleaning up for Him. But then if you were that pious, you'd be off reading some improving book instead of . . . this one.

d. Squelch, cauterize, *crush* your natural feeling of repugnance and wonder whether it wasn't sinful pride that made you feel it. That must be why God has chosen to humiliate you. You're a sinner who always returns like a dog to its vomit, so why shouldn't He send you to the toilets? Afraid your proud, proud spirit will try to shirk this part of your necessary purgation, you volunteer to do *more* of the vilest duties around the shelter—and promise yourself that by *sheer force of will* you won't burn out and drop the project. Or drown yourself in the toilet.

Here are the results:

- If you picked "a": Man up (even if you're a woman), and clean those toilets. The monks who diagnosed this deadly sin say that Sloth can only be conquered by blundering straight through one's tasks, however intolerable it seems. So make it your personal project to see to it that these toilets are the *cleanest in human history*—so sparkling and pristine that the addled people they're meant for will think they're kitchen equipment and be afraid to use them. Picture that scene, using the Ignatian "composition of place." It will cheer you up.
- If you picked "b": If the only reason you can think of for helping desperate people is to lighten your sentence on Judgment Day, that's better than nothing—like going to Confession just once a year, as the rules demand. But the more tasks you think of this way, the harder you'll find it to do them, and the less joy you'll find in this existence. Remember this: if God really meant earthly life to feel like taking the SATs, then why are we so reluctant to admit when our time's up and turn in our booklets?
- If you picked "c": Your attitude doesn't need adjusting and good for you. Now don't give the credit to your naturally upbeat personality or the wisdom and goodness you've attained through all your previous Diligence. It's Grace, which you got for free, so it's bad taste to boast about it—especially in peppy little emails you send your inertful friends. Which only depress them.
- If you picked "d": You probably need to find some other project— one that doesn't provoke you to such exhausting and unsustainable extremes. The frenzy of self-laceration you're starting to feel has a technical name in Catholic theology. It's called a "scruple," and what it leads to is despair. If you do decide to continue at the shelter, remember that if each of these homeless folks is an image of God, then *so are you*. He isn't trying to grind you into mush so He can reshape you into a cosmic ashtray. There's a spirit who does that, all right—he's called "the accuser"—but he plays for the Other Team.

Activities

If after you've measured your soul you find that Sloth is really your strong suit, there are plenty of things you could do to counteract it. But suggesting them seems futile. If you were sufficiently Diligent to take up a to-do list for building the Virtues, you wouldn't need one in the first place. So I'll start small, with a few suggested readings and gentle doses of mild, low-impact activities to help you gradually rebuild the atrophied muscles in question:

❏ If your problem is straightforward Sloth, it is probably undergirded by a sense of weariness and futility. Perhaps a badgering parent or long years of working for Soviet-style bosses have caused you to internalize a kind of preemptive despair. If so, then even simple tasks with obvious, short-term payoffs can loom before you like the stone of Sisyphus, a boulder you'll have to schlep uphill each day just to watch it roll right back down again. If this is how you feel, the answer is irony. Of course each time you organize your bills or shave your legs, in a few days time your work will again be all undone, and you'll face a pile of new invoices and razor stubble. Instead of letting entropy bring you down, try to see it as a kind of cosmic joke—but remember that it isn't on you. In fact, you're in on the joke. Pretend that you're part of an improv skit, and your theme is "Murphy's Law of Thermodynamics." In a Fallen world, everything falls apart, so why should you expect to be exempt? Remember that when Franz Kafka would read his friends his short stories about hapless nebbishes trapped in castles or turned into insects, both the author and the audience laughed out loud. So why not pick up Kafka's stories for *lectio divina*? For my part, I got to sleep each night after tense days in a leftist English department by nodding off to an audiobook of Kafka's read aloud by Lotte Lenya. (Those too Slothful to read to their kids at bedtime should pop in this tape for them instead.)

❏ Adopt a beagle (see Chapter 4).

❏ If you're not profoundly slothful, but instead slog through your days in a dutiful, joyless funk, we can ratchet the uplift a bit: Get a hold of one first-rate book on how to work happier, *Flow: The Psychology of Optimal Experience*.[9] It's written by a man who overcame a handicap few of us could face—a name not even he knows how to pronounce: Mihaly Csikszentmihalyi. Overcoming this crippling obstacle taught what's-his-name the skill of finding joy in the midst of toil and sent him on a quest to discover the

---

9. Mihaly Csikszentmihalyi, *Flow: The Psychology of Optimal Experience* (New York: Harper Perennial, 1991).

qualities shared in common by successful people who are happy in hundreds of different lines of work. His book explains how farmers, astronauts, and African mercenaries (if memory serves) all harness the power of playful creativity to render their workaday tasks more meaningful, moment-to-moment.

❏ If your problem is that subtler form of Sloth that hides behind incessant, exhausting activity, you're better off buying Josef Pieper's classic on the Catholic psychology of work, *Leisure: The Basis of Culture.*[10] First written to warn the Germans right after World War II about the dangers of working hard without working "smart," Pieper's wise and warmly readable book explores the role of festivity, liturgy, and contemplation in the life of busy parents and laymen.

❏ If you're struggling with Acedia, the sense that in the midst of all your work, prayer, and carefully harnessed leisure, a hollowness and spiritual dryness pervades your days, one antidote can be found in the classic work by Stefan Cardinal Wyszynski—the wily Pole who led the resistance to the Soviet domination of Poland and mentored Karol Wotyjla. Suffused on every side by Marxist "humanism" that acclaimed hard work as the key to building a workers' utopia, the Poles knew that in fact they were digging holes, just to fill them up again. (Or as an old Polish joke went, "We pretend to work, and they pretend to pay us.") In *Working Your Way into Heaven: How to Make Work, Stress, and Drudgery a Means to Your Sanctity,*[11] Wyszynski draws on scripture and the stories of the saints to find redemptive meaning even in seemingly futile tasks—such as working in hopelessly inefficient socialist borscht canneries or teaching freshman composition to graduates of American public high schools.

---

10. Josef Pieper, *Leisure: The Basis of Culture* (San Francisco: Ignatius, 2009).
11. Stefan Cardinal Wyszynski, *In Working Your Way into Heaven: How to Make Work, Stress, and Drudgery a Means to Your Sanctity* (Manchester, NH: Sophia Institute, 1998).

Vainglory: The Few, the Proud, the Damned

I teach my students to work with language by showing them how to play with it—just as a psychology professor teaches future therapists how to play with people's minds. Sometimes I combine the methods proper to both disciplines—for instance, when I keep a straight face explaining to my classes the following little-known facts about the English language:

- The proper pronunciation of "comeuppance" hews close to its medieval French cognate. Hence, it's "kom-ooh-PAHNS."
- "Misled" is scientific jargon dating from World War II and is correctly pronounced as "MY-zeld."
- The word "moustache" derives originally from "mustard," which used to get caught in the hair of the upper lip, before the invention of hot dog buns.
- Pig Latin was developed by oppressed Roman swineherds as a code their masters couldn't understand.
- "Gullible" isn't in the dictionary.
- All of the above will appear in questions on the final.

It's amazing what you can get away with thanks to the authority conferred by a Ph.D.—and, more importantly, a lectern. The deadly sin I'm addressing here offers similar opportunities for creative verbal nonsense. In fact, there are so many different meanings and emotional nuances that go with the simple word "pride" that you might well despair of making a sin of the thing. It's as if we can't decide what we think Pride means, so we use it almost randomly—the way college students employ the specific, historical adjective/noun "fascist" to describe everything from professors who mark off for grammar to pants that fit too tightly. Want to have fun at a campus coffee shop? As you're leaving, raise your voice and finish your final sentence with this phrase: "I just think that's really fascist—in the *negative* sense." Make your way calmly but quickly to the exit, before all those heads explode.

A mother holding her newborn is invariably called "proud," just as her child is always "adorable." Now, if you wanted to get pedantic, you could parse all that and ask, "Does mama really partake in the deadly sin that goaded Lucifer to rebellion? Do we really 'adore' her child? Then why aren't we kneeling and swinging incense in front of him?" (There's a word for people whose advanced education drives them to say things like this around women pale from labor. That word rhymes with "fast moles.")

The Marines, who call themselves "the few" and "the proud," clearly mean

something different from the principle of angelic insubordination. Can you really imagine Lucifer and his angels submitting to basic training, with St. Michael as their drill sergeant barking insults and giving them feminized nicknames—responding "Saint, yes Saint," like a scene from Kubrick's *Preternatural Jacket*? The "pride" a warrior takes in obeying legitimate orders is clearly a horse of a different feather.

Then there's black pride, gay pride, and white pride. Each of those combinations, I'll venture, gives the reader a different feeling. Some Yale conservatives in the 1990s, too clever by half, responded to the school's gay pride initiative by printing up T-shirts that went through each of the other Deadlies—as in "Gay Envy," "Gay Lust," and so on.

I'm not sure what point they were trying to make, and I pity the SAT champion who drew the short straw and had to walk around all week in a shirt that read, "Gay Sloth." Indeed, there are so many gay pride events across the country that the very word "pride" on its own has begun to take on that connotation. Perhaps our grandchildren, hearing the story of Satan's fall, will think he stormed out of Heaven in a hissy fit provoked by "creative differences."

St. Thomas Aquinas found himself so flummoxed by the different meanings the mind can give to Pride that he broke the concept down into usable pieces. There's

Superbia, the outsized, metastasizing self-love and willfulness we associate with two-year-olds and Lucifer. St. Thomas saw this dark tendency in the soul as the root of every evil, so he removed it from the list of the Seven Deadly Sins, sequestering it in a category all on its own, under twenty-four-hour lockdown.

Then comes *Magnanimitas*, or greatness of soul—which we display when accepting proportionate praise for a job well done and which drives us to strive after greatness. (For instance,

Q: "Those shoes are so *great*!" A: "They better be—they cost me a month's salary.") Refusing to take any credit for good deeds we've done, to gratefully acknowledge our natural gifts, or to graciously accept a compliment can turn someone who misunderstands Humility into a cringing, obsequious toady—the sort of Christian one would gladly feed to the lions, except he might make the lions sick. St. Thomas's term for this condition was Pusillanimity, or the smallness of the soul.

It's hard to strike the healthy balance between an honest awareness of the good we have achieved and the temptation to preen and strut over gifts we have received. When we do that, we're caught up in a sin the great Dominican called *Vana Gloria*, or Vainglory. We are literally proud of nothing. It is this tendency St. Thomas listed as one of the Seven Deadly Sins, and he no doubt saw plenty of it in his day—feudal lords who vaunted the lands they had inherited as if they'd laid the tectonic plates themselves, ladies whose fleeting beauty turned them into tyrants, and mystics who used their "revelations" as a means of wielding power or making money. In other words, nothing has changed in seven hundred years.

C. S. Lewis did the best job of defining Humility when he summed it up as honesty applied to the self. Anything that distorts our intellectual apprehension of our own nature and moral state is dangerous. It is truth that sets us free, not hype-driven self-esteem or self-deprecating smarminess. All the rest is manipulation, even if we're only doing it to ourselves. As the Irish priests used to tell the boys, "Leave yourselves alone! Don't you know your body is a temple?"

All of which is to say that the vice opposed to Humility is Vainglory, something we New Yorkers know all about. If in Lake Woebegone, every child is "above average," then in New York City, every adult is "almost famous." Each is just "one big break" away from grabbing the world by the yarbles—from creating some artwork, writing a novel, releasing an album, performing a monologue, or founding an organization that will achieve world historical importance and end up being taught in Columbia University's core curriculum.

In most communities, young people start out hoping to change the world, to make their mark, to nurture their private passion until it blossoms in fortune and fame, acclaim and immortality. Then they fail, shut up, get "real jobs," and practice their talents as a hobby. This is especially true of Southerners, who might major in theater at Vanderbilt, move to Brooklyn for five years, and work washing dishes or zipping around with bicycle messages—while taking classes and auditioning for roles, scanning *Variety*, and hanging with other "actors." But after a while, most of them get tired of eating Ramen noodles and making excuses to their parents, then go home and sell real estate in Marietta. They have some kids, do a little community theater—you'll see them fighting attack rabbits in Fort Worth's *Spamalot*, mewling horrifically and hopping around like mangy crickets in the Greenville production of *Cats*—pay their taxes, and grow old gracefully.

We don't grow old in New York; that might entail growing up. Imagine a city where roughly half the population goes through life still somehow convinced that we really will someday end up as astronauts, cowboys, ballerinas, and princesses . . . we just need a better agent. It doesn't help that The City is flooded each year with the scraped-off valedictorians of every community in the country, who pour across our borders, hike up the rents, and get back at the "rednecks" in their hometowns by voting in Democrats to govern mine. When some of them do succeed and settle into the apartments they've bid up to $3,000 per month, they condescend to us natives who live out in Queens with the term "Bridge and Tunnel" (to which the proper response is always, "Yearbook Editor!").

Those who don't ever "make it" are driven to make it up. And that is the essence of Vainglory—making a great show about nothing. We carry on our life's vocation of greatness entirely within the confines of our minds. Some of us get remarkably good at this, creating for ourselves entire critiques of our chosen fields, designed to explain why our talents have been frustrated. These critiques involve extensive reference to "the System," which freezes us out because we are (variously) Catholics, Jews, conservatives, progressives, women, veterans, Italian-Americans, ex-cops, or straight albinos. I'm sure that somewhere in a basement in Maspeth, Queens, there's a floundering fiddle player who blames his blunted career on discrimination against the slothful.

But these are only the pikers. The truly deluded, the absolutely expert New Yorkers, don't blame others for our failure—because we *never realize that we've failed*. We can go on for years serving coffee at Starbucks, telemarketing, cadging sleep grants from the New York State Department of Labor in the form of unemployment checks, never working (much less succeeding) in our fields . . . and it makes no difference at all. We're each really "brilliant" writers, critics, actors, activists, or mimes, and all of our friends are, too. We meet up with them at diners like the Little Poland on Second Avenue, which serves up buzzing flies and a big bowl of "Meat Soup with Husks of Bread" for under $3, to talk about our projects, which are somehow always "incubating."

For instance, let me adduce the following people, drawn exclusively from folks with whom I've traded delusions over the years:

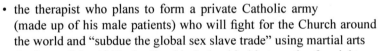

- the sculptor who hasn't sculpted in seven years, who works as a tour guide and introduces himself as "an artist"
- the opera singer who never made it past the chorus, who flounced offstage complaining about "misogyny." She now calls herself a "former diva."
- the Catholic journalist whose principled refusal to work lost him, over time, several primo apartments (they expected him to *pay rent*!) and most of his front teeth. He has planned for some twenty-five years to personally refound the Jesuits.
- the Irish-American violent alcoholic who fancies himself a Sinn Fein freedom fighter—which is easier since he has never been to Ireland
- the chef who got booted from kitchen to kitchen—who explains that his cuisine was simply too sophisticated for New York City. While working as a janitor, he would tell people, privately, he is one of the three best chefs . . . on earth.
- the therapist who plans to form a private Catholic army (made up of his male patients) who will fight for the Church around the world and "subdue the global sex slave trade" using martial arts
- the Staten Island kid who lived in Ireland in his twenties for eighteen months—and has talked with a full-on brogue ever since

I really could go on all day. And I would have to, if I shared with you the delusions that used to keep me going. To people who've never lived in The City, this phenomenon is hard to explain. Or, as my Southern-fried beloved likes to say, "What is *wrong* with you people?"

I've offered various theories. Is there some kind of delusional cloud that hangs over The City? A curse cast by the Manhattan Indians on their way out of the island? Maybe a mild hallucinogen the landlords add to the water to keep us from begrudging our rents? No, in cold fact, I think it's the pressure exerted by the huddled masses of National Merit Scholars sneaking across our border, pushing the rest of us over the side. The East River washes us out into the Long Island Sound. Then we wake up in Atlantis—where each of us gets to be emperor.

Every Statement Made by Satan in the Bible—Set to an Irish Drinking Song

The vice of Vainglory amounts to preening over qualities you either don't have or didn't earn. Like every other sin, Vainglory stems from Pride, but the latter is something more dark and primal. To make this point more clearly, I wrote a merry song about it, inspired by the writings of dissident Catholics who preen about their "courage" in flouting the Church's authority—as if they were courting the visit of Spanish inquisitors. The following paean to Pride can be sung to the tune of the old Fenian rebel song "The Rising of the Moon," although it probably shouldn't be—unless you happen to have an exorcist handy.

Non Serviam, Lord

I'll ascend into heaven, that's where I'll exalt my throne
up above the stars of God, and the covenant's lofty stone.
In the sides of the North I'll ascend above the cloud.
Being like to the Most High, I will sing out bold and proud:
And I'll say, "*Non serviam*, Lord! No, *non serviam*, Lord!
I am not some cringing servant. So, *non serviam*, Lord."

Does Job fear God for nothing? Or hast Thou not put a hedge
around him and his dwellings, and he feels his safety pledged?
Thou hast blessed his work and wealth, and hast watched over his race.
But strike down his good fortune, and he will curse Thee to Thy face.
And I'll say, "*Non serviam*, Lord! No, *non serviam*, Lord!
I am not some cringing servant. So, *non serviam*, Lord."

Why pester me, O Jesus, what have I to do with Thee?
Or since our name is Legion, I should probably say "we."
Art Thou simply being cruel, smiting us before Thy time?
If Thou really must expel us, how about that herd of swine?
And I'll say, "*Non serviam*, Lord! No, *non serviam*, Lord!
I am not some cringing servant. So, *non serviam*, Lord."

Feeling hungry, Son of God? Why not turn these stones to bread?
Or leap down from that Temple—will He let Thee hurt Thy head?
Or see those mighty kingdoms, spread from sea to shining sea—
All their glory will I offer to the one who worships me.
Still I'll say, "*Non serviam*, Lord! No, *non serviam*, Lord!
I am not some cringing servant. So, *non serviam*, Lord."

Kneeling before the World: Vainglory in the Church

So far, the instances of Vainglory we've encountered have seemed less insidious than ridiculous. But the monks who listed this sin among the seven deadlies knew the human heart better than any psychologist, having conducted exploratory surgery on the depths of their own souls with the aid of wise superiors and engaged in systematic meditation and contemplation according to the rules of their communities. In that sense, Ignatian or Franciscan "psychology" has a much better claim to being empirically grounded than any you'll find on a college syllabus.

Vainglory is more than just having a big head. You might start there, with deluded perceptions about your own virtues or talents. But then you need to feed that head, to keep on pumping it full of hot air so it can float past Macy's on Thanksgiving, to the cheers of imaginary crowds. To maintain the illusion, you alter what you do and why, distort your work, and sometimes betray what God created you to do, the better to pimp for "attaboys" from your peers. In short order, you can forget entirely why you started writing, painting, delivering babies, or teaching in the first place. This can even happen to parents when they start to obsess about making their children "outshine" their classmates and neighbors.

Vainglory can operate on a grand scale, infecting nations with the notion that their culture, ideology, or way of life is not simply right for them—but is the final answer for every other country, or at least those neighboring regions with really desirable natural resources they'd like to plunder. We well remember expansionist Nazi Germany and Soviet Russia, but less malevolent countries have inflicted their own share of mayhem in search of "glory" or in service of "the white man's burden." Think of Napoleon's wars against all of Europe, which killed tens of millions, or the cruelties of colonialism.

Vainglory can also infect the Church, or at least her members and her leaders, leading them to neglect or even betray their supernatural mission for the sake of lesser, more tangible goods such as political power, social prestige, or even (most crassly) money. Vainglory in this sense has washed through the Church in the West for at least the past forty years—and produced as its toxic fruit the ugliest scandal in Church history since Christians stopped burning witches: the sex abuse crisis that broke in the 1990s.

Some anguished Catholic observers of this protracted, appalling scandal consoled themselves by saying that the Church was going through a stern purgation, and we should think of it as a kind of Lent. That metaphor works, up to a point. The liturgical season does drag on and on, and if you take it seriously, it can seem to last forever. But it has a definite ending, set down in black and white—the black vestments of Good Friday, the white dawn of Easter lilies and candles. As hard as we try to recapture the grief of the apostles and Our Lady on Good Friday, to join ourselves to Jesus as He cries, "My God, my God, why have You abandoned Me?" there's always a cushion in the back of our minds: we know the story's ending. As we watch with Christ for one hour on Holy Thursday or meditate on His seven last words on Good Friday, at the very lowest point in that bleakest, hostless liturgy, we can't quite forget that "death is swallowed up in victory." We have that advantage over the apostles.

Not so in worldly affairs. Societies, even Christian societies, really have collapsed. Catholic missions to pagan empires that came achingly close to mass success—in Japan, in China—have failed thanks to human mistakes, to hubris or corruption, and ended in massacres. More tragic than those who died horribly as martyrs are those who succumbed to fear, who traded (as most of us would) the integrity of Faith for a few more years of "quantity time." Catholic nations have lost the Faith, as the English did, under slow, relentless pressure from their governments. Still others have weathered persecution nobly, then greeted the dawn of freedom with a yawn. The Faith that sustained my Irish ancestors through the Famine in time of feast seems childish, a bogeyman of the past that adds local color—like the leprechauns.

As Americans, we like to think that we're exceptional, that our nation is some unique, divine experiment, immune to the laws of history. We're not the first nation to think so, and we're unlikely to be the last. But the events of recent years have disproved this charming theory. It turns out we really *can't* impose modernity and liberalism on a civilization of a billion through either force or farce; neither the Pentagon nor Hollywood seem likely to turn the intolerant *Dar al-Islam* into one more interchangeable piece of a globalized, peaceful McWorld. Nor can we live in prosperity forever without *making* anything—trading for cheap imports our cleverness at finagling finances. One needn't think lending at interest sinful, nor reject the market economy to see that the hucksterism that passed for investment wizardry on Wall Street amounted at last to usury. Nor can we count on the order and stability of a society that has undermined its very building block—the family—through sexual revolution, incessant contraception, and easy divorce. Anarchy begins at home.

American Catholics think that we too are exempt; at no point since the Nativist riots of the 1850s have we endured any serious persecution. The closest thing we had to an organized attack on our nation's Catholics was the passage of Prohibition—for which we repaid America by supporting Franklin Roosevelt. To be fair, our bishops helped infuse the New Deal with pro-family policies, and for a few decades there, it looked like we might well make the Democrats into Christian Democrats. It seemed that the fusion of Catholicism and Americanism might well form the wave of the future. There were no other Christian creeds that made a serious bid to provide America's civic conscience; our country's founding Puritanism was so inhuman that it dissolved into Unitarianism. Evangelical Protestantism had plenty of heart but seemingly never grew a brain. Mainline Protestantism degenerated via the Social Gospel into a weak-tea progressive politics—temperance, eugenics, and assorted Wilsonian meddlings.

At the apex of our influence as part of the Cold War anti-Communist coalition, it must have seemed in 1960 that Catholics really were on the verge of assuming the mantle as America's new leadership class. The Kennedys, in their support of the Cold War and their efforts on behalf of civil rights, seemed to serve as the voice of steadfast political prudence and abstract moral principle—the very fusion favored by great Catholic statesmen over the centuries, from Constantine to Charles V, from Lord Acton to Konrad Adenauer. Could Catholics step in and teach America how to balance order and justice, tradition and innovation, the common good and individual freedom?

We know now it was all a delusion. But why did the promise of Catholic America come to nothing? For journalist Philip Lawler, who served as editor of Boston's archdiocesan paper *The Pilot* under Bernard Cardinal Law, the answer is Vainglory (though he doesn't use the word), practiced on a massive scale throughout our nation's Church, from episcopal palaces right down to us pudgepots in the pews. Lawler's book, *The Faithful Departed: The Collapse of Boston's Catholic Culture*,[1] chronicles the rise and fall of Catholic America in the microcosm of Catholic Boston and tries to understand how the high hopes for an "American era in the Catholic Church" (a phrase used by Evelyn Waugh, of all people) came to a squalid end in the abuse crisis of the 1990s. The book has made Lawler enemies and has been banned from the shelves

1. (New York: Encounter Books, 2008).

of some Catholic bookshops—the same kind of stores that won't sell books like . . . this one.

What are they all so afraid of? The truth, it seems. According to the *Dallas Morning News*,[2] while less than *5 percent* of American priests have been accused of sexual abuse, some *two-thirds* of our bishops were apparently complicit in cover-ups. The greatest scandal isn't the sick excesses of a few dozen pedophiles or even the hundreds of priests who had affairs with teenage boys (the bulk of abuse cases). No, it is the Vainglory of wealthy, powerful, and evidently worldly men who fill the thrones—but not the shoes—of the apostles. In case after case, we read in the records of their soulless, bureaucratic responses to victims of spiritual betrayal; these bishops' prime concern was to *save the infrastructure*, the bricks and mortar and mortgages. Ironically, their lack of a supernatural concern for souls is precisely what cost them so much money in the end. Vainglory doesn't pay.

As the learned Fr. George Rutler wrote in *Adam Danced: The Cross and the Seven Deadly Sins,*

> Pilate washes his hands: the ultimate gesture of contempt for people outside, and in the final analysis, the ultimate gesture of contempt for himself. If there are patron saints, there are patron sinners; and Pontius Pilate is patron of proud public figures who will not impose their personal morality on anyone else even when it means the destruction of innocent life by the consent of silence. He has a career and is getting along pretty well. And that's what seemed to count then, too. (11)

Bishops are public figures, and the dozens of American prelates who washed their hands of abuse complaints by shunting the guilty priests off to therapists, and went not to their confessors but their lawyers, were like Pilate looking out for their careers.

Two. Thirds. It takes your breath away. One bishop in New England only escaped imprisonment by cutting a deal with the prosecutor, essentially admitting guilt and allowing the district attorney's office to audit Church decisions, to forfend future cover-ups. So the highest authority governing the Church there is an official of a state that tolerates abortion—and *I'm relieved to hear it*. O great Diocletian, from our own shepherds defend us.

When you read how even bishops of impeccable orthodoxy were willing to overlook the seduction of altar boys, to squirm away from responsible leadership, it's much easier to understand their typical response to complaints from the laity (or from Rome) of liturgical or catechetical problems. Men who have practiced decades of denial about serial

---

2. Brooks Egerton and Reese Dunklin, "Two-Thirds of Bishops Let Accused Priests Work," *Dallas Morning News*, June 12, 2002.

abusers like Boston's Paul Shanley, who close ranks with fellow clergy *addicted to sex with teenage boys* against the "threat" posed by the laity, find it easy to shrug off trivialities like heresy and sacrilege.

In this sense, the clerical abuse crisis is just one symptom of a systemic Church collapse. We all know the statistics of decline in Mass attendance and vocations, the horror stories of seminaries either emptying or turning "lavender," the long lists of Catholic colleges and schools that have shrugged off essential doctrines. What is the root of the problem? Where in Hell did we go wrong?

The problem doesn't boil down to birth control, modernist theology, or fuzzy documents of Vatican II. We can't blame it all on the psychiatrists, the Freemasons, or the nuns with tambourines. Their excesses are merely symptoms. So, in their own way, are the guilty bishops. The illness that has infected them—that might infect you and me—amounts to what Jacques Maritain called (in *The Peasant on the Garonne*) "kneeling before the world." In return, we hope the world will kneel before us. Spiritual directors used to call this craving the sin of "human respect," which is another name for Vainglory.

In his book, Lawler gives a capsule history of the rise of Catholic Boston—a town where Puritans once outlawed the Mass. When masses of Irish immigrants arrived half-starving, they appeared to native Brahmins at best half-human. When the "world" was spurning us, when American Catholics were viewed with suspicion or dwelt in ethnic ghettos, we pushed back energetically. Our sins rarely entailed compromise. It's hard to sell out when nobody's buying.

The Church in Boston—in America—was finally corrupted by success. We recapitulated in less than one hundred years a process that elsewhere took centuries, skipping straight from the catacombs to the corruptions of the Renaissance without all the nifty art. Having built a vast infrastructure of wealth and power through the desperate sacrifices of hard-working immigrants, the Church began to attract as leaders men who treasured such things—powerbrokers, managers, and statesmen—but very few saints.

Where would one find saints, anyway? As Catholic laymen moved up in the world, they chafed at their sense of strangeness in a liberal, Protestant New England, at the Catholic "difference" in which their parents had taken pride. With the rise of the Kennedy family, they had arrived. It was time to leave behind all the shabby, embarrassing baggage, to settle down in the world, and of the world, and for the world, with the Spirit of the World, for a long and comfy common-law marriage. From the grubby, roughneck immigrant families of nine Vinnies or Patricks who'd filled the ethnic parishes and pickle factories, we'd finally made our way into the mainstream, to join the lapsing members of the old American elite—whose Protestant faith and natural virtues were even then dribbling down their pants leg like John Cheever's seventh martini.

At the same time the Kennedys were following Catholic teaching by opposing segregation, they were also gathering liberal theologians to prepare the way for *Roe v. Wade.* Lawler reports,

In July 1964, several liberal theologians received invitations to the Kennedy family compound in Hyannisport, Massachusetts, for a discussion of how a Catholic politician should handle the abortion issue. Notice now that abortion was *not* a major political issue in 1964. . . .

The participants in that Hyannisport meeting composed a Who's Who of liberal theologians, most of them Jesuits . . . Father Robert Drinan . . . Father Charles Curran . . . Father Joseph Fuchs, a Jesuit professor at Rome's Gregorian . . . Jesuits Richard McCormack, Albert Jensen, and Giles Milhaven.

For two days the theologians huddled in the Cape Cod resort town as guests of the Kennedys. Eventually they reached a consensus, which they passed along to their political patrons. Abortion, they agreed, could sometimes be morally acceptable as the lesser of two evils. Lawmakers should certainly not encourage abortion, but a blanket prohibition might be more harmful to the common good. (81)

I don't think that the Kennedys or their pet Jesuits especially hated children. They weren't yet in the grip of Malthusian panic. Instead, as Lawler points out, they were troubled by doctrinal obstacles to their smooth advancement in modern America. These stumbling blocks, these "scandals," could needlessly hold back the progress of Catholics from the ghetto to the suburbs, from ward heeling to the White House. Offering some moderate compromise was surely the "Christian" thing to do.

This didn't set the Kennedys apart from the rest of Catholic elites; instead of serving as America's moral conscience, discerning which causes of social reform were just and which were groundless, our leadership class in the universities was signing on with a "progressive" social agenda across the board. Hence, when the main goals of the civil rights movement had been achieved, our leaders with few exceptions joined the next reform movement, Women's Liberation, which borrowed its central demand—legal abortion—from the population controllers and eugenicists.

And so we have continued, unto today. Having loved the trappings of the Church, her might as a civic and cultural institution, we've forgotten why she was founded—and by Whom. Facing a culture that feared the fullness of Christ, we have proven ourselves great trimmers. We've trimmed a little here and a little there, just enough to prove we're not fanatical, superstitious peasants clinging to outworn dogmas, but sophisticated believers—whose commitment to "social justice" fits very nicely inside contemporary, secular liberalism. We are now officially upper-crust Americans and deeply proud of ourselves for every exquisite Gothic parish, Catholic hospital, or elite liberal arts college we have worked hard to inherit.

Leave out the infrequent, cringe-worthy interventions by distant Rome, and Catholics could easily "pass" for Uniting Methodists. Our modernized, milquetoast Church is made up of the Stuff That White People Like.[3] And most of us like it. Insofar as we really do, we have the bishops we deserve.

The Vanity of Ayn Rand

Once again, in addressing this deadly sin, we dig through the annals of history to find an Olympic-level practitioner, then use him as a piñata. For medicinal purposes only. History's pages are filled with grand examples of vanity—principally rulers akin to Shelley's "Ozymandias":

> I met a traveller from an antique land
> Who said: "Two vast and trunkless legs of stone
> Stand in the desert. Near them on the sand,
> Half sunk, a shattered visage lies, whose frown
> And wrinkled lip and sneer of cold command
> Tell that its sculptor well those passions read

---

3. Available at http://www.stuffwhitepeoplelike.com.

Which yet survive, stamped on these lifeless things,
The hand that mocked them and the heart that fed.
And on the pedestal these words appear:
My name is Ozymandias, King of Kings:
Look on my works, ye mighty, and despair!
Nothing beside remains. Round the decay
Of that colossal wreck, boundless and bare,
The lone and level sands stretch far away."

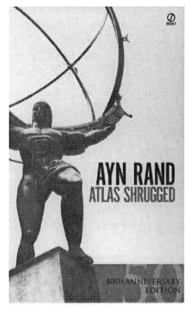

From the global polis of Alexander's dreams, up through fantasies of thousand-year reichs, international proletarian revolutions, and new world orders, we can stroll through the picturesque wreckage, kicking rocks and snickering. Since few of us will ever command a platoon, much less an empire, this seems to me too easy. I'd rather pick an example of Vainglory whose abuses I find accessible—someone like a writer.

It would, again, be easy to pick on random bloggers or trolls who commandeer comboxes, fancying themselves the voice of "the New Feminism" or "real Catholic social teaching." But I fancy myself as above the task of microwaving gerbils. Instead, I'll pick on someone my own size—in fact, much larger—who has sold millions of books, created a political ideology, and even launched what former followers call a cult: the philosopher and novelist Ayn Rand.

First, the obvious stuff: Rand was a programmatic atheist, who sneered at religious believers as self-deluding "mystics." Here's her analysis of Faith, from *Atlas Shrugged*:

A mystic is a man who surrendered his mind at its first encounter with the minds of others. Somewhere in the distant reaches of his childhood, when his own understanding of reality clashed with the assertions of others, with their arbitrary orders and contradictory demands, he gave in to so craven a fear of independence that he renounced his rational faculty. At the crossroads of the choice between "I know" and "They say," he chose the authority of others, he chose to submit rather than to understand, to believe rather than to think. Faith in the supernatural begins as faith in the superiority of others. His surrender took the form of the feeling that he must hide his lack of understanding, that others possess some mysterious knowledge of which he alone is deprived, that reality is whatever they want it to be, through some means forever denied to him.[4]

That's just a letter-perfect description of saints Paul, Augustine, Thomas More, Joan of Arc, Ignatius Loyola, and Edmund Campion, isn't it? Rand should have run their pictures surrounding this paragraph as a "cloud of witnesses."

Goaded by an entirely justified hatred for twentieth-century collectivism, Rand went far beyond classical liberalism and even libertarianism in her disdain for sharing the wealth: while Austrian economists might argue that the corporal works of mercy are best performed willingly by individuals, churches, and civic groups, Rand opposed even private charity on principle (although she made reluctant exceptions, allowing that she might give money to "gifted" children). She condemns "altruism" as a radical perversion of ethics, hence her most famous phrase, "the virtue of selfishness"—an axiom Rand explained this way in her book of that title: "Just as life is an end in itself, so every living human being is an end in himself, not the means to the ends or the welfare of others—and, therefore, man must live for his own sake, neither sacrificing himself to others nor sacrificing others to himself." Elsewhere (in Chapter 14), I address the postmodern, liberal Christian impulse to reject a God-given concern for one's own well-being. (Psychologists call it "healthy narcissism," and it's the reason babies cry and battered spouses flee.) This self-loathing, projected onto politics, results in socialist multiculturalism. If you need a visual, picture a pallid, blue-tinged Anglican bishop staring from the porch of his empty cathedral at the swarms pouring into a London mosque . . . and forcing himself to smile.

Perhaps my early exposure to Rand—whose works I read and whose followers I had to argue with incessantly in college—inoculated me against such religious masochism and made me view with a jaundiced eye the wave of vague, self-flagellating statements that sluice out of the United States Catholic Conference or the Pontifical Council for Justice and Peace. (Those clerics really should be strapped down, in *A Clockwork Orange* style, and forced to read some Rand.)

But Rand's ideal of selfhood amounts to self-deification, fed by the pretense that the individual is wholly self-created, owing nothing to history, ancestors, neighbors, or the future. Think I'm being unfair here? Let's

---

4. Ayn Rand, *For the New Intellectual: The Philosophy of Ayn Rand* (New York: Signet, 1963), 160.

check what Ms. Rand had to say in her play *Anthem*: "And now I see the face of god, and I raise this god over the earth, this god whom men have sought since men came into being, this god who will grant them joy and peace and pride. This god, this one word: 'I.'"

Should you ever get cornered on a long plane ride with a follower of Ayn Rand, and he asks indignantly why he should give a penny of unearned charity to the unfortunate, here's a handy-dandy answer. You might wish to cut it out and paste it to the back of an unwanted business card. (You never know!)

> *Did you invent the English language? Did you develop Common Law, or write the Constitution that protects your cherished rights? Did you build up urban civilization, or invent the technology that lets you live better than what man is by nature—a hunter-gatherer? I didn't think so. It seems to me that you inherited a great deal of social capital that you did absolutely nothing to earn. So now it's time to pass along a little bit of the largesse you received, or else you really ought to strip naked and go hunt wildebeest in the savanna.*

Rand's idea of the autonomy of the individual is so autistic, so clinically isolated from any real, human knowledge of how people grow up in families and cultures, that it recalls the lab experiments with baby monkeys raised by wire mothers. Rand never had or claimed to want children, and neither do her heroes and heroines. A true wire monkey mama, Rand bore fictional offspring who never fall in love, breastfeed, change diapers, or do any of the things that for a moment allow for *the loss of self*. They are all about Apollo, with not a moment to give to Dionysius. Her figments do sometimes engage in sexual activity, but it's almost always a rape—albeit a rape where the steely eyed, Art Deco female genius allows herself, after a struggle, to be overwhelmed by the broad-shouldered, hunky industrial megatycoon. Bodices are ripped with some enthusiasm, before the characters get back down to their real monkey business—ecstatically swapping scorn for the sea of primate mediocrities that surrounds them. It's telling that Rand simply could not visualize and convincingly depict a willing erotic surrender that didn't first need the use of force. No wonder she couldn't differentiate the impulse to engage in willing self-sacrifice on behalf of a needy fellow man from the hatred, Envy, and power-lust intrinsic to every form of socialism—including those who tout themselves as Christian.

Given Rand's picture of the person as self-created, ex nihilo, it's not surprising to learn that she hated giving credit to other thinkers from whom she'd learned—most obviously, Nietzsche. By the time her cult following had grown into a kind of church from which she would literally excommunicate errant sheep, Rand held that there were only two serious philosophers in history: Aristotle and Rand. She thought of her didactic pop novels as the artistic equivalent of Dostoevsky's oeuvre—except that they weren't marred by his "pathological" mysticism and altruism. And indeed, they aren't. All Rand's heroes and heroines are as calculated, and as human, as a mathematical equation.

In teaching *The Brothers Karamazov*, I've noticed that the author gave some of its ugliest characters his very own characteristics: the sensualist buffoon Fyodor shares Dostoevsky's first name; the self-destructive Dmitri spends money as addictively as the author used to gamble it; and the murderer Smerdyakov is, like Dostoevsky, an epileptic. The creator of "The Grand Inquisitor" (the *other* "Grand Inquisitor"[5]) wasn't self-hateful, cringing in abject adoration of the imposed opinions of others—as Rand imagined every believer must secretly be. Instead, he had the Magnanimity and self-confidence to acknowledge his very real flaws. His selfhood wasn't a brittle concrete statuette of Atlas, cherished like a fetish in a self-created church. It was, in fact, a landscape, a vast field he knew he hadn't himself created, with room for many mansions that could welcome countless guests. And at its heart there hung an icon, where burned a lamp, for the great Guest Dostoevsky hoped would take up residence there.

---

5. The graphic novel of that title, by the present author, is conveniently available from The Crossroad Publishing Company.

12

Humility: Please Allow Me to Humiliate You

My favorite thing about the Church's intellectual tradition is the way it grafts the finest parts of worldly, haughty, sexy Hellenic civilization onto the sturdy vine of Jewish monotheism, while snipping off the bits of each that might hinder the hybrid's growth. Early on, we shed circumcision—a painful barrier to entry for Gentile converts with Y chromosomes—then those OCD dietary laws and the stern rabbinic rules against four-color, 3-D holy cards. Conversely, we had to tell the Greeks and Romans who lined up for third-century RCIA classes[1] to abandon the shameless *love for glory* they'd learned from reading about their heroes—literary figures like Odysseus and Achilles and real-life gloryhounds like Julius Caesar, whose high point in life was marching through Rome in triumph, dragging behind him thousands of captured slaves in chains. To classical pagans, the love of adulation was fundamentally wholesome, conducive to acts of courage and Magnanimity, while the Humility espoused by early Christians was an attitude suited at best to well-behaved slaves. In the nineteenth century, Nietzsche, reacting to mealy mouthed, liberal Protestants, would revive this charge against all Christians—and the Jews before them. He termed the "priestly" tradition that came to dominate the West after Constantine a "slave morality" designed to serve the Envy and the lust for power of the weak in their battle against the strong.

Nietzsche strikes me as one of those people who watch nature documentaries and root for the eagle to catch the skunk and kill it. Okay, to be candid, I do that, too. The difference is that Nietzsche objected on principle to the "weaklings" fighting back with the only means nature gave them—a highly developed system of morality—to "guilt" the tall armored men in plumed helmets carrying spears out of selling them into slavery. That's like blaming the skunk for spraying the eagle in the face.

The problem with my metaphor is that it seems to equate Christian Humility with the highly concentrated, vile-smelling musk emitted from the back end of a mammal. Indeed, as we'll see, some documents written by real or aspiring saints do carry a whiff all their own. But seen in the proper context—that is, in the works of St. Thomas Aquinas—we find a definition of Christian Humility that isn't reducible to the grim master-slave dialectic that, in Nietzsche's view, governed history. As the greatest student of Aristotle, Aquinas was the man best suited to rescue what was

---

1. Just kidding. If RCIA had been the Church's mode of teaching converts in the ancient world, then to this day, we'd still be making weather forecasts by cutting open roosters and reading their entrails.

GLORIFYING THE AMERICAN SKUNK

ALL BLACK

SHORT STRIPE

SKUNK FOLLIES

LONG STRIPE

BROAD STRIPE

noblest in the classical tradition and use it to rein in the pious enthusiasm that drove some Christians off the deep end. As Thomas writes,

> Humility has essentially to do with the appetite, in so far as a man restrains the impetuosity of his soul, from tending inordinately to great things: yet its rule is in the cognitive faculty, in that we should not deem ourselves to be above what we are. Also, the principle and origin of both these things is the reverence we bear to God. (*Summa Theologica* II, 2: 161, 6)

In other words, Humility means we train our minds to stay scrupulously truthful to the nature of our own attainments and place in the world, erring where necessary on the side of self-demotion—if only to counteract the fallen human tendency to glory in what is vain. We should do this without going too far, and lapsing into cringing Pusillanimity, or else we're back up inside the butt of the skunk. Have you got all that?

Let's try this another way. We all know the story of the Pharisee and the tax collector in the Temple (Lk 18:9–14):

> But then the tax collector, aware of his own deep humility, looked upon the Pharisee and said, "Lord, I thank thee that I am not such as this man, who fasts and prays and gives alms unto the poor. Rather, in the depth

of my sinfulness is the greatness of my repentance, so am I exalted far above this other man."

Or something like that.

This mash-up of Scripture came to me from Tom Hoopes, my old boss at the *National Catholic Register*, and it points out the perverse uses we can make of Christianity's deepest impulses. I've seen people really do this—for instance, Catholic bloggers who boast about the depth of their former sins and wallow in their specialness compared to dreary, bourgeois churchgoers who've always tried to follow the rules. There's a certain type of penitent who delights in playing the perpetual prodigal son, always deserving of the fatted calf. Just by going one more day without shooting heroin or cheating on their spouses, they think they are forever causing greater joy in heaven than whole cloisters full of holy Carmelites. The trick is to stay the "lost sheep" and never blend in and become one of those boring ninety-nine. . . .

Another instance comes in *American Pictures*, a documentary by Jacob Holdt—an earnest post-Christian Dane who has misread far too much Kierkegaard. I saw this dog and pony show in college, but now it's used worldwide as part of gunpoint "diversity training." In it, Holdt retold how he sought out the lowliest, most oppressed people in America, and he lived among them to learn their stories. There was clearly a humane, even theological impulse behind this quest, and Mr. Holdt had me walking right along with him—until the Dane followed his sentiments into what he called "the most despised of subcultures, the black drag queens of San Francisco."

As he traipsed along behind these glittery, towering transvestites, this well-meaning young man spoke about them in the language of the Gospels, implicitly comparing them to the woman caught in adultery, the prodigal son, and any number of other penitent sinners. Except, of course, what the drag queens wanted wasn't healing and repentance but uncritical social acceptance of their lifestyles and stylin' lives. You can diagnose the sentimental cancer that is liberal Christianity as the metastasized impulse to accede to such demands, replicating unhindered by natural law or revelation.

All of which is to say that Humility isn't a Virtue you're meant to boast about—and simply being abject doesn't mean that you're the meek who'll inherit the earth.

A lot of felons are pretty abject in prison, and it's often the child molesters and rapists in there who get treated the worst. Cry me a river.

Maybe we shouldn't be too impatient with folks who misunderstand Humility, since even the way certain holy people talk about it emits more heat than light. When canonized saints go on at length about how they're the lowest of sinners, it can serve as a wholesome reminder to those of us tempted to lazy smugness. Or it just might induce a bout of scrupulosity so severe that it leads us to give up. If even Mother Teresa trembled for her salvation . . . really, what's the point? Pass me that six pack over there.

Of course, when the topic of Humility comes up, the elephant in the bathtub—or, at least, the holy card crudely taped to the dashboard of the minivan—is the Litany of Humility. Penned by the deeply spiritual Cardinal Merry del Val, a faithful servant of the great St. Pius X, it would seem to come highly recommended. And pious folks I've known still swear by it. But give it a read, and see why instead I swear *at* it:

The Litany of Humility

O Jesus! meek and humble of heart, *Hear me.*
From the desire of being esteemed,
    Deliver me, Jesus.
From the desire of being loved . . .

From the desire of being extolled . . .
From the desire of being honored . . .
From the desire of being praised . . .
From the desire of being preferred to others . . .
From the desire of being consulted . . .
From the desire of being approved . . .
From the fear of being humiliated . . .
From the fear of being despised . . .
From the fear of suffering rebukes . . .
From the fear of being calumniated . . .
From the fear of being forgotten . . .
From the fear of being ridiculed . . .
From the fear of being wronged . . .
From the fear of being suspected . . .
That others may be loved more than I,
 Jesus, grant me the grace to desire it.
That others may be esteemed more than I . . .
That, in the opinion of the world, others may increase and I may decrease . . .
That others may be chosen and I set aside . . .
That others may be praised and I unnoticed . . .
That others may be preferred to me in everything . . .
That others may become holier than I, provided that I may become as holy as I
 should . . .

A Catholic shrink I once knew said he kept this prayer out of the hands of the
clinically depressed; indeed, the speaker in this prayer sounds like he's already
afflicted with that disease. I'd also keep it away from spouses of any kind of addict,
and pretty much every teen—except for beauty queens and quarterbacks. Just reading the thing, I can feel the serotonin draining out of my head. What is more, St.
Thomas teaches that it's wrong for us to practice Humility when it tempts others to
sin. That means that accepting abuse and resigning yourself needlessly to suffering
an injustice might, in fact, be un-Christian. Nowadays we call it "enabling."

To be sure, it's critical for Christians to slip the snares of Vainglory—the yearn-
ing for undeserved praise and the tendency to take personal pride in things God
handed you on a silver platter. Many instances of ethnic, racial, or national pride
amount to one form or the other. I'll never forget the racialist who pointed to New
Hampshire's White Mountains and said to me, smiling, "See those mountains?
White men built those mountains." ("See those pyramids? African Americans built
those pyramids.")

But the sentiments in the litany seem less a rejection of such nonsense than a
comprehensive denial of most of the natural impulses God built into our psyche. To
make this point more fully: If it's good to wish all these things for one's self, then
one should equally wish them for one's children. I challenge the reader to go through
the earlier litany and substitute for "I" the words "my son" or "my daughter." Hence,

"that others may be loved more than my son, Jesus grant me the grace to desire it." That kind of takes the red paint right off the Schwinn bike, now doesn't it?

Of course, there's a way to give this litany a more charitable reading, and here I think we might come upon the truth behind the holy card: In the first part of the prayer, you're asking Christ to deliver you from *desire* and *fear*—desire for good but inessential things and fear of all sorts of suffering (and suffering, in itself, is objectively evil). Now God can bring good out of evil, but that doesn't mean we should go out and canonize Judas, no matter what *National Geographic* says. Our Lord in Gethsemane wasn't pumped up about the prospect of His suffering. He hadn't pestered a spiritual director into letting Him volunteer to die on a cross. He sweated blood in dread of what was coming and begged the Father to spare Him. We should follow His example. The Church encouraged martyrs to be steadfast; she steadfastly discouraged people from seeking martyrdom. There was a whole school of heretics in the early Church called the Circumcellions, who made their name by rushing out and taunting Roman officials until they got themselves fed to the lions. Happily, this kind of heresy tends to persecute itself.

Insofar as we ask God to free us from anxiety over the future, we're acting like penitent packrats who bring in a professional organizer to help us throw out half our stuff. Likewise, by unloading extra baggage such as attachment to the easy and pleasant, we're freeing ourselves for service. If I really cannot bear to fly coach, that means I usually can't afford to travel. Likewise, if the only time you can bear to witness to the Gospel is among like-minded folks who will nod and pass the donuts, your usefulness to the Kingdom is . . . limited. In this light, I can see why St. Ignatius insisted that his Jesuits try to cultivate what reads to me like a punishing version of Humility: actively wishing to suffer as Jesus did. By freeing men up from wholesome natural impulses, you can make them psychologically almost bulletproof—which is why the Church's persecutors, from the Samurai to Elizabeth I's professional priest hunters, were always most scared of the Jesuits. They'd been through Humility boot camp. And they needed it, having come (as Ignatius insisted they should) from only the smartest, strongest, and potentially proudest young men in Europe—men like Edmund Campion (see Chapter 14).

Still, for most of us, a little bit of such humiliation goes a long way. St. Thomas teaches that Humility is a subdivision of the Virtue of Temperance—the rational estimation of one's true merits, seen in the cold light both of one's sins and of God's many gifts. A consistent awareness that all of our good acts are only possible (after the Fall) thanks to actual graces and that our very existence is contingent on God's deciding each moment to keep us from falling into the Void . . . all this should be quite enough to keep the average man from succumbing to Vainglory. ("See our great country? Catholics founded our country.")

I think the good cardinal's litany should be reserved for future missionaries to Burma and patients with a formal diagnosis of narcissistic personality disorder. It's not so much a Humility nutrient as Humility chemo. And I'm kind of vain about my nice brown head of hair.

The Politics of Humility: Monarchy

On February 1, 2008, the *Orlando Sentinel* reported that the Church had recognized the final miracle required to make a saint of the last Habsburg emperor, Karl I. It seems that a Florida Baptist from Kissimmee, at the encouragement of a Catholic friend, invoked Karl's intercession for help with metastatic breast cancer. As the *Sentinel* notes, "A judicial tribunal convened by the Diocese of Orlando and officially

concluded Thursday has found that there is no medical explanation for the woman's dramatic recovery, and more than half a dozen doctors in two states—most of them non-Catholics—agreed." That makes two miraculous interventions attributed to Karl, enough for the pope to certify that Karl is in heaven. As I wrote of Karl in *The Bad Catholic's Guide to Good Living,*

Karl is known for abolishing flogging, dueling, and other abuses in the army he briefly commanded, restricting the use of poison gas and civilian bombing, and attempting to decentralize power among the ethnic groups of his polyglot monarchy, which he came to rule in 1917. Karl insisted on eating the same rations as an ordinary civilian—refusing even white bread, which he handed out to his troops. His court photographer reported seeing the newly-crowned emperor visiting a battlefield full of corpses—and collapsing into tears. Karl murmured, audibly: "No man can any longer answer to God for this. As soon as possible I shall put a stop to it."

Almost immediately, Karl began attempts to negotiate a "peace without recriminations" to end the criminal slaughter of World War I. He was the only sovereign in Europe to attempt such a peace. Had he succeeded, the world might never have witnessed a Bolshevik or Nazi regime, a Holocaust, a Ukrainian famine, a Dresden or a Hiroshima.

Karl's clarity and charity, alas, were no match for the war parties that ruled in London and Berlin, Paris and Washington, from 1914 to 1918. President Woodrow Wilson insisted personally on the dismemberment of the Austrian monarchy, as one of America's war aims. Fighting dragged on another fateful year—giving Lenin the chance to seize power in Russia—before it ended with the collapse of Germany and Austria. The victors' peace imposed by the Allies sowed the bitterness that would someday bring the Nazis to prominence. The weak republics carved out of Austria's corpse would all, one day, fall first to Hitler's armies—and then to Stalin's. So went this world "made safe for democracy."

Exiled on the wintry island of Funchal with his young family, Karl soon succumbed to disease and died while still a young man. The night before he passed, he whispered to his wife, Zita: "All my aspiration has ever been to know as clearly as possible the will of God in all things and to follow it, and precisely in the most perfect manner." By the Church's infallible judgment, he succeeded. (168)

As I bang the kettledrum for the Habsburgs again, I want to set two scenes, one from a fine and under-rated movie, the other from my first visit to Vienna. The powerful historical drama *Sunshine* stars Ralph Fiennes as three successive members of a prosperous Jewish family in Habsburg Budapest. The film was so ambitious as to try to portray the broad sweep of historical change— and, as a result, it was not especially popular. The historical dramas we moderns tend to like are movies like *Braveheart* or *The Patriot*, which recount the tale of a single hero and how he wreaks vengeance on the villains with English accents who outraged members of his family. *Sunshine*, on the other hand, tells the vivid story of the collapse of Euro-pean civilization in the course of a mere forty years. The Sonnenschein

family are the witnesses and the victims, as the creaky multinational monarchy ruled by the tolerant, devoutly Catholic Habsburgs gives way through reckless war to a series of political fanaticisms—all of them driven by some version of collectivism, which the great Austrian political philosopher Erik von Kuenhelt-Leddihn in *Leftism Revisited*[2] calls "the ideology of the Herd."

From a dynasty that claimed its legitimacy as the representative of divine authority at the apex of a great, interconnected pyramid of Being in which the lowliest Croatian fisherman (like my grandpa) had liberties guaranteed by the same Christian God that legitimated the Kaiser's throne, Central Europe fell prey to one strain after another of groupthink under arms: from the Red Terror imposed by Hungarian Bolsheviks who loved only members of a given social class, to radical Hungarian nationalists who loved only conformist members of their tribe, to Nazi

2. (Washington, DC: Regnery Publishing, 1991). This neglected classic of Catholic political thought is out of print but available used. I read it at sixteen, and it's the one book that most formed my own thinking. Perhaps that's more of a warning than an endorsement.

collaborationists who wouldn't settle for assimilating Jews but wished to kill them, and finally to Stalinist stooges who ended up reviving tribal anti-Semitism. The exhaustion at the film's end is palpable: in merely the amount of time that separates Lyndon Johnson from Barack Obama, the peoples of Central Europe went from the humble, kindly Kaiser Franz Josef through Adolf Hitler to Josef Stalin. Call it Progress.

Apart from a heavily bureaucratic empire that spun its wheels preventing its dozens of ethnic minorities from cleansing each other's villages, what was lost with the Austro-Hungarian monarchy? The last political link Western Christendom had with the heritage of the Holy Roman Empire. That empire, Charlemagne's cocreation with the pope of his day, had symbolized a number of principles we could do well remembering today: the empire (and the other Christian monarchies that once acknowledged its authority) represented the lay counterpart to the papacy, a tangible sign that the state's authority came not from mere popular opinion or the whims of tyrants but an unchangeable order of Being, rooted in divine Revelation and natural law. The job of protecting the liberty of the Church and enforcing (yes, enforcing) that law fell not to the clergy but to laymen. The clergy were not a political party or a pressure group—but a separate estate that served as a counterbalance to the authority of the monarchy. No monarch was absolute under this system but held his rights in tension with the traditional privileges of nobles, clergy, the citizens of free towns, and serfs who were guaranteed the security of their land. The Reformation destroyed the Church's power to resist the whims of kings[3]—who gained from Luther the option of pulling their nations out of communion with the pope. In the Middle Ages, no king wielded anything like the monarchical power of a U.S. president. Of course, no medieval monarch confiscated 25 to 40 percent of his subjects' wealth or drafted their children for foreign wars. It took the rise of democratic legal theory, as economist Hans Herman Hoppe pointed out in *Democracy: The God That Failed*, to convince people that the state was really just an extension of themselves: a nice way to coax folks into allowing the state ever-increasing dominance over their lives. What's worse, if monarchy tempts rulers to Vainglory, it at least encourages Humility among the people. Democracy incessantly tempts each citizen to the Vainglory that once consumed only rulers.

A Christian monarchy, whatever its flaws, was constrained in its abuses of power by certain fundamental principles of natural and canon law; when these were violated, as often they were, the abuse was clear to all, and the monarchy often suffered. (In extreme cases, kings were excommunicated or deposed.) "Checks and balances,"

---

3. Today, priests in Germany receive their salaries from the state, collected in taxes from citizens who check the "Catholic" box. So much for the independence of the clergy.

such as we treasure in our republic, actually developed under monarchies—for instance, in the British parliament, which balanced the rights of commoners and nobles against the king's. There were comparable institutions in medieval Spain, France, and Germany. Such checks on royal authority—which was quite limited in the Middle Ages, since kings depended on taxes voluntarily agreed to by their parliaments—maintained a mostly healthy balance of power among the different "estates" of society. Members of various classes were guaranteed their rights by custom, and property was generally sacrosanct from confiscatory taxation.

The House of Austria ruled the last regime in Europe that bound itself by such traditional strictures and that took for granted that its family and social policies must pass muster in the Vatican. By contrast, in the racially segregated America of 1914, eugenicists led by Margaret Sanger (see Chapter 1) were already gearing up to impose mandatory steriliza-tion in a dozen U.S. states (as they would succeed in doing by 1930), while Prohibitionist clergymen and Klansmen (they worked together on this) were getting ready to close all the bars. As historian Richard Gamble wrote in the indispensable history of America's intervention, *The War for Righteousness*, in 1914 the United States was the most "progressive" and secular government in the world—and by 1918 it was one of the most conservative. We didn't shift; the spectrum did.

The Steinhof.
Courtesy of photographer Andrea Schaufler.

Dismantled by angry nation-alists who set up tiny and often intolerant regimes that couldn't defend themselves, nearly every inch of Franz Josef's realm would fall first into the hands of Adolf Hitler, and then into those of Josef Stalin. Today, these realms are largely (not wholly) secularized, exhausted by the enervating and brutal history they have suffered, interested largely in the calm and meaningless comfort offered by modern capitalism, rendered safer and even duller by the buffer of socialist insurance. The peoples who once thrilled to the agonies and ecstasies carved into the stone churches in Vienna can now barely rouse the energy to reproduce themselves. Make war? Making love seems barely worth the tussle or the nappies. Over in America, we're equally in love with peace and comfort—although we've a slightly higher (market-driven?) tolerance for risk, and hence a higher birthrate. For the moment.

On my first trip to Vienna, I spent an afternoon exploring the most beautiful Catholic church I have ever seen—the Steinhof, built by Jugendstil architect Otto Wagner and designed by Koloman Moser. An exquisite balance of modern, Art Deco elements with the classical traditions of church architecture, this church is proof that we could have built reverent modern places of worship, ones that don't simply ape the past. And we still can. A little too modern for Kaiser Franz, the place was funded, the kindly tour guide told me in broken English, by the Viennese bourgeoisie. (Since my family only recently clawed its way into that social class, I felt a little surge of pride.) Apart from the stunning sanctuary, the most impressive element in the church is the series of stained-glass windows depicting the seven spiritual and the seven corporal works of mercy—each with a saint who embodied a given work. All this was especially moving given the function of the Steinhof, which served and serves as the chapel of Vienna's mental hospital. (It wasn't so easy getting a tour.) As the guide explained, the church was made exquisite intentionally to remind the patients that their society hadn't abandoned them. As Housman almost wrote, "Moser does more than Sig Freud can/to reconcile God's ways to man."

We see in the chapel the spirit of Franz Josef's Austria, the premodern mythos that grants man a sacred place in a universe where he was created a little lower than the angels—and an emperor stands only in a different spot, with heavier burdens facing a harsher judgment than his subjects. No wonder the humble Franz Josef slept on a narrow cot in an apartment that wouldn't pass muster on New York's Park Avenue, rose at 4 AM to work, and granted an audience to any subject who requested it. He knew that he faced a Judge who isn't impressed by crowns.

As we left the Steinhof, I asked the guide about a plaque I'd seen but couldn't quite ken, and her face grew suddenly solemn. "That is the next part of the tour." She explained to me and the group the purpose of the Spiegelgrund Memorial. It stands in the part of the hospital once reserved for children with mental or physical handicaps. While Austria was a Christian monarchy, such children were taught to busy themselves with crafts and educated as widely as their handicaps permitted. The soul of each, as Franz Josef would freely have confessed, was equal to the emperor's. But in 1939, Austria didn't have an emperor anymore. It dwelt under the democratically elected, hugely popular leader of a regime that justly called itself "socialist." The ethos that prevailed was a weird mix of romanticism and cold utilitarian calculation, one that shouldn't be too unfamiliar to us. It worried about the suffering of *lebensunwertes Leben,* or "life unworthy of life"—a phrase we might as well revive in our democratic country that aborts 90 percent of Down Syndrome children diagnosed in utero. So the Spiegelgrund was transformed from a rehabilitation center to one that specialized in experimentation. As the Holocaust memorial site Nizkor documents,

> In Nazi Austria, parents were encouraged to leave their disabled children in the care of people like [Spiegelgrund director] Dr. Heinrich Gross. If the youngsters had been born with defects, wet their beds, or were deemed unsociable, the neurobiologist killed them and removed their brains for examination. . . .

Children were killed because they stuttered, had a harelip, had eyes too far apart. They died by injection or were left outdoors to freeze or were simply starved.

Dr. Gross saved the children's brains for "research" (not on stem cells, we must hope). All this, a few hundred feet from the windows depicting the works of mercy. Of course, they'd been replaced by the works of modernity.

We're much more civilized about this sort of thing nowadays. In true American fashion, our genocide is libertarian and voluntarist, enacted for profit and covered by insurance—although it is, like Dr. Gross's crimes, hidden away in clinics.

I thought of the children of the Spiegelgrund again, as I spent the next morning in the Kapuzinerkirche, where the Habsburg emperors are buried and the Priestly Fraternity of St. Peter says a daily Latin Mass. There I learned that the burial of a Kaiser culminated in a ritual of Humility, one performed for every Habsburg monarch for hundreds of years.

At his death, Franz Josef's body was carried in state to the doors of the Capuchin crypt. There his lord chamberlain knocked and asked admission for "Franz Josef, Emperor of Austria, King of Hungary, of Bohemia, of Galicia, of Lodomeria, of Illyria, Archduke of Austria," and so on.

The friar answered, "I do not know him."

The lord chamberlain knocked again, this time on behalf simply of "Franz Josef, King-Emperor."

Again, "I do not know him."

At last, the lord chamberlain begged admission for "Franz Josef, a poor sinner who begs God for mercy."

At this knock, the door was opened.

Role Model for Humility: The Anonymous Capuchins

Now for another group of famously cryptic Capuchins—those who serve and lay at rest at the Church of the Immaculate Conception in Rome. It's a haunting little brownstone parish that stands incongruous on the chic Via Veneto like the skull that always winks out of a painting of "Vanitas." There's *vita* here, all right, but I wouldn't call it *dolce*. The church is fairly ordinary by Italian standards—which means it contains so many lovely and reverent baroque artworks that, in the United

States, it would serve as a site of national pilgrimage. Underneath it lies a crypt that draws in tourists eager to see entire chapels, altarpieces, and ceilings and walls encrusted with carefully placed human bones.

There's always a line, and a basket invites donations—which is only fair, since the place is a tourist magnet, appealing to different drives than those that goad us to the Trevi Fountain. Here you throw in coins with the wish that you never have to return, that you never need join in the fate of its founders—the vowed obedient, impoverished celibates whose Humility was so extreme that they deeded their last remains, the final sad reminders of mortality, their bones, to be pulled apart and made into the ornaments for the rites of their religion. This is all the more appropriate for a faith whose emblem is an instrument of torture reserved for slaves. If the cross, the first-century equivalent of a lynching noose, can be transfigured from gore to glory, then so can a room full of skulls. What could be more appropriate, in fact? Perhaps more parishes should adopt this mode of décor. It might cut down the number of strictly nominal Catholics who insist on lavish church weddings.

My observation about the cross applies to Protestants and Orthodox with equal force; while neither of them engage in iconography quite as graphic as Catholics in depicting the sufferings of Christ, nor do they shrink from the shadow of the Cross. The lyrics of the Lutheran hymn "O Sacred Head Now Wounded," and the icon of "Extreme Humility" dip nearly as deeply into the pathos of the God-Man as the most Lenten Latin image.

Courtesy of photographer Tessier (Creative Commons License).

Of course, the crypt's initial effect is macabre, and some of the visitors come mainly for kicks and giggles. How odd to see a skull surrounded by two shoulder bones that look like wings, to make a grinning Angel of Death. How clever, in a twisted goth way, are the vertebrae glued together into a chandelier . . . and the thighbones that form the Sacred Heart.

It's harder to muster a chuckle over the full-sized standing skeletons vested as friars. By the time you come to the fourth chapel, where two skeletal arms, one robed and one bare, cross to form the Franciscan emblem, most of the folks are quieter. On my visit, I reassured one set of tourists that the souls depicted sitting in flames were not in Hell but Purgatory—hence the saints reaching down to pull them out. That lightened the mood a little.

In the final room, where the altar is warded by a fully vested Grim Reaper, waving a scythe made out of bones, there is nothing left to say. You are ready to head for the door—which is locked, so you must retrace your way through the bone rooms you've already visited, in search of fresh air and some escape from these grim reminders of our common, onrushing fate. The wisest visitors make their way into the church upstairs, whose famous monuments are to the son of that secular savior of the West, Jan Sobieski of Poland, and to Padre Mariano, a (literally) Venerable Capuchin preacher of the 1970s who was nicknamed "the TV priest." What a relief to leave behind all those skeletons—apart from the one inside you, you can't help reflecting—and to kneel in the warmth and welcome of the Presence of the Lord who conquered it all.

It is only this sort of hope—which strains through the needle's eye to spy the camel and crawls up the tree of thorns to wrestle with death, then hounds him into the depths of the earth to harrow Hell itself—that can sustain in the darkest of times, which some say are just ahead of us. When the Vicar of Christ talks of the West as caught up in a "Culture of Death," we might be forgiven for believing him. If we go further along the road of disdaining the sanctity of life and the integrity of the family, no humanistic nostalgia or secular patriotism will carry us along. The hour is now too late, the dark too thick, the fog too full of *mal-aria*, and our enemies too mixed in with our friends—while our old weapons melt away or fall from our enervated fingers. No upraised fist, or straight salute, or peace or dollar sign will drive out the chill from these bony digits. Even clenched in prayer, their flesh feels all too thin. It may be that all we leave behind in the end are our dry bones, in the gaze of impious eyes. But at the very least, we can see to it that our skeletons make up angels.

Trademark-Busting Cosmo-Style Quiz™ *#6: Where Do You Fall on the Spectrum from "Delusions of Grandeur" to "Cringe-Worthy Self-Loathing"?*

Since it's truth that sets us free, the key to attaining Humility is stark self-honesty. That demands a strong, well-developed conscience. Now, there has been plenty of confusion over the past few decades about what this word even means. To cafeteria Catholics, "conscience" is the still, small voice of a Rogerian therapist from Santa Monica, telling you, "It's okay. You're a good person. The things you want are good. Jesus would want you to have them—and have them more abundantly" (even if one of those "things" you want is someone else's spouse). On the other side of the barricade, conscience looms like a punitive superego, corroding any claim you might stake on earthly happiness, goading you into scruples that lead to despair: "Suffering is holy and redemptive. Jesus suffered. He sent you that migraine for a *reason*. Offer it up."

Now, as etymologists out there might have noticed, conscience includes the root "science," which even we English majors know has something to do with knowledge. In fact, the best translation of the word means inner, even internalized knowledge. The best way to grow and tone this muscle is through regular exercise—perhaps through the nightly use of a work like Timothy M. Gallagher, OMV, *The Examen Prayer: Ignatian Wisdom for Our Lives Today*.[4] Building up the habit of looking at yourself honestly will make it almost easy to see your virtues—if only along the way.

It might also make you a little more gracious about accepting compliments instead of engaging in the puritanical practice of insisting that the person praising you is deluded or simply lying. The side effect of this atrocious habit is to goad the well-meaning speaker into piling on the praise, almost begging you to accept it. This can be stomach turning to observe:

"You look fabulous in that outfit!"

"Oh, this old thing? It just shows off how fat I am. . . ."

"You are not fat. I'd kill for that figure."

"Kill what, a buffalo—then eat the whole thing? I look repulsive."

"You do not!"

And so on, for what seems like hours. A healthy conscience, lean and toned, will prove a much better guide, one that tells you candidly whether or not to leave the house in those chartreuse Speedos.

Here's a thought experiment that will hone your skill at sniffing out the "vain" in Vainglory.

---

4. (New York: Crossroad, 2006).

The Quiz

You've completed some creative or artistic work that has taken you many hours. It could be anything at all: your front yard garden, a picture you're drawing, a story you've written, or those awesome flames you painted around the wheel well of your family's aging Volvo. A friend comes across your achievement and praises it lavishly. You react as follows:

a. Smile slowly, comparing your own work to that of neighbors, rivals, or enemies. That flower arrangement really does remind one of certain parts of Versailles, now doesn't it? Your picture recalls Van Gogh, except without the melodrama. Your literary style has all the punch of Hemingway, sans his needless macho posturing. Your car is not only cooler looking than your brother-in-law's new Lexus, but it's also safer in a crash. You know this is true—you looked up the accident statistics and take partial credit for them, as if you were its Swedish engineer. You preen like the character of Mozart in the movie *Amadeus*, and feel as if you're talking to Salieri. "Aw shucks," you say. "This was easy. You should see what happens when I really make an effort."

b. Nod earnestly, and explain how much work you put into the project. "This kind of thing doesn't come naturally to me," you insist. "Like everything, it's 10 percent inspiration and 90 percent perspiration." Remind the listener how you poured your heart and soul out on the endeavor, and silently compare yourself not to Michelangelo but to the humble, nameless builders of the medieval Gothic cathedrals. Judge the work not by its outcome but by how many Saturday afternoons you poured out completing it, and treasure it for decades regardless of what anyone thinks of the thing. It's part of you—just like one of your children. So you're going to cosset and control it, keeping it from any possible harm—just as you do with your children.

c. Look at the finished project alongside your friend, attaining a certain distance from the thing. It's out in the world now, entirely out of your hands, and you can't really believe you're responsible for it. You see some flaws, of course, and they make you wince—but the virtues of the thing seem independent of you. You wonder at it a little, trimming leaves or kicking the tires. Didn't it somehow always already exist? You feel more as if you'd *found* the thing rather than made it. You say, "Thank God it's finished," but you're secretly kind of sad.

d. "That's very kind of you," you sigh, and pat your friend on the back. Then you point out all the flaws you fear he might have already noticed, and kick yourself for workmanship that you now see as kind of shoddy. In fact, you really can't stand having this botched project looked at for very long, so you hustle your friend out of there—and decide not to try this kind of task ever again. Why embarrass yourself that way? Leave this sort of thing to the geniuses or the professionals. (Damn them.) Then you go back to watching *The Real Housewives of Yoknapatawpha County*.

Here are the results:

- If you picked "a": You might just be delusional—a fact you can gauge from the reactions of genuine geniuses or at any rate of professionals. If your best work makes no impression on them, don't take refuge in reading old, hostile reviews of Beethoven's symphonies. Chances are, you really do suck. On the other hand, perhaps you are some sort of genius. The MacArthur Foundation has been pestering you for years, but you won't return their calls. You walked offstage from Carnegie Hall in a huff, rejected the Nobel Prize in French (just like Sartre), and put the poet laureate job on hold till you finish the score of your next oratorio. And the flames on that there Volvo really could make the cover of *Car and Driver*. If any of that is true, or even if you really do have some overpowering talent that takes folks' breath away . . . so what? Will any of that get you into heaven? Not at this rate, anyway. Think hard about how little you did to earn your gifts—which is, come to think of it, the reason we call them "gifts." It's not like you sat in the womb and listed them in some kind of registry. And just try exchanging them for something practical, like a blender. It's almost as if they weren't really yours.
- If you picked "b": You're suffering from the Puritan form of Vainglory, which values good, honest sweat over dodgy, papist vagaries like "inspiration." You're tacitly accepting here Karl Marx's "labor theory of value," which prices an item based purely on how hard and long some guy had to work to make it. So a laptop crafted by a recluse alone in his basement, in his underwear, is much more valuable than one produced efficiently by engineers and robots (never mind how well the laptop works).
- If you picked "c": You may have attained the healthy attitude that 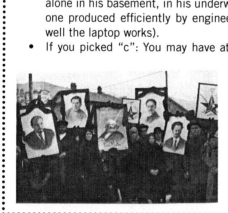 marks a humble, talented craftsman. The fact that you feel a distance from the thing made suggests that you're aware of exactly how much (or how little) you personally contributed—on top of all the natural goodness you found from the hand of God, just lying around for you to use it.

You realize that "creation" for anyone under the sun is really just a matter of creative rearrangement, and your genuine achievements aren't likely to turn your head—for instance, by convincing you that now you're an expert on public policy, qualified to testify before congressional committees on global warming, the safety of vaccination, or the optimal budgetary appropriation for government support of the arts.

- If you picked "d": You're sounding like the kind of person who put the "serf" in "servile." Consider how the self-flagellation in which you're in the habit of engaging keeps the focus on yourself. Instead of looking at the work that you've accomplished and giving God the proper credit, you're fixed on its flaws and how you're to blame for them. Preoccupation with yourself, even if you're only beating yourself up, is still a devil's trap, and it leads to a crushing sense of futility, to resentment, even to Envy. Step back and try to be grateful to God you didn't screw up even worse than you did. Then notice the good in what you made. If you have to, pretend it was made by somebody else—let's say by your friend. Would you really judge it this harshly? Now pretend you're a friend to yourself.

Activities

If you're shadowboxing with fantasies about the extent of your own attainments or tempted to give yourself credit for things that you got handed on a platter, it's critical that you shift the focus of your thoughts outward instead of inward.

❑ You can start by engaging delusional ideas—for instance, that you are Mozart—with cold compresses of reality. But move quickly on to thinking of God rather than man. Whatever it is you're good at, try doing the part you find hardest and dullest. Keep doing it till you're exhausted—remember that God finds it easy, and so do plenty of people whose skills are different from your own. And that's okay. *It's not about you.*

❑ If you're a musician, look into the mathematical roots of music theory and consider how they reflect the divine order of the cosmos. A gardener? Dig into some technical works of botany, treating them as *lectio divina*. Allow yourself to be staggered at Creation's lavish complexity and grateful that you can play a part in tending it. A car buff? Try slogging through a freshman textbook on mechanical engineering. And so on.

❑ You might also benefit from a specialized form of the examination of conscience. Make a list of the skills or attainments of which you're proudest. (This part should be fun.) In a notebook, put each one at the head of a blank page. For each one, write down not how good or great you are but how you got that way. What qualities were you *born* with, and from whom do you think you *inherited* them? What *teachers* were important to you, and what did you *learn* from each? What books did you *read*, what *mistakes* did you make, and how many times did you earn *rejection*? To whom are you most *grateful*?

❑ Conversely, if you find to your surprise that you have been sniveling, it's time to tote up, in the same kind of notebook—make it a nice, leather one, and use a fancy pen—the activities that you find easy and even fun. Through which of them have you given pleasure to other people? (Keep it clean here, folks.) Are there talents God has given you that somehow ended up getting buried? Remember how good you were at calligraphy back in grade school? Could you bone up on that again and volunteer to write invitations for charity fund-raisers? Could you practice and sing a little better in church? Or, at any rate, a little louder? What gifts could you dig up and put in the sunlight? That's the best way, really the only way, of writing a "thank-you" card to the beloved Friend who gave them.

Envy: I See You in Hell

I approach each Deadly Sin from a single, solid standpoint: that of Fallen man, lying in a ditch, who'd like to leave the mud but is unsure it's worth the climb. You might call it the "Marsh-Wiggle's Eye View." Lovers of C. S. Lewis's *Narnia* books will remember these glumly fatalistic frog-men from *The Silver Chair* and the figure of Puddleglum. A deeply dysthymic swamp-dweller, Puddleglum does yeoman's work in the story, helping rescue the captive Prince Rilian and restore good government to the coup-ridden realm of Narnia. He manages all this without betraying his native pessimism or even breaking a smile.

I don't know if Lewis was trying to inspire children of the melancholic temperament or simply to offer a hero for spiritually sluggish moderns. But at most of the parishes I've attended throughout my life, the pews have been groaning with Marsh-Wiggles, who rise for the Gospel reluctantly, sometimes sighing, and wince as they drop their weekly $1 into the basket. The only prayer that they answer with any enthusiasm is, "The Mass is ended, go in peace," to which they practically bellow, "Thanks be to GOD!" as they head for the doors. Of course, my sample is far from scientific. I'm sure that there are parishes full of tambourine-rattling, glad-handing singers of ditties like "On Eagle's Wings." I wouldn't know. I've always avoided the charismatics, secure in my own identity as a deeply phlegmatic Catholic—the kind that seeks a mystical union between his buttocks and the pew.

As Puddleglum might point out, with this chapter we reach a low point—with the one sin St. Thomas Aquinas considered entirely devoid of anything good, namely Envy. He defined this vice concisely as

"sadness at another's good." Put that way, this vice seems to amount to an almost pure form of malevolence. As always, St. Thomas makes the critical distinctions that save us from dangerous scruples:

> Such sadness may happen in four ways. In one way, when you grieve at another's good inasmuch as therein you have cause to fear for yourself, or for other good men. Such sadness is not envy, and may be without sin. Hence Gregory says: "It often happens, without loss of charity, that an enemy's downfall delights us; and without reproach of envy, his elevation makes us sad: because by his fall we think that some are raised up, who deserve to be raised; and by his advancement we fear that many may be unjustly oppressed."[1]

So it's okay to cackle savagely when candidates with evil views get only 19 percent of the vote and leaders with wholesome programs fully compatible with our Faith take power. Not that this ever happens, but it's nice to know the theory, just in case hockey catches on in Hell.

Aquinas continues,

> In another way we may be saddened at another's good, not because he has the good, but because the good that he has is wanting to us; and this is properly emulation. If this emulation is about the goods of virtue, it is praiseworthy, according to the text: "Be emulous of the better gifts." But if it is about temporal goods, it may or may not be sinful.

So when your best friend drops *way* more pounds through his exercise program than you do through your TV programs, your "sadness" might be good, bad, or

---

1. Joseph Rickaby, S.J., trans., *Aquinas Ethicus: Or, the Moral Teaching of St. Thomas. A Translation of the Principal Portions of the Second Part of the Summa Theologica, with Notes* (London: Burns and Oates, 1892), article I. Available online at http://oll.libertyfund.org. All subsequent citations are from the same article.

indifferent—depending on for what (or for whom) you wish you could lose the weight. If I might ask . . . is he or she *married*?

On the next point, St. Thomas for once parts company with Aristotle:

> In a third way a man is saddened at another's good, inasmuch as the person to whom the good comes is unworthy of it. [Such sadness concerns] riches and such-like gifts, as may accrue both to worthy and unworthy. This sadness, according to the Philosopher, is called righteous indignation, and is a point of virtue.

Sounds logical, doesn't it? So do we have permission to resent the comfy lifestyles of worldly, wealthy neighbors? Alas, not so fast, insists Aquinas, who rebukes

> those who have not an eye for eternal goods. But according to the teaching of faith, the increase of temporal goods in unworthy hands is directed by the just ordinance of God either to the correction of the enjoyers of them or to their condemnation; and such goods are as nothing in comparison with the good things to come, that are reserved for the good. And therefore such sadness as this is forbidden in Holy Scripture, according to the text: "Be not emulous of evil-doers, nor envy them that work iniquity."

But it's the final, fourth brand of "sadness" that St. Thomas condemns as the pathogen Envy:

> In a fourth way a man may be sad at the goods of another inasmuch as that other surpasses him in good things; and this is properly envy, and is always evil, because it is grief over that which is matter of rejoicing, namely, our neighbour's good.

So while other vices amount to exaggerations or distortions of wholesome appetites—for marital bliss, glory, or justice—pure Envy craves *evil for its own sake*. We're not just talking jealousy here; in the sinful sense, jealousy means that we see what other people have and wish we had the same or a little bit better. I might see Brad Pitt and Angelina Jolie together on television and somehow convince myself that I deserved a wife that voluptuous, with even puffier lips. I might think of the goofiest things Pitt has said over the years and imagine how much more entertaining I would prove by the poolside—if only I could somehow get to the side of their pool, past all that security. . . . My feelings would add up to jealousy and covetousness, marking me as a creepy, potential stalker. But it need not entail any Envy.

For that to enter the picture, I'd have to follow the details of their marriage and take delight in the troubles they encountered—to gloat over gossip columns describing their public quarrels, to chuckle when Brad lost a coveted role or Angelina put on some weight. Likewise if I consoled myself for the glamour and luxury they enjoy by chronicling their spiritual deficits, in the manner of certain pious scolds I've known. *Yeah, enjoy those Mediterranean beach vacations, Brad. Come Judgment Day, you're headed for someplace a whole lot hotter.*

Now, you needn't be a solitary bachelor crank to enjoy such consolations. Envy is less like chemotherapy than aspirin—an all-purpose pain reliever. I've known married, orthodox Catholics with large families who compensate for the fact that they drive a battered, crap-brown minivan crammed with squabbling toddlers by speculating about the contraceptive habits—and spiritual state—of richer folks with fewer kids. These pious folks mutter, "That Prius should read, 'I ♥ the Culture of Death.'"

I've known working-class Catholics to visit a parish in a posh neighborhood, then spend the Mass pricing people's personal appearances: "Surely, Lord, those implants could have been sold and the proceeds given to the poor."

I don't know anyone personally—I steer clear of people like this—but the Internet is full of "social justice" activists who resent the hard-won, quite recent prosperity of the First World, in general, and our country, in particular. They lobby for wholesale foreign aid and open borders to rectify a perceived injustice they can neither define nor delimit. They just know that it's massive, that the claims of the global poor must always be answered and the "selfishness" of the wealthy sternly rebuked.

The financially "privileged" have essentially no rights, and the only Christian thing for them to do would be to turn over their ill-gotten gains and go live in some favela. That would serve them right. . . .

How about Latin Mass Catholics whose bishops have shunted them off to mental hospital chapels or funeral crypts—who mutter with grim satisfaction at the news that the diocese got slammed with another abuse suit and will have to close a "modernist" parish in the suburbs? I personally have taken pungent delight in reading how apostate religious orders are now devoid of vocations and chuckled at the thought of elderly heretics frying up cat food.

There really is nobody out there whose life doesn't look a bit brighter when his neighbors are viewed through jaundice-colored glasses. Millionaires are free to envy billionaires, and billionaires envy vampires, since the latter never have to die—unless, of course, some envious mortal sneaks up behind them with a stake. . . .

Even deeply spiritual people can benefit from Envy. We've all read in stories of the saints how their principal persecutors were often their superiors or their fellow monks and nuns. We've read about John of the Cross, or Bernadette of Lourdes . . . and we've always sided with the saint. But let's turn things around for once. Just imagine what it would be like to spend your life in a scratchy habit, having taken on the "evangelical counsels" of poverty, chastity, and obedience—thereby renouncing the three consolations that make fleshly life worth living in the first place. You've done all that: check, check, check. You're spending your life behind bars, and you've put yourself there on purpose.

Now who toddles in, but some bizarre, prophetic figure whom God visits personally or to whom He sends His mom. The whole world is begging this person for her prayers or waiting for his next book. This busybody buttinsky may even be trying to reform your religious order. (In John of the Cross's case, he was depriving Carmelites of their shoes.) What's left to do but to wonder if his inspirations are really authentic? The devil comes garbed as an angel of light, you know. Best to test his sincerity from time to time to see how humble he really is. Sure, you'll be inflicting some suffering in the process—but isn't that spiritually edifying? You're helping him get to Heaven. Heh, heh, heh.

In a convent or cubicle, comparing your own achievements and enjoyments with other people's is perfectly natural—in the same sense that death is natural and for the same historical reasons (e.g., the Fall). And it serves a purpose. Envy keeps the economy moving, keeps us piling on the debt that cannot be seen to fund the purchases we flaunt. Envy is patriotic, since it helps us expand our government. It helps move wealth from selfish private hands into the coffers of the commonwealth, where honest citizens can stake their equal claims to a share of the stash. Envy comforts the lonely, consoles the slacker, and fills the prodigal and the shiftless with good things, while the rich it sends away empty.

It's a damned shame that Envy's a deadly sin—the deadliest of the seven, the Deadly Sin that goaded Lucifer, who envied the glory of God. What in Hell would we do without it?

Lilies That Fester: Spiritualized Envy

If you haven't read *The Screwtape Letters*, you should. In fact, put this book down right now, get hold of C. S. Lewis's harrowing look inside of the mind of a "designated tempter" (he's just like a guardian angel, except . . . the opposite), then pick me up when you are finished. It's key to advancing in the spiritual life to know, deep down in your bones, just what you're up against. We face, in our attempts to cooperate with Grace, determined attempts at sabotage by the most brilliant intellect ever created. As St. Cyril of Jerusalem warned, "The Dragon is by the side of the road, watching those who pass. Beware lest he devour you. We go to the Father of Souls, but it is necessary to pass by the dragon."

As we scramble up from the fallenness we're born in, weighed down by all the neuroses, habits, and rationalizations we've picked up through the years, blown hither and thither by the windbags who dominate our culture, the ground we walk is strewn with booby traps. As we try to ascend from ordinary worldliness, our efforts do not go unnoticed. The cold Spirit who threw away beatitude watches us like a scientist goading rats toward electric shocks. He's driven to persecute us by a galling, eternal Envy of the happiness we were promised, which he perfectly remembers, craves, and hates. While we were still wallowing down in the mires of sensuality or resentment, he could snicker and turn his back. But as we clamber to the middle heights on the way to true friendship with Christ, we begin to attract his attention. Our cases cease to be cold, and our files are sucked through the vast, pneumatic ducts of Hell to the desks of more talented tempters. That's when the real "fun" begins.

For a certain type of Catholic, this is when his sincere outrage at the crazed, depressing hedonism that rules the airwaves and the Internet can screw him up into a Puritan, even a world-hating Gnostic. I've read ultra-Traditionalist authors who are so appalled at the modern West's sterile sex cult that they've blundered into heresy—like the elderly lady author who wrote in the Catholic paper the *Remnant* that sexuality hadn't simply

been corrupted by the Fall. Sex, she opined, was the *result* of the Fall, imposed by an angry Creator to mock man's attempts at becoming "like unto God" by driving him to rut like the other beasts. Needless to say, this writer trashed attempts by Pope John Paul II to recover a healthy reverence for sex; in fact, she rejected St. Thomas Aquinas's teaching that marital union is the ordinary means of grace for the sacrament. Such assertions, she scoffed, were merely an attempt by misguided Christians to baptize the "pagan sex cults" of the ancient world. To this, the orthodox answer, of course, is that those very cults were themselves a perversion of the holiness God intended to attach to the marital act. . . .

But why bother arguing? We're not facing here an intellectual difficulty but a spiritual snare, which captured the author and threatens us. Outraged at the sinful abuse of a Created good, she rejects its proper use—imputing evil to those who enjoy it. Married couples who claim that their lovemaking brings them closer to each other and to God? She dismisses them as self-deluded neopagans. Much better, she says, to admit that even marital intercourse is typically at least venially sinful (something St. Augustine said, in a momentary backslide to his Manichaean years) and try to minimize the damage. Close your eyes and focus on procreation. . . .

Another type of Catholic traumatized by the sex wars becomes a different sort of scold—adopting those few tenets of feminism that haven't been solemnly condemned and using Catholic moral teaching as a scourge with which to flog men, in general, and male sexuality, in particular (see Chapter 1). If you ever meet someone who calls herself (or much, more creepily, *himself*) a "new feminist," prepare to be

power-hosed with this stuff. Such a person may think he's "evangelizing the culture" by adopting its idols and then trying to baptize them, but real feminists aren't impressed; they assert, with perfect justice, that full and unrestricted "reproductive rights" (birth control and abortion) are central tenets of feminism. Without them, the situation between the sexes, thanks to the biological consequences of *sex*, will forever be unequal. Since feminism, like Marxism, is focused on obsessively *weighing the power relationships* among people and stoking Envy among the weak, claiming to be a "pro-life feminist" makes as much sense as calling yourself a "free-market Marxist."

Again, you can try to argue all this and point out that the Fall affected both sexes equally, but you won't get very far. You aren't dealing with bad ideas so much as wounded pride, shriveled hopes, long-treasured grudges, or the scars left on the person from his own or others' sins—all helped to fester by a Tempter who learned that spiritualizing Envy is a sure-fire way to steer aspiring saints from holiness back toward hellfire.

The tendency toward spiritualizing Envy extends far beyond the bedroom. It's common for Catholics who've climbed free of gross materialism (see Chapter 7) and tried to cultivate a Christlike love for the poor, to lurch without even noticing it into a slow, burning resentment for the "rich." It's easy to snipe at the leftist academic who rants about his old classmates from college who chose to be stockbrokers, then shows up at class reunions wearing his Sunday worst so he can scoff at their snazzy suits. More insidious, and more to our point, is the dark temptation that drives initially well-meaning Catholics—often addled by the unprincipled and silly social justice documents churned out by hapless prelates—to set themselves up in *judgment over others*. Which is, as I seem to recall, one of the few things Christ specifically told us not to do (Mt 7:1).

We never know, really—unless he is running for president—how much of someone's income he gives to charity. Nor can we tell whether the posh person in the next pew (whose Italian suit distracts us all through the Canon) is wearing clothes he bought for work, which he needs to live out his vocation. Is it any of our *business* if someone who has worked hard and saved his money buys a house that's larger than we think he needs? What possible *spiritual good* can come from dwelling on such questions or congratulating ourselves for our relative penury? At best, this kind of thinking tempts us to the deadly sin of Envy. At worst, it can lead us to act unjustly—on a small scale, by loathing our neighbor whose only sin was to succeed and, on a large scale, by adopting coercive politics that claim, in the name of justice, the right to confiscate other people's money. I've known souls who started by trying to cultivate a Franciscan love of the poor and even of the freedom St. Francis[2] found in "Lady Poverty," who ended up hating wealth and then the wealthy. From a holy, ascetic aversion to the snares of worldliness, they stumbled into a dark, malicious resentment of the consolations enjoyed by others. Caressing their moral superiority

---

2. St. Francis threw off worldly wealth but warned his monks of the danger of begrudging those who hadn't. Those followers of his (the Fraticelli or "spirituals") who went on to condemn private property as sinful were condemned as heretics.

muscle in solitary ecstasy, they're having far more fun than the hapless golf players over at the country club, whom now they hate.

Let's remember which Spirit dwells in poverty, cold, and darkness, consumed by rage at the calm beatitude of the saints. It is he who takes delight in short, unhappy lives attended by illness, hunger, and toil. In the last century, social and political programs whose origin lies in Hell helped spread these stern "blessings" to tens of millions who otherwise might have enjoyed modest prosperity. If you care to read about these people and their fate, you can look them up in *The Black Book of Communism*.[3] Diluted, generic versions of this colossal, concentrated evil are still on sale at political drugstores, under brand names like "social justice," "multiculturalism," and "diversity." We all know their side effects, both for society and the soul.

The Amazing Catholic BS Generator™

This is the kind of subject one writes about with Kinky Friedman (see Chapter 2) blasting in the background, so that's how it is meant to be read. Otherwise, the experience might prove a little too painful. So crank up "Homo Erectus," grab a bourbon, and I'll explain to you the workings of the Catholic BS Generator™. It's the only explanation I can think of for how the deadly sin of Envy worms its way into the nooks and crannies of Catholic discourse, undetected and rarely challenged. Some 90 percent of references to "social justice" came straight out of this machine, and the word "solidarity" or "compassion" in the title of a document is pretty much the equivalent of a trademark. As in "U.S. Catholic Conference Joint Statement on Compassion and Solidarity with the Marginalized.[BS]"

The BS Generator was invented in the 1960s, but it didn't come from Ronco, the folks who brought millions of bloodshot, white-knuckled insomniacs the joys of the Pocket Fisherman. In fact, there's no single tinkerer who can claim sole credit for

---

3. Mark Kramer et al., *The Black Book of Communism* (Cambridge, MA: Harvard University Press, 1999).

the BS Generator. Like eugenics and the A-bomb, it was developed by a team. Its function is to take the complex and deeply considered doctrines of a two thousand-year-old, divinely revealed religion and turn them into dinosaur-shaped nuggets. Like chunks of squirrel, they taste a little like . . . chicken.

Our BS Generator is distinct in structure, design, and output from competitors that serve other faiths. The Evangelical Balderdash Fulminator helps divorced

pastors of megachurches churn out press releases supporting reckless wars and the rape of nature—*since the devil planted them T. rex fossils, and Jaysus is comin' soon!* The B'nai B'rith *Drek Fabrik* produces whole magazines devoted to proving how heterosexual marriage laws caused the Holocaust. The Mormons. . . . Okay, that's just not fair.

But I'm kind of partial to our own papist device. It does my Catholic heart proud to see what we've come up with. It whirs at every level of discourse, from the bloviations of bishops, down through Catholic columnists, to ordinary bloggers and pastors in the pulpit. Large sections of those helpful documents produced by America's bishops in the 1970s and 1980s on economics and politics were clearly squeezed out of the BS Generator, as were their more-recent statements on immigration.

In *The Faithful Departed*, Philip Lawler (see Chapter 11) shows how the BS Generator enabled various bishops to write earnest thank-you notes to pedophile priests, praising them for their "ministry"—and vague, reassuring letters to anguished parents that spoke of "compassion," "therapy," and "legitimate concerns."

Here's how the BS Generator works: presented with a complicated problem that requires balancing the interests of groups with competing claims, it will draw selectively on biblical references and Church documents to churn out rhetoric that simultaneously

1. clouds essential distinctions in a mauve emotive haze;
2. suits the user's political sympathies, institutional interests, or unspoken Envy;
3. presents the speaker as a gentle, vulnerable soul who's acting only out of compassion, whose motives it would be wantonly cruel to question;
4. casts his opponents as blind, cruel, or hypocritical;
5. pretends it is not attacking anyone but gently and bravely pointing to "deeper truths," hence any polemical reply amounts to beating up on Jesus.

I saw the BS Generator operating full throttle in an exchange I had with a group of other frustrated commentors and one Catholic columnist over illegal immigration.

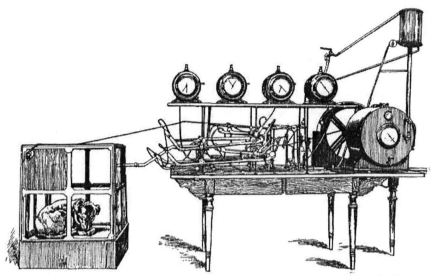

SMALL RESPIRATION-APPARATUS IN THE MUNICH PHYSIOLOGICAL INSTITUTE.

In that article and in his comments on my own article, in cringe-worthy, moralistic prose, the writer excoriates, in turn, the following:

- America for causing poverty in Mexico
- Europe for causing poverty in Africa
- All middle-class Americans for living a "sinful lifestyle." (I guess that includes my sister, who works sixty-hour weeks as a nurse treating illegal immigrants who get free medical care from the taxpayers. After all, my sister has cable TV.)
- Any American concerned about the social problems caused by immigration
- All the residents of Scottsdale, Arizona

When commentors responded to these wild attacks with facts, logical syllogisms, and direct quotations from binding Catholic teaching, the writer responded with the mewl of a wounded bully, "Why are you so hostile? Why are you addressing me as if we are fighting?" Why, indeed?

In case they don't have one at your parish, here's how to build a Catholic BS Generator from ordinary items you'll find around the house.

All the moving parts are ordinary words, wrenched out of context and used to suit a polemical purpose. When arguing with someone, be sure to use the following terms at regular intervals in your sentences

(don't worry about the grammar): *voiceless, afflicted, disadvantaged, marginalized, pastoral, handicapped, undocumented, diverse, needy,* and *displaced.*

Anything you are defending, characterize with words like these. For instance, tenured homosexuals living in Cambridge, Massachusetts, pouring the money they don't need to spend on diapers into overseas investments are *really* "individuals whose personal choices of whom to love have rendered them *marginalized* and *voiceless* in a *heterosexist* world." A drug lord scheduled for deportation back to Colombia is, in fact, "a *displaced, undocumented* Latino business owner subject to America's draconian drug laws." A Somali refugee who's collecting disability for a minor injury while working side jobs off the books can come across as "a *handicapped* African American struggling to support his *needy* family." A pedophile priest who molested your son is really, the bishop explains, "a brother in Christ *afflicted* by a serious mental *handicap* with which he struggles prayerfully with the *pastoral* support of our Christian *community.*"

Conversely, if you need to attack someone or something, employ any or all of these pejoratives: *comfortable, bourgeois, secure, smug, materialistic, consumerist, careerist, racist, xenophobic,* and *suburban.* Hence, a family where both parents work to pay Catholic school tuition so their kids won't get stabbed by gangbangers are really "*middle-class suburbanites* whose attitudes are centered on a fear of *diversity.*" See how it works? Anyone who has worked hard, built a career, and moved to a city where you can't afford an apartment can be characterized as "a *comfortable materialist* engaged in the *consumerist* pursuit of a worldly lifestyle incompatible with Gospel values." And so on.

Remember that you, too, are *marginalized* and *disadvantaged* by your courageous embrace of the *needy* and *voiceless,* uttered in bold defiance of a *smug* and *materialistic* society, which cruelly and in plain violation of the commandments of Jesus Christ won't give you a stipend so you can sit around all day in your Spiderman pajamas writing blogs in a nice *suburban* house in Scottsdale, Arizona.

Stalin's Trollop: The Envy of Lillian Hellman

In analyzing Envy, we must look beyond the obvious. It's true that this sin is specially tempting to life's apparent "losers"—to those with fewer natural gifts of talent and treasure, of looks or smarts. But Greed isn't limited to the rich, nor is Envy owned by those enumerated in Marty Haugen's catchy, godless Communion hymn, "Gather Us In." (I quote from memory.)

> Gather us in, the ugly and stupid
> Gather us in, the drunk and insane
> Those whose brains by Meth are polluted
> We are the ciphers who blather in
>   vain. . . .

Envy is a festering spiritual sore equally common among the elite, at least those afflicted by what Catholic anthropologist René Girard[4] called "mimetic desire." We see what others have and crave it—but a slightly higher-end model. And if we can't get it, we'll settle for dragging our rivals down through gossip, office politics, or friv-

LILLIAN HELLMAN

PENTIMENTO

olous litigation. From the courts of Renaissance Europe to the soirees of Hollywood, the "insiders" of society have displayed capital sin as vividly as the habitués of any Ozarks trailer park, and often with deeper malice.

C. S. Lewis warned of a genus of Envy linked closely to elitism. In any given social group, one hungers to join the ranks of the insiders who make up its Inner Ring:

> I believe that in all men's lives . . . one of the most dominant elements is the desire to be inside the local Ring and the terror of being left outside. . . .
>
> I have no right to make assumptions about the degree to which any of you may already be compromised. I must not assume that you have ever first neglected, and finally shaken off, friends whom you really loved and who might have lasted you a lifetime, in order to court the friendship of those who appeared to you more important, more esoteric. I must not ask whether you have ever derived actual pleasure from the loneliness and humiliation of the outsiders after you yourself were in: whether you have talked to fellow members of the Ring in the presence of outsiders

---

4. Nota bene to those of you who happen (God help you) to be enrolled in grad school for literature: Girard is a world-famous literary critic who reverted to the Catholic Faith. But the critical establishment doesn't seem to have realized it yet, so you can rely on him as a source for your academic papers without earning an ideological "F." Make full use of him before he's sniffed out and stuffed down the memory hole like Cleanth Brooks and Robert Penn Warren. And for God's sake, find a more hopeful line of work. There are coal mines hiring in Kentucky. . . .

simply in order that the outsiders might envy; whether the means whereby, in your days of probation, you propitiated the Inner Ring, were always wholly admirable. I will ask only one question—and it is, of course, a rhetorical question which expects no answer. In the whole of your life as you now remember it, has the desire to be on the right side of that invisible line ever prompted you to any act or word on which, in the cold small hours of a wakeful night, you can look back with satisfaction? If so, your case is more fortunate than most.[5]

With his typical psychological insight into evil, culled from a lifetime spent among academics, Lewis here points to what we might call the Envy of *influence*, a trait that links the socialite lounging by poolside with the ambitious chimpanzee keen on toppling a higher status male or the meerkat mother who commandeers the "mansion" by eating another's young.

Which brings us to Lillian Hellman. A playwright of modest talents, she first made her name in 1934 with the drama *The Children's Hour*, which depicted a vicious boarding school girl who covers for her misdeeds by falsely charging her headmistresses with lesbianism. Hellman's depiction of self-serving viciousness and callous lying might seem like the keen insight of a literary moralist—until we sit down next to Lillian on the divan and get to know her a little better.

Born to wealth in New Orleans, Hellman attended and dropped out of both New York University and Columbia University before moving to Hollywood, where she attached herself to the successful dipsomaniac, Marxist detective novelist, and screenwriter Dashiell Hammett. Their affair continued for more than thirty years, and while Hellman was rarely faithful, she gained an iron control over Hammett's career. Hammett paid tribute to Hellman in the figure of Nora Charles—an elegant, glamorous amateur detective who'd be played in the movies by Myrna Loy.

He was clearly besotted. As Rhoda Koenig of *The Independent* (UK) wrote of Hellman,

---

5. C. S. Lewis, "The Inner Ring" (Memorial Lecture, King's College, University of London, 1944), available at http://www.lewissociety.org/innerring.php.

She was no beauty, even when young (when old, it was said she looked like George Washington, or Casey Stengel, the manager of the Mets baseball team), but never let that stop her from having plenty of men—rich men, successful men, men several decades younger. Well into her seventies she was the talk of Manhattan for not only purring huskily to young men at parties but flashing her silk knickers. (October 3, 2001)

The next time you have a problem with Lust, there's a visual that should help you.

A youthful convert to orthodox Communism, Hellman never wavered in her loyalty to the Moscow Party Line. She whitewashed the artificial famine in Ukraine (see Chapter 3), praised the grotesque Purge Trials, and backed Stalin's alliance with Hitler. She called on the U.S. government to deny asylum to Stalin's rival, Trotsky—

who fled instead to Mexico, where Soviet agents assassinated him. Honoring the Hitler-Stalin pact, she joined the Communist-sponsored Keep America Out of War Committee (which promptly dissolved when Hitler invaded Russia) and lauded Stalin's invasion of neutral Finland.

When the House Committee on Un-American Activities, founded in 1938 to hunt down elusive Hollywood fascists, turned its gaze in 1947 on the abundant Communists serving the "workers' cause" at the Polo Lounge, Hellman took the grandstand. In a later memoir, she'd claim that she told the Committee, "I cannot and will not cut my conscience to fit this year's fashions."

And that much was true. She ordered her conscience straight from Moscow. As she stood up for the inalienable right of cosseted screenwriters to get rich writing scripts they'd vetted with Soviet spies, Hellman oozed approval of Communist puppet regimes from Eastern Europe to China. She denounced Roger Straus (of Farrar, Straus, and Giroux) for publishing Alexander Solzhenitsyn's work. In fact, she created her own little KGB in the publishing world, keeping hostile books out of print and hounding her enemies. As Koenig recalls, "When a journalist wrote a piece she disliked, she told him that if he didn't print a retraction she would tell his employer (this was when such things mattered) that he frequented gay bars. It was no coincidence that the plot of all Hellman's hit plays turned on blackmail."

In 1967, Hellman served as executor for the estate of her old friend Dorothy Parker. According to the Web site of the Dorothy Parker Society,

Her will was plain and simple. With no heirs, she left her literary estate to Dr. Martin Luther King, Jr. She'd never met the civil rights activist, but always felt strongly for social justice. She named the acerbic author Lillian Hellman as her executor. . . .

Within a year of her death, Dr. King was assassinated, and the Parker estate rolled over to the National Association for the Advancement of Colored People. To this day, the NAACP benefits from the royalty of all Parker publications and productions.

Hellman went to court to fight the NAACP over Parker's literary estate. Hellman lost in 1972 when a judge ruled that she should be removed from executorship. Hellman was adamant that she get Parker's money, and came out of the mess painted as a racist. She was sure the will was supposed to give her a huge sum. Hellman said, "She must have been drunk when she did it."

Nor was Hellman much more faithful in disposing of Parker herself:

Parker didn't want a funeral, but Hellman held one anyway, and made herself the star attraction. . . . Parker was cremated June 9, 1967, at Ferncliff Crematory in Hartsdale, New York. Hellman, who made all the funeral arrangements, never told the crematory what to do with the ashes. So they sat on a shelf in Hartsdale. Six years later, on July 16, 1973, the ashes were mailed to Mrs. Parker's lawyer's offices, O'Dwyer and Bernstein, 99 Wall Street. Paul O'Dwyer, her attorney, didn't know what to do with the little box of ashes. It sat on a shelf, on a desk, and for 15 years, in a filing cabinet.

Hellman restored her fortunes with a series of gossipy, name-dropping memoirs that centered on her heroic struggle for social justice and her glamorous Hollywood romances. The memoirs were riddled with half-truths, smears of anti-Communist liberals, and outright fabrications. Hellman's boldest lie came in the second volume, *Pentimento*, where she claimed that she'd spent the 1930s smuggling money into Europe via an underground agent named "Julia" to rescue Jews and dissidents from the Nazis. With Hellman's help, a film was made of the story, starring Vanessa Redgrave—which raised one little problem: the real Julia, a New York psychiatrist named Muriel Gardiner, saw the movie and went to the press. She'd never gotten any help from Lillian Hellman—although they'd shared the same lawyer, who probably passed her story on to Hellman.

Hellman's torrent of tall tales irked the novelist Mary McCarthy, whose carefully crafted works that admitted to being fiction barely paid her rent, so on the *Dick Cavett Show* in 1979, McCarthy said of Hellman, "Every word she writes is a lie, including *and* and *the*."

Hellman answered this wisecrack with a libel case. As Carl Rollyson writes, "Hellman filed a lawsuit, engaging as her counsel a close friend, Ephraim London, who charged her no fee. Hellman wanted to ruin McCarthy by driving up her legal fees, and she made no secret of the fact that she was out for blood" (*New York Sun*, November 25, 2005).

Hellman pursued the case for five long years, until she finally died in 1984. Koenig comments,

> How ironic . . . her last act the persecution of a fellow writer. Then living in New York, I never much cared for Mary McCarthy, but was outraged that no one was helping her. "Why don't we all say that Hellman is a liar?" I asked the editor of a literary magazine. "If everyone wrote the same thing, she couldn't sue us all, and what we said could be used by the defence." He patted my hand and smiled.
>
> "It's very simple," he said. "Everybody's afraid of Lillian, and nobody really likes Mary."

14

Pack a Magnum in Your Animus

The answer to Envy isn't, as many moderns think, self-loathing Servility. Instead, the Church suggests we should cultivate the Virtue of Magnanimity. Taken literally, this means we should *expand our souls* and acquire the virtuous habit of reaching out toward great things, to achievements that advance the good. If Envy amounts to looking at others and wishing to drag them down, Magnanimity requires that we see others and wish them well. This applies even to our enemies, whom we shouldn't give the power to drag us down to their level. If you need a visual here, imagine that a band of idiots starts pelting you with dog turds. Is the answer to drop to your hands and knees to scramble for the same kind of ammo? In most cases, no.

Nor is it quite enough to walk off sniffily, dripping contempt—but secretly fuming, planning higher-order, tidier vengeance. Instead, we're called by Christ to shrug off insults, forgive, and (when it's prudent) *forget* the slights we suffer. Instead of repaying injuries with interest, we should expand and elevate the objects of our attention and, in a high-minded spirit, wish the best for everyone—even our enemies.

And the best thing for anyone, of course, is eternal salvation. So that's the place to start, by "praying for those who persecute you." You might have to do this with gritted teeth at first, and don't become scrupulous or surrender if your sentiments never fall in line with your will. Twenty years later, your stomach might still knot up and your fists clench when you remember that grammar school sociopath who dunked your head in the toilet, the pastor who ripped out your parish's Gothic altar, or the college boyfriend who dumped you to marry your wealthy, widowed mom. There's no need to confess this.

Remember that anger at evil isn't sinful—in fact, it's rational and right, and suppressing it is a sickly symptom of Servility. The sin starts when you stop there—and pretend that the person can be summed up, entirely and for eternity, by his sin. That's the kind of "judging" Christ means when He says, "Judge not, lest ye be judged." (Mt 7:1) We're meant to register and learn from sins we witness, make notes to ourselves that help us avoid being victimized, and sometimes to call the cops. What we can't do is wish for the wholesale destruction of our enemies, as Prince Hamlet did when he caught his murderous uncle praying—and deferred his execution, for fear that if he killed him on the spot, the old man would go to Heaven. Even the old-school IRA[1] did better than that, typically waiting to assassinate its enemies until

---

1. In the 1920s. By the 1970s, they were a band of murdering Marxist thugs.

they emerged from confession on Saturday afternoons. If terrorist gangs can keep some vestige of charity, maybe we can, too. Think of it as starting small, and make this affirmation every morning: "*Just for today*, I will be as charitable as the IRA." Just for today.

St. Thomas follows Aristotle's lead in defining Magnanimity as the orientation of the soul toward great things rather than petty, and honorable actions instead of squalid ones. But Aquinas had to wrestle with the unembarrassed love that pagan Greeks took in public glory—seeing it as the reward due to men of greatness, which they could rightly seek. Inspired by the examples of Homer's heroes such as Achilles who preferred a short life with glory to a long life without it, Greek leaders and Roman generals expected lavish public triumphs in their honor, and in the end, Roman emperors demanded to be worshiped as living gods. Much as we love our classical inheritance, I'm afraid we Christians must draw the line somewhere short of this, and St. Thomas found the way to square the circle. As Mary M. Keys of Notre Dame observed in a stellar essay on the subject,[2] Aquinas rescued Magnanimity—the crowning human Virtue, according to Aristotle—and baptized it by pairing it with Humility. We should glory in what goodness or greatness we really do have, attributing it to God—and humbly admit our sins and flaws, accepting the blame for them ourselves. In looking at others, we can hate the sins for which they're responsible but love the sinners as creatures of God.

This might not sound easy or pleasant, but in fact, it's not so bad. Let's use an extreme example, one where human evil reaches perhaps the greatest depth imaginable. That's right, again I mean Lillian Hellman. Having just picked our way through the medical waste dumpster that is her legacy and used calipers to hold up for your instruction each atrocity, I'd find it easy and fun to picture the fate that likely awaited her in eternity. (Were I poor Mary McCarthy, this might prove irresistible—but I wouldn't consider her culpable.) In fact, I was tempted to do just this, using Photoshop to place Hellman squarely inside one of Gustave Doré's engravings of the *Inferno*, perhaps as one of the Harpies. Perhaps you're disappointed that I didn't.

Sorry, guys. There's a moment when proper disgust at sins shades over into sinful hatred of the sinner, and whenever I cross that line I feel the damp brush of a cold and leathery wing. The same Enemy of the human race who chuckled over each of Hellman's malices would take delight in mine. By gloating or raging at her, I would, in some small way, become more like her. Flip back to her picture, folks. You really don't want to go there.

What's more, once we've learned all we can from studying an evil, fixing our attention on it is time poured down a very dark hole, into sheer perversion and negation. If we turn from a sinner's acts to her nature as a thwarted child of God, we're turning back toward the light. Whatever lingering disgust or righteous anger we feel, we're starting to think about God, instead of a scary-looking actress.

---

2. Mary M. Keys, "A 'Monkish Virtue' Outside the Monastery: On the Social and Civic Value of Humility" (working paper, the Religion and Culture Web Forum, University of Chicago, May 2004).

Against Unselfishness

If you wish to obey Christ by loving your enemies, you'd best make sure that you're not one of them—for instance, through a sickly lack of self-love. In an otherwise excellent book on Catholic social teaching, *Human Goods, Economic Evils*,[3] economist Edward Hadas made a statement that goaded me to think more deeply about this question. After rightly trashing the utilitarianism of Jeremy Bentham, Hadas declared, "A more Christian analysis suggests that men should search for the greatest good, which involves a *profound denial of all selfishness and self-interest*" (emphasis added).

At first blush, this suggests that Christian ethics really are something like Ayn Rand's (see Chapter 11) caricature of "altruism," which she pillories at tedious length throughout her novels. To move many notches up the scale of literary quality, this is the variety of Christianity that motivates the self-extinguishing clergymen in Jean Raspail's prophetic novel, *The Camp of the Saints*—who welcome the conquest of the West by Moslems and Hindus, all in the name of selflessness. It is the same "unselfishness" that C. S. Lewis's devil advocates in *The Screwtape Letters*.

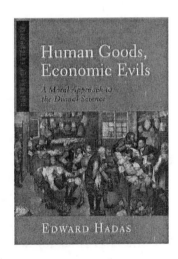

If I could add a few qualifiers to Hadas's language, such as "denial of unjust selfishness" or "distorted self-interest," I could adopt his statement and move on. But given his use of "profound," I don't think he'd let me, and because of that the point is worth arguing.

Are Christians really called to a profound denial of all self-interest? In the most fundamental task that faces any of us, seeking eternal salvation, our first motive is the pursuit of eternal happiness with God. This is no hedonistic or shallow search for satisfaction but the proper functioning of a human will as it seeks the goal for which it was created, which God Himself surrounded with rewards that redound to the self and to no one else—since God doesn't need us. The alternative, damnation, is equally hedged around with punishments that one will endure by oneself. It seems that the divine

---

3. Edward Hadas, *Human Goods, Economic Evils* (Wilmington, DE: Intercollegiate Studies Institute Press, 2007).

economy itself is set up based on the assumption that man will pursue happiness and shun unhappiness, and this is as it should be. In the writings of the most mystical of saints, we occasionally find a saint who actually ceases to care about the happiness of heaven—so pure is his love of God. However, that is a difference of emphasis, not a contradiction. Where mystics like the Quietists have arisen who actually professed that they did not care whether their souls were damned or saved, they were excommunicated. A certain eternal self-seeking is not just permitted; it seems to be commanded. Jesus was not averse to offering punishments and rewards—a fact for which Nietzsche condemned Him.

Let's move to more controversial ground: the natural order. If man is to reject all self-interest, this must include every sphere of life—including the realm of eros. On a radically altruistic analysis such as this, none of us should seek out the company of people whose conversation we enjoy or wed those to whom we are attracted. Instead, we ought to mortify such selfish inclinations and seek out the loneliest person we can find. We should mortify biology and find a spouse among the ugliest and least marriageable—lest the taint of selfishness attach itself to the sacrament.

Equally, I cannot see why we should prefer the interests of our own children or family members over those of strangers or of our countrymen over foreigners. Strictly applied, such a standard would dynamite the Christian notion of subsidiarity, which ranks our obligations as proceeding outward from the self, with the greatest claims upon us made by those who are nearest (relatives and neighbors). Perhaps one could make a case that in strict justice we owe our own children nutrition before we owe it to strangers, but in dispensing it we would always have to be careful to disentangle any motives of personal affection or attachment and strive not to take undue pleasure in it.

I am reminded here of Charles Dickens's character Mrs. Jellyby (of *Bleak House*), whom Jim Forest of the Orthodox Peace Fellowship summed up brilliantly as

> a woman living in London who resolutely devotes every waking hour to a project in Africa that she refers to as the "Borrioboola-Gha venture." Her goal is the resettlement of impoverished Britons among African natives, all of whom will support themselves through coffee growing. Mrs. Jellyby is convinced that no other undertaking in life is so worthwhile or would solve so many social problems, in both Africa and England, at a stroke . . . a person so wedded to her work that she has no time

for her husband or their several children, with the exception of Caddy, her eldest daughter. When we meet Caddy, we see her conscripted as her mother's secretary. Ink-spattered Caddy puts in nearly as many hours as her mother in the daily task of answering letters and sending out literature about Borrioboola-Gha. Unwilling conscript that she is, Caddy has come to hate the very word—Africa—or any phrase that has the remotest suggestion of idealistic causes. For her, "cause" is another word for the ruin of family life.

Meanwhile Mr. Jellyby is a man on the edge of suicide. Though he is still surviving his despair as the book closes, in our last glimpse of him he is resting his head despondently against a wall.

In the book's postscript, we learn that the Borrioboola-Gha project failed after the local king sold the project's volunteers into slavery in order to buy rum. Far from being deterred by this grim outcome, Mrs. Jellyby quickly finds another cause to occupy her time, "a mission with more correspondence than the old one," thus providing new vistas for a permanent campaigner.[4]

Does it sound like I'm addressing a problem confined to nineteenth-century novels, cutting down a straw man in a forest where no one will hear it fall? I wish I were. The first time I discussed this issue with a dear friend, she confirmed that she too had been troubled by the question of selfishness: "I've always wanted to adopt, and I still intend to. But for a long time I wondered if it was even moral to have my own children, when there are so many unwanted children out there whom I could raise instead."

To which I responded, "That's kind of creepy and sick, don't you think? Is 'I'd like to adopt' a morally licit reason for avoiding pregnancy?" She allowed that it probably wasn't. Not everyone would agree. A decade ago, I wrote an article addressing a book by Bill McKibben, *Maybe One: A Case for Smaller Families*, which argued that Westerners did not have the right to reproduce themselves in a world troubled by hunger. The book's position can only be described as demographic masochism. The whole discussion reminded me of the

---

4. Available at http://www.incommunion.org/2006/02/19/mrs-jellyby-and-the-domination-of-causes.

words of a spiritual director, who told me, "Jesus said to love your neighbor as you love yourself. But what if you hate yourself?"

Let me carry this reductio just one step further—into the absolute ethical contradiction to which it leads. If all self-interest is evil, then what does it mean when I perform an act of kindness to someone? Let's say, I volunteer to shovel out his driveway. Whose interests am I serving? His. If he accepts that offer, whose interests is he serving? His own. In other words, he is being selfish. Which is evil. Indeed, by even offering him this service, I am in essence serving as a near occasion of sin, a temptation to self-interest on his part. In which case, the kindest thing I could do— thinking of his eternal salvation—would be not to make the offer. Unless, of course, I was sure he would be virtuous enough to refuse. Of course, continuing the regress, he might reluctantly accept, if only to allow me the chance to do something virtuous—just as the woman I did not want and who did not want me might unselfishly accept my marriage proposal, so each of us could make a lifelong sacrifice. In such a world, everyone would be holding the door for others, who would smile but refuse to walk through them. And no one would get anywhere.

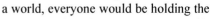

More realistically, the people who accepted this notion of unselfishness would be holding the doors for the selfish ones, who would prosper enormously in the absence of anyone defending their legitimate, just self-interests. Any claim of weakness by the unscrupulous would be immediately met with a wave of self-accusation by the scrupulous, who would avoid the crippling guilt by giving in to every demand. All of which pretty well describes current ethnic politics in America and Europe.

Instead of such a frankly hopeless standard, Christians are better off accepting the fact that they have selves with legitimate interests, which they should pursue— but keeping a skeptical eye, focused by justice and charity, on the excesses of selfishness that tempt us constantly. We need not make some universal moral calculus that determines if each of our actions is motivated by the greatest good of the greatest number. Instead, we must walk through the thicket of mixed and conflicting motives, asking always for the Grace that perfects, but does not abolish, nature.

How Would Mary Drive?

A subdivision of the Virtue of Magnanimity is the quality we dub simply, perhaps nostalgically, as kindness. I first tried to write on this topic on an inauspicious day—April 15. But I was soon engaged instead in an essay arguing that American taxpayers are worse off than medieval serfs. I let that field run fallow, distracted as I was by current events. And isn't that right there a microcosm of the problem—the way ephemera and chatter can drive the Virtues straight out of our thoughts? Indeed, the list of Virtues I haven't properly cultivated usually rings in my mind, like the tally of gorgeous foreign cities I've never visited, and evokes the same reaction: Temperance, Humility, Dubrovnik, Prague, Chastity, Venice. Yep, I'm adding them to my bucket list. On the flip side, I run through the Deadly Sins and they remind me of places where I lived but wished I didn't: Wrath, Lust, Midtown Manhattan, Sloth, and a steamy dorm room under the bleachers of Louisana State University's Tiger Stadium.

Whatever problems we have with lusty thoughts, I'm willing to bet that any man who drives in traffic spends less time picturing Taylor Swift in a French maid's outfit than he does daydreaming about hurling hand grenades at his fellow motorists. One guy who'd blocked an entire lane of traffic in Nashua, New Hampshire, greeted my toot of the horn by leaning his crew cut out of the cockpit and threatening to "get outa this car and rip your head off," and I knew that if he came within ten feet of the front of my car, I would use every ounce of steel in my 1990 Chevy to send him flying through the air at thirty miles per hour. In which case I would be writing these chapters from prison. But it seemed like my only option at the time since, you know . . . I don't own a handgun.

Of all the "hard sayings" in the Bible, the one I have the most trouble with is "turn the other cheek" (Mt 5:38–42). For

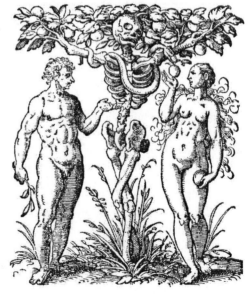

one thing, we aren't wired this way, and I doubt that this is entirely the fruit of Adam's Fall. Most animals aren't pacifists but rather defend themselves from harm. The only exception I can think of is apes or dogs in hierarchies that meekly accept abuse from higher-ups, merely cringing or showing their bellies to beg for mercy. Is that what God wants of us?

Somehow, I can't believe that this is the answer to a question I often ask myself: what would unfallen Adam do (WWUAD)? That's a worthy inquiry, since it helps us distinguish between the demands of natural justice (WWUAD) and the higher call of Grace. We need a higher call, since our darkened reason is all too ready to tell us what our fallen will would like to hear—that the guy who's making me late for work really does deserve to spend the rest of his life in one of those paraplegic scooters. And it's my job to put him there, to stop him before he blocks traffic again.

The upward call we find in Jesus's words is (just barely, just sometimes) enough to counteract the gravity into the gutter exerted by our fallen will and goad us to act perhaps as well as Adam would have, without even breaking a sweat. Or as Our Lady would have, untainted as she was by the sin of our first *schlemiel.* I imagine the Blessed Virgin piloting a dirt-brown minivan with Rosary bumper stickers through clotted New Hampshire traffic, equably navigating the jittery teens, slow-motion retirees, and Obamadites in pro-choice Volvos. As a model for ordinary Christian behavior, I think that Mary works a good deal better than Christ Himself—since few of us are really called to serve as itinerant rabbis, much less wonder-working sacrificial redeemers who make astounding and innovative theological claims, arguing from personal authority.

What's more, Our Lord was only meek and mild, so far as I can see, for a week or so of His life—at other times, needling Pharisees, confronting demons, and purging the Temple of liturgical abuses. (What would Jesus do to the drum kit in the sanctuary?) The Second Person of the Trinity knew how to dispense tough love when it was called for.

We can practice Kindness by imagining *what Mary might do* in a given situation. That makes a nice Ignatian starting point, anyway—to visualize her facial expression, the tone of voice she'd use, the wry humor and sober solicitude that got her through difficult days. Her most famous prayer, the Magnificat, was called a

poisonous instance of Envy by the French pro-Catholic atheist Charles Maurras, but an unjaundiced eye sees something very different. Our Lady exclaims,

> He hath scattered the proud in the conceit of their heart.
> He hath put down the mighty from their seat, and hath exalted the humble.
> He hath filled the hungry with good things; and the rich he hath sent empty away.

Her sentiment in this prayer isn't grim satisfaction at the rectification of historic inequalities. It's simple awe—wonderment at the power of God to overturn the carefully built-up, crushing hierarchies man sets up in his Vainglory, the world where we learn to be proud of ourselves for being born prettier, richer, smarter, or whiter than other people. Our Lady, a peaceable Jewish nobody living in the middle of nowhere under foreign occupation, looks at what the Lord has done for her—and her reaction to it boils down to "Wow."

And that's the key to kindness, I think. As Chesterton said, we need a sense of wonder that anything exists at all and that so many good things have rained down upon us undeserved: the natural beauty that man hasn't yet chewed up; the innocence of animals; the penitence of children; the peace and relative order still remaining in our country and the liberties we have left; the clarity that comes from struggling against the passions; the blessings of mental health; and the fact that J. S. Bach was ever born in the first place, much less that his music pours forth freely from the HD radio I saved up to install in my nineteen-year-old clunker.

That's enough, if I think about it, to let me offer unearned mercy to the lunatic in the SUV who's threatening my life. I can drive away with a smile. Which only, by the way, makes him madder. Some virtues are their own reward.

Misguided Compassion: The Reigning Vice of Our Time

Periodically, I hear or read of a film that's a "must-see" for Catholics. Depending on who's recommending it, I'll find out that the film is essential because it does the following:

- affirms the sanctity of life (*Bella*)
- celebrates the fundamental goodness of every person, even the simplest (*Forrest Gump*)
- dramatizes a sacramental vision of life (*Babette's Feast*)
- tells the story of an important saint (*Thérèse*)
- depicts priests or religious as multidimensional people worth taking seriously (*Into Great Silence*)
- shows practicing, sacramental Catholics who are neither unlettered peasants nor Mafia kingpins, but likeable, smart Americans (*Return to Me*)
- powerfully tells the story of a conversion (*The Third Miracle*)
- gives "our side" of historical events that are typically slanted to fit some Black Legend or Whig Authorized Version (*A Man for All Seasons*)
- shows Catholics resisting the Nazis (*The Assisi Underground*)

These are all important benefits, even if not all of the aforementioned are important films. It's hard enough to find entertainment these days that's not embarrassing to view in mixed company (let's leave out the question of letting the kids watch). It's a bonus if such a film is not just inoffensive but actually paints a world that we, as believers, can recognize. When I finished watching my favorite film of those I listed, *The Third Miracle*, the only way I could describe the experience to a friend was to say, "Imagine if all your life you'd been watching movies that pretended gravity didn't exist—where people just floated around like Peter Pan. Then finally, *finally*, somebody makes a movie where objects fall to the ground and people have to use stairs. That's what this movie does for religion."

I'd like to commend a movie that offers none of those happy attributes: *Longford*. While it isn't profane or "dirty," one of the main characters is an infamous child murderer, so I wouldn't suggest you pop it in and gather the kids. It's not a feel-good movie about the Church, since its Catholics are clearly in trouble. But *Longford* is essential viewing for Christian grown-ups of every variety, since it tackles what Mother Angelica called the reigning sin of our time. It's not a Deadly Sin but instead a perversion of the virtue of Magnanimity. It isn't exactly a heresy, although it gives heretics aid and comfort. A sharp, if hostile, observer—Friedrich Nietzsche—looked at Christianity and thought this error (admixed with Envy) lay at the very heart of our ethics, which led him to label ours a "slave morality." And wherever this vice takes over a Christian's heart, slave morality is precisely what we're practicing.

This vice is Misguided Compassion. That was the good sister's term for it, although St. Thomas might have gone medieval on this vice by describing it as Generosity and Magnanimity corrupted by neglect of the governing natural virtue, Prudence. An easier way to say all that is simply "mercy without justice." As we all know, that's not real mercy at all, and it's not what we expect from Christ on Judgment Day. As a lover of Byzantine and Medieval art, I've seen plenty of images depicting Our Lord enthroned as judge of the human race—and He isn't the Buddy Jesus depicted in the dreary 1990s comedy *Dogma*.

The movie *Longford* depicts Misguided Compassion gone horribly, wildly out of control—to the point where it ruins lives and destroys the good name of decent people, all to serve the purposes of a manipulative criminal who wishes to make a mockery of justice. But the story it tells could serve as a microcosm of the postconciliar crisis in the Church and the current futility of Catholic political activism in America. (Have I sold you yet? Are you ready to Netflix the DVD and pop the kettle corn?)

Frank Pakenham, the seventh earl of Longford, was a kind and pious man. Born a British aristocrat, he flouted public opinion by converting to Catholicism in 1940. An accomplished historian, loving

husband, and nurturing father—one of his many overachieving children is historian Antonia Fraser—Lord Longford was also active in politics. Long a member of the British House of Lords and a convinced socialist, he led campaigns against pornography and gay activism, in the face of widespread mockery in the press. It didn't help, I guess, that he insisted on conducting widely publicized fact-finding tours in strip clubs, with journalists in tow. Did I mention that Longford lacked the virtue of Prudence?

Educational reformer, chronicler of the Irish war for independence, visionary moral crusader—for none of these things do Englishmen remember the Earl of Longford. Instead, they know him as the British lord who tried to get Myra Hindley out of jail. Hindley's name is still a watchword for hellish cruelty. She was convicted in 1966 along with her lover Ian Brady for jointly kidnapping, sexually abusing, torturing, and murdering five children—whose anguished cries they tape-recorded. The Moors Murders, and the subsequent trials, were the media sensation of the middle 1960s, and neither Hindley nor Brady showed remorse at their public trial. The two were sentenced to life in prison.

And that's where poor Longford came in. As a deeply religious Catholic, the earl made a point of visiting prisoners—which, you might remember, is one of the corporal works of mercy. What you might also recall from Catechism class is that it *nowhere says you have to try to get guilty prisoners out of jail.* That distinction eluded the good Lord Longford, who responded to a letter from Myra Hindley requesting a visit.

As the film depicts their dawning, fawning friendship, it is clear that Hindley is a brilliant manipulator, skilled at reading Longford's character and telling him what he most wants to hear: She is deeply, profoundly sorry for what she did. She was an abused child, seized and dominated by a strong, sadistic lover, who forced her to take part in the murders. Oh yes, and she is deeply attracted to Longford's Catholic Faith. Would he consider sending her some Catholic books, including her in his prayers, and returning for future visits?

Soon Longford is traipsing back and forth between the House of Lords and a dingy women's prison, listening wide-eyed to Hindley's fabricated accounts of her spiritual progress and flattering himself for his attraction to "the most despised, most marginalized members of society." What he leaves aside is the fact that some people are marginalized and despised for very good reason. Looking only at Hindley's suffering at the hands of her (rightly disgusted) fellow prisoners, he sees her as a kind of Christ figure, and he proceeds to take her on as his personal cross. Convinced that she has been rehabilitated— forgetting that prison's first and most urgent task is punishing guilt and offering victims and society justice—he launches a campaign to win her parole.

The results are predictable, and they play out in the film like a slow-motion wreck of the Little Engine That Could. Longford squanders his political influence, nearly wrecks his marriage, humiliates his family, outrages and pains the parents of the murdered children, and becomes a public laughingstock. Even when Hindley's accomplice shows Longford letters where she mocks him and makes light of her repentance, the earl continues his efforts, which, thankfully, are futile: At story's end, we see Hindley dying in prison, admitting that her conversion was a sham— reminiscing about the murders, which taught her "that evil can be a spiritual experience, too." Indeed, it can be.

The first thing this movie reminded me of was the story of all those bishops whose criminal folly reassigned "penitent" sex abusers to parishes. Then I thought of the Anglican Archbishop of Canterbury, smiling vaguely as he endorsed the use of Islamic sharia in England. After that, I remembered those clerics and columnists who blathered on throughout the 1980s about the "seamless garment" that somehow made support for legal abortion morally equivalent to favoring budget cuts in Medicaid. And I thought of the time a papal speechwriter compared rejecting economic migrants to destroying unborn children. And so on, through the long detour so many

Christians took through genuine slave morality. By the film's end, I began to favor the death penalty—for Longford.

Then the movie's message turned and smacked me in the face. I remembered the times I had won cheap grace by engaging in fake compassion—the kind that disregards the truth, vitiates Justice, and treats the virtue of Prudence as something stuffy or unheroic. (You and I are *above* such worldly concerns.) Specifically, I remembered how I'd listened to a long series of implausible, heartrending sob stories from someone who craved my time, attention, and treasure—and dangled before me the prospect that she might "come back into the Church."

The prospect of "saving" a soul, of leading someone to Christ, is a heady temptation indeed—one designed to fool those who've conquered more straightforward sins. (Dorothy Sayers famously wrote in the introduction to her peerless translation of Dante's *Purgatorio* that Satan is at his most dangerous when he attacks us through our virtues—and that if he could elicit one emotion from us toward himself, it would be . . . *pity*.) Such a heavenly prospect as "landing" a convert can overwhelm rational judgment, blind you to contrary evidence, numb the self-protective instinct, shunt aside prudent counsels to "avoid evil company," and end up in scandal and squalor.

In my case, I introduced this potential "convert" to close and trusted friends—friends who trusted me and expected that I would use good judgment in choosing my associates. The least outrageous outcome? She bilked two of my close friends out of thousands of dollars. By the time I accepted the truth, the list of people who deserved my apologies was long.

So I have no room to throw stones at the Earl of Longford. His vice is as commonplace now as vengeance was in the age of dueling or bigotry during the Crusades. A predominant sin, the one that rules an epoch, is rarely obvious to those who were raised to find it natural, normal—even praiseworthy. It's like a toxic ozone that hangs over our heads, clouding our thoughts and blurring the light of day. It takes works of art to blow away the fog. *Longford* is that kind of artwork. For my penance each Lent, I'll watch it again.

A Soul Too Big for England: St. Edmund Campion

In a pleasing contrast to the bumbling attempts at Magnanimity of Viscount Longford comes the case of St. Edmund Campion—perhaps the greatest soul ever produced in England. Campion's biographer Evelyn Waugh recounts that Campion was a stellar Oxford scholar, poet, and playwright, who showed the same youthful promise as John Donne. Had Campion not joined the Church that Donne abandoned, there is no telling what masterworks Campion might have written. And which of us wouldn't rather end up in the Norton Anthology than the Roman Martyrology?

Well, Edmund, for one. Young Campion gave up a cozy college sinecure paid for by Protestant nobles and left Elizabeth's England to join the Jesuits. Even as the "Virgin Queen" literally tightened the screws on Catholics and sent priest-hunters to scour the country, Edmund trained for a mission he knew would almost certainly end on the scaffold—with his entrails slowly drawn out before his eyes. . . . You get the picture, which is one I should like to hang in my local Episcopal parish, but it ain't magnanimous to kick folks when they're down.

While he might have served the Church with a nice, clear conscience sending eloquent pamphlets across the Channel—which I'd think the sane course of action, but my soul is travel-size—Campion could not forget the hundreds of thousands of English Catholics who lived deprived of Holy Communion and Confession, paying massive fines rather than go to Protestant services, watching the Faith

of their fathers slowly strangled at the hands of political hacks. While he recognized the quite legitimate good of keeping his organs inside his body, Campion's soul had grown too large for his health. If saying Mass or shriving souls was now an act of treason, he would make the most of it. He returned in secret to England on June 24, 1580, and started his underground ministry, aware that he might quickly be arrested. If that happened, he would be tortured by Elizabeth's highly efficient secret police,

who, in such cases, racked captive priests for "confessions" admitting that they'd been sent by the pope to assassinate the queen. (Few rulers have deserved it more, but that's for another book.)

Not certain of what he might end up inventing under torture, Campion composed what we'd now call a press release and had it sent all over England shortly after his arrival. This document, now called "Campion's Brag," makes bracing reading—at least for those of us whose experience of "persecution" consisted of getting shunned in Gothic dining halls for publishing pro-life essays in the *Yale Daily News*. In the Brag,[5] Campion expresses the humility in which every Jesuit once was trained: "I would be loath to speak anything that might sound of any insolent brag or challenge, especially being now as a dead man to this world and willing to put my head under every man's foot, and to kiss the ground they tread upon." This puts the reader off guard, but then Campion challenges any and every Protestant intellectual in the country to open debate:

> I know perfectly that no one Protestant, nor all the Protestants living, nor any sect of our adversaries (howsoever they face men down in pulpits, and overrule us in their kingdom of grammarians and unlearned ears) can maintain their doctrine in disputation. I am to sue most humbly and instantly for combat with all and every of them, and the most principal that may be found: protesting that in this trial the better furnished they come, the better welcome they shall be.

Then Campion threatens a flood of men who will follow in his wake:

> Many innocent hands are lifted up to heaven for you daily by those English students, whose posterity shall never die, which beyond seas, gathering virtue and sufficient knowledge for the purpose, are determined never to give you over, but either to win you heaven, or to die upon your pikes. And touching our Society, be it known to you that we have made a league—all the Jesuits in the world, whose succession and multitude must overreach all the practice of England—cheerfully to carry the cross you shall lay upon us, and never to despair your recovery, while we have a man left to enjoy your Tyburn, or to be racked with your torments, or consumed with your prisons. The expense is reckoned, the enterprise is begun; it is of God; it cannot be withstood. So the faith was planted: So it must be restored.

---

5. Available online at http://www.ewtn.com/library/mary/cambrag.htm.

This brashness was enough to make the document a national sensation and kick off the witch hunt that ended with Campion's arrest thirteen months later. Eager to gain a celebrity convert, Campion's old patrons arranged for him to meet with Queen Elizabeth. She promised that he'd be made a bishop and given an income, a wife, and a palace, if only he'd renounce the silly business about the pope. Campion magnanimously urged the queen to save her soul instead.

QUEEN ELIZABETH.

After that, the petty Anglican appointees enjoying the pulpits and priories built by their Catholic ancestors vented their spleen by forcing Campion to engage in debates, just as he'd challenged them. Before each event, he was tortured for days at a time. Then he'd he appear alone, physically broken, dressed in the Tudor equivalent of an orange prison jump suit, to face down teams of Oxbridge academics (complete with their books) in public disputations about the Faith. And Campion still won—or at least the Anglicans thought so, since they canceled the debates and sped up the process leading to his execution. He was convicted in a trial that would have made Joseph Stalin smile.

It was then that the last part of "Campion's Brag" came into play, the sentiments he'd repeat upon the scaffold, when he would not pray with the Anglican chaplain furnished—although he would pray for him. As Campion had written, so he died:

> If these my offers be refused, and my endeavours can take no place, and I, having run thousands of miles to do you good, shall be rewarded with rigour, I have no more to say but to recommend your case and mine to Almighty God, the Searcher of Hearts, who send us His grace, and see us at accord before the day of payment, to the end we may at last be friends in heaven, when all injuries shall be forgotten.

Souls don't come in a bigger size. That's triple-XL, available only at Big and Tall soul shops. Be warned: they're hazardous to your health.

Trademark-Busting Cosmo-Style Quiz™ #7: Where Do You Come Down on the Spectrum from Schadenfreudian to Sap?

Considering our role models in this chapter, the contrast between an envious and a magnanimous soul could hardly be starker if it were painted on the face of the moon. That's not a bad way to visualize the issue at hand: which way is your face turned—toward the sun or the sterile expanse of space? Envy is the dark side of the moon, and the more we're facing the light, the brighter we appear. Take the following quiz to see if you're a full moon like Edmund Campion or a tiny crescent moon like the emblem of a major world religion that shall remain nameless.

The Quiz

Here's your hypothetical: At your job, you have a colleague—let's call him Mr. Wonderful—whose talents and tasks are starkly different from your own. You're not direct competitors (which would muddle things), except in the vaguest way, so he's no threat to your job. You're plugging away just fine in your position, and from time to time, your work gets the praise it deserves. It's the same with him and has been for years.

Then something happens. A project he's working on becomes enormously successful, seemingly through happenstance. Suddenly, Mr. Wonderful's work is attracting all kinds of internal attention and bringing in significant new business. He starts disappearing for long lunches at chichi restaurants with your boss and is given a nice private office—which you pass each day en route to your cubicle. Your cube, which used to feel like a comfy den where you worked contentedly, now seems to close around you like a veal pen, and you start to feel strangely possessive about that red Swingline stapler on your desk.

Mr. Wonderful is still perfectly friendly to you, but now in what seems a slightly swaggering way that makes you suspect he's trying to be magnanimous about his success. And you really, really hate that. You feel like he's tossing you bits of goodwill that you're expected to catch in your mouth like dog treats, then wag your tail. But that's exactly what you do.

In the course of things—you were doing opposition research on the guy, just admit it—you turn up some embarrassing secret about his past. Nothing creepy or criminal, but an incident or character trait that would take some of the gilding off Mr. Wonderful's halo and slow down his canonization. Let's say you accidentally found a bottle of his schizophrenia medication. What do you do with this information?

a. First of all, you treat yourself to a dinner worthy of François Mitterrand (see Chapter 5), which you eat alone with a notepad, making a list of which executives at the firm would find this information most unsettling. Next, you isolate the two or three biggest gossips in the company—the same people who gave you all the details on the boss's ugly divorce and gorgeous trophy wife, including the cost of her cosmetic surgery. You decide which of these "friends" to confide in. Then you take her to this very same restaurant, ply her with steaks and mojitos, and in a soft, compassionate voice tell her how much you *admire* Mr. Wonderful for his *courage* and *willingness to heal*. The whole time you act as if you thought this blabbermouth from the mailroom already knew Mr. Wonderful's secret. When she starts to literally paw at you for more details, you dispense them distractedly, as if they were already common knowledge. When you "discover" that she hadn't a clue, you pretend that you're embarrassed. You swear her to secrecy and apologize profusely. You do your best to blush and refuse to eat dessert. You've "lost your appetite" (in fact, you're stuffed to the gills and giddy). You let her box up your soufflé and take it home. She scarfs it down in the cab.

b. You take secret delight in learning this fact about Mr. Wonderful but immediately suppress it. Aware of the dark and deadly source of the satisfaction you're taking in this knowledge, you decide never to mention it, and you congratulate yourself on acting so magnanimously in this case. Still, it's a fact worth knowing, something you might someday be forced to use—but only in self-defense, of course. Should this fellow ever turn his growing power against you and treat you unjustly, it might in fact become important for folks to know all the facts about his mental stability. But the likelihood of that seems small. In fact, at the rate he's moving up, he'll probably soon cease to notice you. Then you'll be safe, and you won't need to use this fact. So you tuck it away in a little velvet jewelry box and try not to think about it too much. After a quick examination of conscience, you can't find any sin here. You can see the red light on God's control panel cease to flash and His hand recede from the celestial "Smite!" button. You're in the clear. Exhausted, you go home and microwave a burrito in your underwear.

c. You feel the same sick thrill of delight that anyone would, but it nauseates you. Even if Mr. Wonderful were in fact persecuting you—which he isn't (he doesn't bother)—you know that employing tactics like these would be beneath you. They ought to be beneath anyone. No job is worth slithering into the sewer like this, you decide. In fact, you promise yourself that you'll quit before you let this knowledge influence your thoughts or behavior in any way. Then you pretend that the news is something you accidentally overheard someone saying in Confession—which it's a mortal sin to reveal. You make a special effort to appreciate Mr. Wonderful's contribution to the company—without sucking up to him. That's also beneath you. You cook your own dang dinner for a change.

d. The news delights you in a different way. Instead of seeing this as a weapon you might use against your rival—whether or not you deign to—you seize upon it as a "humanizing" flaw, something that makes Mr. Wonderful no longer threatening but sympathetic. Just another struggling, broken, lonely soul. The kind of person who needs a friend, whose suffering has deepened him beyond the ordinary run of unreflective, *bourgeois* functionaries you're forced to work among. He's kind of interesting now, a little Bohemian, maybe a frustrated artist. You start to cultivate his company, approaching him with a much more solemn air, as if you'd met for the first time at Alcoholics Anonymous. You volunteer to run menial errands for him and take him to the healthiest vegan bistro in town—where you feel free to unload on him your own secrets and fears. He's no threat to you, after all. I mean, with *his* problems. . . .

Here are the results:

- If you picked "a": You're a real piece of work. You should probably be working as a "community organizer" forcing public schools to fire teachers who don't speak Hmong, or a tort lawyer suing family doctors into bankruptcy. A long and prosperous future awaits you, and an interesting eternity. If this scenario sounds even remotely plausible, it's time to shift your gaze away from Mr. Wonderful and to something more interesting: why not try the Creator of the universe—Who, it is important to remember, maintains you from moment to moment in existence by conscious choice. He could, if He stopped thinking of you for a moment, let you drop like a match in a urinal. The thought's kind of bracing, isn't it? He could drop Mr. Wonderful in there too—along with the whole staff of the company and the waiters over at Café Pretentious, where you've made yourself a nuisance sending back the bottled water. So why not focus on the One who has really got the power and try winning favor with Him? It seems He has for the moment given Mr. Wonderful some temporal success, which He doesn't trust you with. Your colleague will be held accountable for his excellence someday, as you'll be for your relative mediocrity. Use it as best you can, in the time you have left, to placate the only Boss that really can burn you.
- If you picked "b": You're a very careful person. No sense in taking chances in life, now is there? You were given a set of talents and saw there was no sense in squandering them on some job you never dreamed at age twenty you might be doing at forty. You put in your

hours, of course, and fulfill every jot and tittle of your job description, but the rest of your time is your own. Not that you use it much, but at least it's safe. You can see the spot where you buried it, back behind the house. Every few weeks you poke it with a spade, just to be sure. Can I offer a suggestion? As a change of pace, why not try looking at the next task that comes before you as if it were the *last thing you'd get to do on earth?* As if your whole human worth would be judged by the excellence or flatulence you attained? Try this once, and see how it feels. Hold the results in your hand, as if you'd carved them out of ivory until your fingers bled. An interesting sensation, isn't it? The whole time you were doing it, you know what you forgot about? Mr. Wonderful. And yourself.

- If you picked "c": You've got the right response, looking for "glory" not in attaboys from colleagues but in the proper ordering of your soul. You probably work very well at your job, despite all the distractions. Think of the glamour Mr. Wonderful's enjoying as a little consolation God sent him, perhaps as recompense for his past suffering, and remember it might be fleeting. You have no excuse to ruin his fun—and no reason to, come to think of it. His happiness doesn't detract from yours one bit. Nor would it really make you happier if he failed. When you have your own glory days, down the road, remember to treat them ironically, at once enjoying them and shrugging them off. All is vanity. Enjoy it while it lasts.
- If you picked "d": Your future lies not in business or entertainment but in politics, perhaps as an activist on behalf of "nonprofits" that garner handsome government contracts or get money from the basket through the Catholic Campaign for Human Development. You've already got a homemade BS Generator fully operational in your shed, and you dish out open-handedly what it emits. You've put the "puss" in pusillanimous. But think about this: your weakness, Mr. Wonderful's psychiatric issues, the wounds and scars and anguish you find so endlessly interesting—they're really kind of dull. They're evils, natural evils resulting from the Fall, but in themselves they're like flies in the Jell-O mold some putz brought to a neighbor's wake. Suffering is only of value to God when it's willingly offered in union with Christ's on the cross. Otherwise, it's just a miserable waste. Artists and writers who've actually suffered from alcoholism or depression would tell you that their afflictions never helped their craft or made them deeper, stronger, or wiser. Mr. Wonderful would tell you that too, if you intruded on his confidence. Unless he simply punched you in the face.

Activities

In Chapter 12 I airily dismissed the Litany of Humility. And I really don't think it's much use in combating Vainglory—since a vain man who undertakes that prayer is all too likely to find himself preening about his newfound Humility, mouthing the prayer without really meaning it. But if you're infected with full-on Envy, such a litany might come in handy. Your task isn't simply (like the vain man's) to correct a delusional perception of your own abilities. Instead, you need to redirect your will from a deep-seated malice that aims to drag down your fellow man to suffering in this life and damnation in the next. That's a tall order, pal. Giving yourself the beat-down entailed in the Litany of Humility would make an excellent first step. Since Envy begins with invidious comparisons between your gifts or good fortune and someone else's, it might help to focus your mind not on that other's guys' merits and debits, but on your own. To address this sin more specifically, here are some affirmations you might want to write down on little fortune cookie slips and stick in your wallet, or write on Post-It Notes to place on every mirror in your house. Taken together, I have a name for them:

The Litany of Reality

- ❏ "I do not deserve to exist." No, really. If you disagree, come up with five good reasons right now why you *in particular* (as opposed to anyone else) had a right to be created out of nothing, maintained in existence by the incessant attention of an omnipotent deity, and protected from falling into Hell for any one of the mortal sins you've committed since the age of reason. Remember to use a number two pencil.
- ❏ "I didn't deserve to be born in a country with working toilets." (Assuming, of course, that you were. If you're reading this book in North Korea, please skip to the next bullet point.) The orderly, fundamentally prosperous society in which most of us live really is the sediment left behind by millions of people working hard and postponing gratification, playing by complex civic rules, and risking their lives in combat. If some of those people accumulated wealth, they did so largely by offering goods and services to their fellow citizens, who paid for the stuff because they wanted it. What private wealth some people leave to their children is nothing compared to the social health our ancestors stored up for us. We (and certainly you) did nothing to earn it. If Envy goads you to tear it down, you're acting like a spoiled kid who pees in the public pool.
- ❏ "I really haven't worked as hard as a lot of people." For instance, a large swathe of the folks whose possessions or achievements send you into occasional fits of resentment. If you need to, do some

research on the years of schooling, arduous work schedules, and truncated personal lives that add up to wealth and advancement in our post-Edenic world. Remember all the time you spent pursuing your artsy hobbies (or playing online computer games) while the "elites" you're so angry at were spending their twenties grinding their way through WestLaw or Wharton.

❏ "God only gave me a few talents, while He gave other people more." If your answer to that stark reality is to take your meager stash and go bury it out back—for instance, by pouring your energy into Envy—remember what He has in store for you. If I might quote the Bible verse best loved by Republicans: "For the one who has will be given more, and he will have more than enough. But the one who does not have, even what he has will be taken from him" (Mt 25:29).

❏ "It's not up to me to judge what other people deserve. There's probably some good reason, which I'll never find out this side of the grave." On Judgment Day, those sinners who really have abused the gifts God gave them will suffer a worse fate than even you could cook up for them. How would you like to join them in the Lake of Fire? No? Then stop confessing other people's sins and focus on your own.

Believe it or not, working through this set of sobering facts will help your soul to grow, not shrink. The illusions Envy uses to prop up the ego act like crutches or leg braces on a healthy limb—they impair proper function and lead to atrophy. Once you toss them aside, like a miracle tourist at Lourdes, you'll find that the real you—the one God created and loves—will grow healthier and stronger. Pretty soon, you'll actually find yourself wishing your enemies well in the long run. Which is to say, you'll hope that they go to Heaven. As soon as possible.

From *The Bad Catholic's Guide to Good Living*

March 17

Patrick: Bobbing for Potatoes

If there's one thing the long-suffering people of Ireland came to be known for, it was their ability to transform misery into joy. Listen to Irish music: the songs that aren't about hopelessly unrequited love are tales of rebellions gone astray, betrayals by trusted allies, and drinking entire barrels of beer on board a sinking ship. Irish wakes—held in the home, around the body, which is frequently plied with the deceased's favorite brand of whiskey—end with friends of the deceased hiding the body from the family, who then have to ransack the house to locate the corpse so it can be buried.

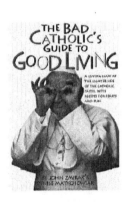

In this spirit, we'd like to suggest a way to celebrate the great Apostle of Ireland, St. Patrick, that doesn't involve green beer, paper shamrocks, or tipsy parades full of scheming politicians. This year, invite your Hibernian friends to a Potato Famine Party.

Of course we don't intend to make fun of the people who suffered in the great famine, which struck Ireland between 1845 and 1850, leaving millions dead or malnourished while a complacent British government debated the merits of free market economics. Hundreds of thousands died, while millions were forced to emigrate, half-alive, in "coffin ships" to Boston, New Brunswick, New York, and other ports. Instead, we propose this party to honor their endurance and faith—and offer those who died the Irish wake they never had.

Your party should embody the great Christian theme of earthly suffering—interrupted by a sudden explosion of joy. To make this work, it should begin as miserably as possible: try to create the atmosphere of a ramshackle, nineteenth-century

Irish hut. Strew your floor with straw, hang your walls with old-fashioned religious pictures, and drape the entertainment center with burlap potato sacks. Dress the hostess, host, and kids in peasant clothes and cover your coffee table with fresh-cut moss. As guests arrive, greet each with a deep, long sigh, and a roll of the eyes. When they ask, "How are you?" answer, "As best as can be expected" or "I'll be offering it up." Smudge the children's faces with a little charcoal and give each one a can to beg the guests for change "for charity's sake." Make sure each can bears a big green cross and is clearly labeled "IRA."

To set the mood, your hidden CD player should be set on a continuous loop of Irish dirges, and the hostess should lead the guests in a "keening" contest, encouraging each arrival to practice the deep, guttural howl in which legend attributes to banshees, the female ghosts rumored to haunt the Irish countryside. If your friends seem disinclined to keen, just wait until they get a load of the food.

Of course, you'll serve only potatoes. But you won't serve enough of them. To reinforce the scarcity theme, make sure there's only one potato for every two guests, who'll have to compete if they wish to eat. You might propose arm wrestling, a hurling match, or the traditional Irish party game of bobbing for potatoes *in the water where they were cooked.* Blindfold the guests with gray, moist rags and encourage them to seek out their potato with their teeth. (Make sure the skins are still on and that the water has cooled.) Let the winners wash down their dinner with bad American beer (such as Killian's "Irish" Red), served lukewarm. Then go back into the living room to keen about your hospitality.

When guests begin to head out the door, shaking their heads and vowing never to return, it's time to spring on them the sudden explosion of joy: change the music to jigs and reels and lively songs by modern Irish groups (the Cranberries, Rogue's Progress, and the Pogues come to mind), and pull out your carefully hidden stash of excellent Irish alcohol, such as Guinness, Magner's Cider, and Black Bush Irish Whiskey. Quickly save the party by serving an array of gourmet Irish food—such as cold baked salmon with dill, au gratin potatoes, warm cabbage salad with bacon, and buttered Irish soda bread. Give each of your guests one of the "contest" potatoes to take home as a keepsake—and hope they don't hurl it at your windows as they drive away.

Apart from the boiled potatoes, today's menu is composed mostly of cold dishes so that you can fool your hungry guests. The seafood and apple crisp can be put in the oven at the last minute. Serve the meal buffet style. We've chosen traditional Hibernian dishes, which were popular in medieval Ireland—before it was conquered and the English took all the . . . (*insert tipsy, semicoherent, thirty-minute rant about ancient historical wrongs here*). Made from ingredients abundant in the Emerald Isle and promoted by the Bord Bia (Irish Food Board), these recipes are part of the culinary renaissance now sweeping Ireland.

CELEBRATE

Steamed Lobster and Crabs with Herb Butter
Oysters on the Half Shell
Vegetable Platter of Pearl Onions, Radishes, and lightly dressed Baby Greens
Salt Roasted Shrimp in the Shells (see recipe)
Apple Oatmeal Crumble (see recipe)

Salt Roasted Shrimp in the Shells

Preheat oven to 550 or as hot as it will go.
  Rinse and pat dry shrimp.
  Cover large baking pan with salt.
  Distribute rosemary on salt.
  Toss shrimp with coriander and pink peppercorns.
  Lay in an even single layer on salt.
  Roast for 8–10 minutes. Shrimp will turn pink. Toss gently to cook other side.
  Cook another 2–5 minutes. Serve on a platter garnished with rosemary branches.

Makes 2–4 servings

Apple Oatmeal Crumble

Preheat oven to 375 degrees.
  Lightly butter 1-1/2 quart casserole dish.
  Simmer raisins and whiskey on low until whiskey is absorbed and the raisins are plump.
  Meanwhile quarter, core, and slice unpeeled apples. Toss with raisins in baking dish.
  Mix together oats, sugar, and salt. Beat in butter and work until evenly combined.
  Spread over apples evenly. Bake for 45–50 minutes. Allow to cool briefly before serving allowing crust to crisp.

Makes 6 servings

From *The Bad Catholic's Guide to Wine, Whiskey and Song*

Opus One and Opus Dei: Worldwide Conspiracy in a Glass

If there's one thing that makes people happier than finding a forgotten bottle in the cupboard or a six pack in the fridge, it's finding out that world events are dominated by an evil conspiracy. It's hard to explain why such a discovery proves so consoling, but it does: Some 35 million people shelled out cold, hard cash to buy *The DaVinci Code*—most of them Christians, eager to read a tale which portrayed their entire religion as a scam cooked up by a Roman emperor and perpetuated by a spectral order of murderous, albino monks. Clearly, they were not picking up this book because it depressed them. Such books give readers the free and easy feeling that they needn't lift a finger to change the world—it's all so futile anyway. ("What can you and I hope to do, against the likes of . . . Them? So let's go rent *Jackass* again.")

At the same time, however, there's a Gnostic thrill that comes with finding out sordid secrets, the feeling that you are now privy to the seamy underside of life, one of only 35 million or so "insiders" who know the score. As you come across bits of supporting evidence, it's fun to forward them to skeptical friends, with snarky commentary like, "Oh, and I suppose *this* is a coincidence?"

In the past it was Jews, Jesuits, Masons, or Communists who bore the brunt of suspicion—though sometimes (somehow) it might be all of them at once. The Nazis persecuted all of these groups—perhaps, as evil conspirators themselves, they wanted to preempt the competition.

In subsequent decades, the usual suspects have sometimes come in for blame in one place or another. Sometimes a grain of truth in one allegation was built up into a mock-pearl of great price: for instance, the fact that a few American Communists at once worked for civil rights and spied for Joseph Stalin[1] gave J. Edgar Hoover the license he needed to spy on the patriotic Rev. Martin Luther King. One of the present authors grew up hearing from his mother extensive warnings about the "secret Soviet plot to seed Catholic seminaries with Communists." One evening, when he brought his coauthor home for Thanksgiving, she regaled them both with a long lecture on why African-American panhandlers *should never be given money*. As Mère Zmirak explained,

> I heard this from an FBI agent on television—she was a colored woman herself. And she worked for J. Edgar Hoover. She said it doesn't matter if the beggar is dressed as a priest or a nun . . . don't give them a dime. Because they are all, *all* raising money to buy guns and ammo for the Race War.[2]

An awkward dinner. The turkey was dry.

Such theories are thankfully less respectable today. Instead, the focus of suspicion has shifted to the likes of Opus Dei. A Spanish apostolate founded in 1928 in Spain by Rev. Josemaria Escriva, Opus Dei hearkened back to the theology of St. Benedict, incorporating spirituality in one's everyday life and work.[3] Having seen the effectiveness of Masonic groups in attracting people and working together—even grown boys love a secret—Escriva decided to cloak the group in a bit of mystery. His constitutions for the group ask initiates to "always maintain prudent silence about the names of other members, and not to reveal to anyone that you belong to Opus Dei." Such practices have fired the imaginations of critics ever since, as has the group's success in attracting highly educated and successful members. What is worse, the organization doggedly upholds traditional Catholic teaching, and some of its members still employ old-fashioned penances, like flagellation. All this seems terribly unwholesome to outsiders, who darkly suspect that the practice is *not* meant to generate sexual pleasure. It's all so *sick*. . . .

---

1. A close friend of the authors—a Red Diaper baby who later found Christ—recalled to us that her grandmother did both, and she later saw FBI documentation proving it.
2. Only slightly more awkward was his attempt to take his mother along with some friends through New York's Chinatown. She refused to get out of the car, averring simply, "I haven't trusted THOSE people since Pearl Harbor."
3. At least that's what They want you to think.

DaVinci Code typist Dan Brown chose Opus Dei as the villain of his novel, rightly guessing that modern readers would thrill to read of the evil machinations of a secretive, well-funded group from Spain—Inquisitionland![4]—which carried on doctrines and customs that can only be described as "medieval." Even better if the truth these conspirators sought to suppress was that Jesus Christ was not really the founder of a Church but merely a misunderstood male feminist, a soccer dad, who was always supportive of his life-partner's career—in this case, as the embodiment of the Divine Feminine. It all worked wonderfully, to the point where Brown achieved the closest thing to canonization available to the living: Tom Hanks starred in the movie. To your average multiplex moviegoer, that's like making a film about the Bible where Jesus plays Himself.

Intriguing theories about Opus Dei aren't limited to readers who revise their religious beliefs based on novels they read while "going Greyhound." A cottage industry has grown up around the group, spinning ever more elaborate and sinister webs of intrigue around these shadowy Spaniards. If you troll the Internet for half an hour, you can turn up some amazing revelations about the group.

For instance, according to Web reporter Wayne Madsen, who claims to be a former NSA analyst, Opus Dei is a "shadowy and sinister Roman Catholic group [that is] running an espionage and political assassination team in the United States." (One that apparently can't shoot straight enough to hit Dan Brown, but never mind.)

In the book *Their Kingdom Come: Inside the Secret World of Opus Dei*, British journalist Robert Hutchison calls Opus Dei "a Mafia shrouded in white." He asserts that the group assigns its members to infiltrate intelligence agencies, newspapers, banks and political parties, and cultivate connections with organized crime. This power, once amassed, will be used to stifle reform within the Church and provoke a confrontation with Islam that would culminate in a revival of the Crusades. Nice work, if you can get it.

Nor are Moslems the only target. The Opus Dei menace is homing in on gay wedding planners, according to blogger Bob Geiger, of *Democrats.com*. In the article "Is Brownback Bringing Opus Dei Into The Senate?" Geiger slams the Catholic convert senator for opposing same-sex marriage with arguments drawn from the Princeton University-based Witherspoon Institute. That group, according to Geiger, is

> linked to Opus Dei, a strict, religious group that some former members have described as a cult. . . . [C]ritics in academia—which include former members who sometimes go through "deprogramming" upon exiting Opus Dei—charge that organizations like the Witherspoon Institute are just veiled attempts by Opus Dei to spread its influence in top-tier academic circles.

A think-tank trying to exert influence by giving money to professors and sending out press releases. . . . Will these monsters stop at *nothing?*

---

4. Also briefly the name of a failed pre-Vatican II theme park in Ohio.

Another resolute critic of Opus Dei is Miguel de Portugal, a self-proclaimed visionary who makes it his life work to spread apocalyptic warnings over the Internet. Among his claims is that Opus Dei is at once backing prolife neo-Nazis in Argentina and selling abortifacients in Spain, infiltrating the FBI[5] to cover up its involvement in the Anthrax attacks and smuggling massive quantities of *ganja*. And one more thing: Remember when Pope John Paul II canonized Opus Dei founder Rev. Josemaria Escriva? To most of us, that was like all such canonizations an exercise of papal infallibility. To Miguel de Portugal it was in fact the "abomination of desolation" warned of in the Apocalypse. Just in case, you know, you were wondering.

Nor is the world of wine immune to the many-tentacled reach of global conspiracies. While it's true that octopuses cannot survive on land, and rarely appear in vineyards, that does not mean that winemakers are safe.[6] Witness the tangle of accusations that surround the vintner Robert Mondavi. A Stanford graduate with a business head, Mondavi came from a long line of Italian winemakers, and in 1966 established his own winery in Napa Valley. Unlike most of his competitors, he sold his wine by variety (such as Sauvignon Blanc) rather than simply labeling it by region (such as Napa). He also strove to raise the standards of California wines to equal or rival European brands. Mondavi's innovations proved so successful that he was soon able to buy up some of his rivals and prevail in blind-taste test competitions against the finest imports from France.

Indeed, the wines produced by Mondavi and his imitators have begun to displace the products of ancient family vineyards in France and Italy—to the outrage of traditionalists. In fine American fashion, the Mondavi winery makes use of high-tech techniques and consultants to turn out wines that suit the tastes of influential critics like *Wine Spectator's* Robert Parker—whose 100-point wine ratings get prominent play in wine shops, and can make or break a vintage. Such wines can best be described as "big," with potent flavors and lots of "fruit." Indeed, the most overwhelming of these wines are sometimes ridiculed by cognoscenti as "fruit bombs." It was wines like this, recommended by critics such as Parker, that won most Americans away from drinking Mateus and great big jugs of Ernest & Julio Gallo.

But that doesn't mollify some critics. As *New York Times* food critic Eric Asimov has written (May 20, 2006),

> Parker's critics have asserted that his power is so great, and his taste so monochromatic, with a preference for powerfully concentrated fruity wines, that some producers around the world feel compelled to customize their wines for his palate. These "Parkerized" wines have proliferated,

---

5. Okay, so that part is true: Two O.D. members include former FBI director Louis Freeh and current jailbird Robert Hansen—who used the money he got from his Soviet spymasters to pay tuition for his daughters at the Opus Dei school Oak Crest in Virginia. One of us used to date a graduate who knew the Hansen family. She assured us that Oak Crest no longer gives discounts to parents who pay in rubles.

6. Please. You people are *so* naïve.

they say, and as a result wines from all over the world, made from different traditions and from different grapes, taste the same.

Instead of big, obvious tastes created with the help of chemists, some wine aficionados prefer the subtle, complex flavor acquired by wines made in the traditional way, where the taste is redolent not of expertise but of the sun, soil, and shade that attended the earth where the grapes were grown. They worry that the prevalence of a narrow set of tastes will homogenize the variegated wines of the world and reduce the ancient art of wine-making to yet another scientific field dominated by Americans—who will promptly get bored and outsource the entire industry to China.

As critic James Bowman writes, a number of these wine activists have embraced conspiracy theories, suggesting that winemakers like Mondavi and critics like Parker work hand in hand, forming an axis of oenophiles to extend their domination across the wineries of the world. In the otherwise excellent 2005 documentary *Mondavino*, Bowman finds a troubling political undertone:

> That the Mondavis' conspiracy against the world's wines is linked to the grand unified conspiracy theories of the left is sufficiently attested to by the fact that both Parker and the representative of the Rothschild winery of Bordeaux which is collaborating with the Mondavis on the their up-market, Opus One, brand have the same photo of Ronald Reagan holding up a glass of wine prominently displayed in the room where they are interviewed.[7]

Here at last we find the smudgy fingerprints of conspiracy: the *Rothschilds* are involved. This family, which first acquired its wealth serving as the bankers to royalty, is perhaps the single most abused bloodline in Europe.[8] Anti-Semites and Marxists alike could come together in hating this family; the former because they are Jewish, the latter because they helped keep monarchies afloat. Indeed, as Hannah Arendt pointed out in *The Origin of Totalitarianism*, the various branches of the Rothschilds, who worked in London, Paris, Vienna, and Berlin, were often employed as unpaid diplomats by their governments—who might not trust their own ambassadors but could rely upon the Rothschilds. The family knew that war was bad for business and frequently strove through its various branches to patch up quarrels among the nations; the last Rothschild peace initiative

7. *The American Spectator*, May 31, 2005.
8. One of the authors has actually dated a member of the House of Rothschild—the New York-based Gregoire de Rothschild—and found him perfectly charming, with excellent taste in wine. He never, at least in her presence, exerted undue control over world events.

was launched in 1914, as various Rothschilds shuttled all over Europe trying to avert the outbreak of World War I. That war brought down three monarchies, which used to do business with the family, and forced them to concentrate on their vineyards—once a sidelight started to turn out some decent kosher wine.

But their honest dealings never won the Rothschilds any gratitude among narrow nationalists, who suspected the loyalty of Jews, aristocrats, and clergy—each of whom had dangerously "international" connections. As Rothschild critic Myron Fagan[9] asserts,

> Adam Weishaupt was a Jesuit-trained professor of canon law, teaching in Engelstock University, when he defected from Christianity to embrace the Luciferian conspiracy. It was in 1770 that the professional money lenders, the then recently organized House of Rothschild, retained him to revise and modernize the age-old Protocols of Zionism, which from the outset, was designed to give the Synagogue of Satan, so named by Jesus Christ, ultimate world domination so they could impose the Luciferian ideology upon what would remain of the human race after the final social cataclysm by use of satanic despotism.

For instance, by making better wine. In 1978, Baron Philippe de Rothschild, owner of Château Mouton-Rothschild in Pauillac, France, met with Robert Mondavi to discuss a joint venture that would wed French tradition, American technique—and presumably, Luciferian ideology. The winery they started, Opus One, produced what was perhaps the first "ultrapremium" American wine, introduced in 1984 at $50 per bottle—more than double the price of comparable California vintages. As Steve Pitcher wrote in *Wine News* (Feb./Mar. 2000), the price reflected the work that had gone into the wine:

> Opus One is meticulously "hand massaged," with frequent topping of barrels and six rackings during its 18 months in barrel, making it extremely labor intensive. The wine is moved only by the gentle force of gravity; mechanical pumps are banned. In the first-growth tradition, the $700 French barrels are never reused. And, at a cost of more than $29 million, the Opus One Winery ranks as one of the world's most expensive single-product facilities.

The wine was an immediate and enduring success, which of course awakened suspicion. Was it merely an *accident* that a vulgar American corporation was working with scions of an ancient banking family to dominate the worldwide wine

---

9. A playwright and journalist, who "launched a one man crusade to unmask the Red Conspiracy in Hollywood which had set about to produce films that would aid that One World Government [sic] plot," according to the often surprising educational site: http://educate-yourself.org.

market? Surely, there must be more to the story than that—some Hidden Hand squeezing the grapes. . . .

And indeed there was. According to the always-informative Web resource Illuminati Today Index (www.scoreboard-canada.com), that hand belongs to Opus Dei. The intrepid anonymous author of the Sept. 3, 2006, expose "Dorothy Bush-Koch Linked to Rothschilds and Opus Dei through Devil's Wine" reports with alarm that Dorothy Bush-Koch, sister of the president, is married to a man named Robert "Bob" Koch, himself also a president—albeit only of the Wine Institute, an industry lobbying group. But who should turn up among the members of that secretive vintners' cabal? None other than both the Mondavis and the Rothschilds. Even worse, the site reports,

> The winery itself and the name of its prime product "Blood Red" have given rise to suspicions of satanic ritualism and architecture. The Baroness Rothschild who now heads this particular enterprise also has a joint venture with the Chilean winery Concha y Toro—or Seashell and Bull—in Chile. That Winery is openly run by Opus Dei. Its favorite brand is Cassilera del Diablo or Devil's Cellar. The silver wrapping on the cork has the outline of a devil. Rather odd for a group that claims to be doing God's Work as the name Opus Dei implies in Latin. . . .
>
> A QUESTION WITH AN ANSWER WE MAY NOT WANT TO KNOW: Does the Catholic Church use Opus One for Mass?

We checked on this, and the author is absolutely right: Concha y Toro's CEO is indeed Eduardo Guilisasti, 53, of Santiago, Chile, and he does belong to Opus Dei. As to the more critical question of which parishes serve up Opus One (now $149 a bottle) at Mass. . . . we're still out there looking. If any of our readers turn up such a church, please send us the name and driving directions.

The Bad Catholic's Guide to Good Living: A Loving Look at the Lighter Side of Catholic Faith, with Recipes for Feasts and Fun. 978-0-8245-2300-8.

The Bad Catholic's Guide to Wine, Whiskey, and Song: A Spirited Look at Catholic Life & Lore from the Apocalypse to Zinfandel. 978-0-8245-2411-1.

Support your local bookstore or order directly from the publisher by calling 1-800-888-4741 for customer service.

To request a catalog or inquire about quantity orders, please e-mail info@CrossroadPublishing.com

About the Author

John Zmirak graduated from Yale in 1986, where he studied religion and literature. He completed his MFA and Ph.D. in English at Louisiana State University, where he focused on Southern literature—especially the novels of Walker Percy. He is the author of five books, including *The Bad Catholic's Guides to Good Living* and *The Bad Catholic's Guides to Wine, Whiskey, and Song.* He wrote the graphic novel *The Grand Inquisitor* and edited *Disorientation: How to Go to College Without Losing Your Mind.* He writes regularly for InsideCatholic.com and other periodicals and is currently writer-in-residence and assistant professor of literature at Thomas More College in Merrimack, NH. He is the proud father of two beagles, Susie and Franz Josef.

Related Reading

Angelo Stagnaro
THE CATECHIST'S MAGIC KIT
80 Simple Tricks for Teaching
Catholicism to Kids

ISBN 978-0-8245-2518-7

The first and only book on Gospel magic, The
Catechist's Magic Kit by Gospel magician Angelo
Stagnaro brings the wonder of magic into the Catholic
classroom. This creative tool for Catholic instructors
teaches the fundamental pillars of the Catholic faith
through 80 enchanting magic tricks. Each trick is easy
to learn and perform, and corresponds to a specific
passage of the Catechism of the Catholic Church.

This book is approved for Catholic catechesis
and was granted the Imprimatur.

Support your local bookstore or order directly from the publisher at
www.CrossroadPublishing.com

To request a catalog or inquire about quantity orders, please e-mail
sales@CrossroadPublishing.com

The Crossroad Publishing Company

Additional Reading

**Gregory K. Popcak, Ph.D.
GOD HELP ME! THIS STRESS
IS DRIVING ME CRAZY!
Finding Balance Through God's Grace**

ISBN 978-0-8245-2598-9

Reduce anxiety and stress by discovering God's healing grace.

In this book you'll find:

- Real-life stories and anecdotes showing how you can deal with stress.
- Checklists, quizzes, and questionnaires to help you identify your own situation.
- Clear explanations of the latest psychological research on stress
- Insights into how the sacraments enrich your life.
- Reminders of why God is more powerful than even your deepest trouble.

Support your local bookstore or order directly from the publisher at
www.CrossroadPublishing.com

To request a catalog or inquire about quantity orders, please e-mail
sales@CrossroadPublishing.com

The Crossroad Publishing Company